D0938401

The FBI &

American Democracy

The FBI
& American Democracy

A BRIEF CRITICAL HISTORY

Athan G. Theoharis

 University Press of Kansas

Published by the University Press of Kansas (Lawrence, Kansas
66049), which was organized by the Kansas Board of Regents and
is operated and funded by Emporia State University, Fort Hays
State University, Kansas State University, Pittsburg State University,
the University of Kansas, and Wichita State University

Library of Congress Cataloging-in-Publication Data

Theoharis, Athan G.
The FBI and American democracy : a brief critical history /
Athan G. Theoharis.
    p.   cm.
Includes bibliographical references and index.
ISBN 0-7006-1345-5 (cloth : alk. paper)
1. United States. Federal Bureau of Investigation—History.
2. Intelligence service—United States—History.
3. Internal security—United States—History.
4. criminal investigation—United States—History.
5. Abuse of administrative power—United States-History.
I. Title.
HV8144.F43T49 2004
363.25'0973—dc22   2004006077

British Library Cataloguing-in-Publication Data is available.

Printed in the United States of America

10 9 8 7 6 5 4 3 2 1

The paper used in this publication meets the minimum
requirements of the American National Standard for Permanence
of Paper for Printed Library Materials Z39.48–1984.

TO SAM,

who deserves better

Contents

Acknowledgments

I have incurred numerous debts in the course of my many years of research involving the FBI. I do want to thank in particular the following individuals who shared either FBI files that they had obtained or their own specialized knowledge of FBI activities—John Stuart Cox, Herbert Mitgang, David Burnham, Steve Aftergood, Kenneth O'Reilly, David Williams, Ellen Schrecker, John Donovan, Patrick Jung, Cathleen Thom, Christopher Gerard, Stephen Leahy, Susan Dion, John Elliff, Mark Gitenstein, Mike Epstein, Gary May, Seth Rosenfeld, John Henry Faulk, Alger Hiss, Harrison Salisbury, Don Edwards, Tony Mauro, Anthony Marro, Morton Halperin, Kai Bird, Victor Navasky, Douglas Cassel, Harold Weisberg, M. Wesley Swearingen, David Luce, Richard Criley, Percival Bailey, Kenneth Waltzer, Sigmund Diamond, Steven Rosswurm, Charles Martin, Jon Wiener, John Fuegi, Dan Simoniski, Theodore Kornweibel, Sam Walker, Ray Dall'Osto, W. H. Ferry, John Studer, Holbrook Mahn, Allan Witwer, Alex Charns, James Rowen, Laura Kalman, Jessica Wang, Boria Sax, Barton Bernstein, Robert Griffith, Timothy Ingram, David Kendall, Ira Shapiro, Lewis Paper, and David Thelen. Marquette University—particularly Joyce Hunkel—has provided invaluable support to my research and writing (in Joyce's case, patiently assisting my feeble efforts to master word processing). FBI personnel in the FOI/PA section have patiently processed my numerous Freedom of Information Act requests; I do want to acknowledge specifically the helpful assistance of Robert Watson, Susan Rosenfeld, Linda Kloss Colton, and John Fox. I thank the Field Foundation, the Warsh-Mott Fund, the C. S. Fund, the Fund for Investigative Journalism, the Webster Woodmansee Fund, the Albert Beveridge Award, and the National Endowment for the Humanities for their financial support, which helped defray the hefty processing fees incurred in the process of obtaining FBI files. The Franklin and Eleanor Roosevelt Institute, the Harry S Truman Institute, and the Lyndon Baines Johnson Foundation helped fund my research at presidential libraries. I owe a special debt to Michael Briggs, editor-in-chief of the University Press of Kansas, who convinced me that, while a comprehensive history of the FBI could not be written at present, a briefer survey could enhance our understanding of the role that the FBI played in America in the twentieth century and continues to play in the twenty-first. Last, my own work has been influenced by the example and commitment to social justice of my wife, Nancy, and my children and their partners—Jeanne, Scott, George, Julie, Elizabeth, and Chris.

Introduction

Twice in the recent past—first in the years 1974–1976 and then in the years 2001–2004—the role of the FBI became a major policy issue. In the years 1974–1976, political and public opinion leaders decried FBI abuses of power and violations of First Amendment and privacy rights dating from the mid-1930s. A different issue surfaced in the years 2001–2004—that, as a result of their commitment to a law enforcement agenda, cautious bureaucrats at FBI headquarters had failed to anticipate and, thereby, avert the devastating terrorist attacks of September 11, 2001. While arising out of seemingly different concerns, both these two issues generated essentially the same response. In neither case did political and public opinion leaders institute changes based on the principles of limited and defined powers and public accountability. The underlying premise was that FBI officials should have the discretion to anticipate potential threats to the nation's security and that FBI operations should not be confined to investigating violations of federal statutes.

When created as the investigative division of the Department of Justice in 1908, the Bureau of Investigation (renamed the Federal Bureau of Investigation, or FBI, in 1935) was composed of just 34 agents stationed in Washington, D.C. By 2003, the FBI had expanded to 11,776 agents and 16,080 support staff stationed at either FBI headquarters in Washington, D.C., one of the fifty-six field offices (and adjoining four hundred resident agencies) in the nation's principal cities, or one of the forty-six legal attaché offices (legats) housed in U.S. embassies in foreign capitals ranging from Mexico City to Kuala Lumpur. (See appendix A.)

The FBI's creation and initial expansion were the by-product of a rejection of a states' rights tradition that held that law enforcement should be a local and state responsibility. At various times after 1908, Congress enacted laws expanding the definition of interstate commerce crimes—and, thus, the FBI's responsibilities. Nonetheless, the bureau's explosive growth in the years after the twin crises of World War II and the Cold War was due less to these laws and more to the fact that, as we will see shortly, FBI operations were, after 1936, no longer confined to investigating violations of federal statutes and included as well noncriminal "intelligence" investigations.

Presidents and their attorneys general increasingly turned to the FBI in a quest to anticipate foreign-directed threats to the nation's internal security. Because they no longer believed that the nation's international role should be confined to responding to direct military attacks, presidents increasingly thereafter pursued a more activist, interventionist international role. They had a companion interest either in obtaining advance intelligence about or curbing the plans of those U.S. citizens and alien residents who might attempt to undermine support for policies intended to expand the nation's economic, political, and military commitments overseas—and, particularly, in ascertaining whether radical activists and organizations (variously defined as "subversive" or "terrorist") were directed or influenced by either foreign powers or foreign movements.

The goal of anticipating threats to the nation's internal security led to the abandonment of an exclusively law enforcement mission—and of the principle that the subject of an investigation meet a standard of a "probable cause" to suspect violation of federal laws. Rather, spying, sabotage, and terrorism needed to be anticipated, discerned through monitoring a suspicious individual's political views (not overt conduct). And, since subversives and terrorists operated by stealth and subterfuge, investigators similarly had to rely on inherently intrusive and invariably illegal investigative techniques (wiretaps, bugs, break-ins, mail opening).

Intelligence investigations were not intended to result in prosecution and were to be conducted in secret—thus negating the safeguards of the judicial system meant to preclude or deter abuses of power. This was so because such investigations either led to the uncovering of information illegally or did not establish that the targeted individual had violated a federal statute. At the same time, intelligence investigations often uncovered information about a targeted subject's political and personal conduct. Both these factors led FBI officials over time to seek alternative means to use such information to contain "subversive activities"—for example, by disseminating derogatory personal or political information to the White House, to other intelligence agencies, or to verifiably reliable reporters, members of Congress, or congressional committees. In the process, the FBI's mission became, in effect, one of political containment.

FBI officials were able to pursue this course of political containment because their operations were shielded from critical scrutiny. The crises of World War II and then the Cold War provided the cover for this shield of secrecy as members of Congress and the public in general feared that openness and accountability would undermine the nation's security interests. Ironically, the secret conduct of intelligence investigations did not just invite abuses of power; it ensured that senior FBI officials would not be subject to critical scrutiny over how effectively they had met a desired goal of anticipating internal security threats.

At two critical times, despite having launched massive intelligence investigations, FBI officials failed to anticipate first espionage and then terrorism. The first of these incidents involved Soviet intelligence operatives who, during the 1930s and 1940s, successfully recruited American Communists (and other liberal antifascists) holding sensitive government positions. The Soviets' objective was to obtain classified records (pertaining to State Department policy, U.S. military production, and military technology, including the World War II atomic bomb project). The second involved the suicide bombing operation of September 11, 2001, when nineteen resident aliens affiliated with the Al Qaeda terrorist network commandeered four commercial jets, flying two into the World Trade Center, one into the Pentagon, and one into a field in rural western Pennsylvania, and resulting in the deaths of 2,973 and billions of dollars in property and related economic losses.

Beginning in the mid-1930s, the Roosevelt administration sought to contain a perceived threat to U.S. security posed by Nazi Germany and the Soviet Union, worried by the possibility that fascist and Communist movements within the United States might act as agents of these foreign powers. This concern led the president in August 1936 to authorize FBI intelligence investigations of "the Communists and of fascism in the United States" insofar as fascist and Communist movements "were international in scope and that Communism particularly was directed from Moscow." Roosevelt's successor, Harry Truman, shared this concern about the "subversive" orientation of American Communists, with the result that, between 1936 and 1952, FBI appropriations increased by more than 1,800 percent (from $5,000,000 to $90,665,000) and FBI personnel by approximately 1,000 percent (from 609 agents and 971 support staff to 6,451 agents and 8,206 support staff). In addition, through secret directives issued either by the president or unilaterally by the FBI director, FBI agents were authorized to employ such investigative techniques as wiretaps, bugs, break-ins, mail covers (whereby the names and addresses of the sender and the recipient of a letter were recorded from the envelope), and mail intercepts (whereby the contents of letters were photographed). Exploiting this secret authority, FBI agents wiretapped the Soviet embassy, Communist Party headquarters, and the residences of Communist activists or suspected Communist sympathizers; bugged Communist meetings; and broke into the warehouse of the Soviet Government Purchasing Committee, the national and branch offices of the Communist Party, and the residences of American Communists to photograph their records (including correspondence, membership and subscription lists, and financial reports).

FBI Director J. Edgar Hoover regularly briefed the White House between 1940 and 1945 on the results of the FBI's counterespionage operations. In his reports, Hoover unqualifiedly affirmed that the FBI was fully conversant with the plans and objectives of both fascist and Communist operatives. For example, in 1940, he advised the White House that, through "constant observation and surveillance [of] a number of known and suspected Agents of the German, Russian, French,* and Italian Secret Services," FBI agents were able to "maintain a careful check upon the channels of communication, the sources of information, the methods of finance and other data relative to these agents." Hoover reaffirmed this success in 1941, advising the White House that FBI agents kept "under observation and constant study the operations of the German, Italian, Soviet and Japanese Agents" and knew the "identities of all major representatives of" these governments. He concluded by emphasizing that "their activities are under constant scrutiny." FBI agents continued to monitor Soviet officials and American Communists even after the United States entered the war, despite the fact that the United States and the Soviet Union were military allies. In a monthly "general intelligence survey in the United States" that was sent to the White House, the FBI director detailed FBI findings related to fascist and Communist activities within the United States. Significantly, the section of these reports covering "Communist activities" described only efforts to influence public opinion, recruitment efforts, legislative strategies, and efforts to influence labor union and civil rights activities, citing *no* example of a Soviet or an American Communist espionage operation.

Belying Hoover's assurances, and despite the FBI's massive surveillance of both Soviet officials and American Communists, Soviet operatives stationed in the United States during the 1930s and the World War II period did obtain sensitive classified information about U.S. foreign policy plans,

---

* The French had surrendered in June 1940 and a profascist government established in Vichy.

military capabilities, and military technology. The FBI even failed in a particular case where FBI officials had advance intelligence about a planned Soviet espionage operation and the specific individuals who would oversee it.

From a wiretap of Communist Party headquarters, FBI officials were alerted to a conversation in which the Communist Party chief, Earl Browder, forewarned Steve Nelson, a Communist activist residing in Oakland, California, about a pending sensitive operation. FBI agents thereupon bugged Nelson's residence and, through this bug, intercepted and recorded an April 1943 meeting between Nelson and Vassili Zubilin, the third secretary of the Soviet embassy. Zubilin was recorded giving Nelson a large sum of money for the "purpose of placing Communist Party members and Comintern agents in industries engaged in secret war production so that information could be obtained for transmittal to the Soviet Union." When briefing the White House about this discovery in May 1943, Hoover assured the president that the FBI was taking "steps" to identify "all members of the Communist International (Comintern) with which Steve Nelson and Vassili Zubilin are connected, as well as the agents of this apparatus in various war industries."

That month, FBI officials launched an intensive investigation that lasted until 1945 and was meant to identify the participants in this planned espionage operation. FBI agents not only monitored Zubilin's and Nelson's movements but also extensively used wiretaps, bugs, break-ins, mail covers, and mail intercepts. The ensuing investigation expanded through concentric circles as, from their surveillance of Zubilin and Nelson, FBI agents identified other suspects with whom Zubilin and Nelson came into contact. The FBI investigation received a further break with Hoover's receipt in August 1943 of an anonymous letter, written in Russian and postmarked Washington, D.C., identifying by name other Soviet officials stationed in the United States who were involved in espionage operations directed against the United States.

This FBI investigation, code-named COMRAP (an acronym for Comintern Apparatus), had the initial advantage of allowing FBI agents to focus on specific individuals rather than indiscriminately monitoring all Soviet officials and all American Communists. FBI agents also had access to privileged telephone and room conversations, confidential correspondence, and confidential records (obtained through wiretaps, bugs, break-ins, and mail intercepts). Nonetheless, by 1945, not a single instance wherein either a Soviet official or an American Communist stole or acquired classified information had been uncovered. FBI agents had established only that American Communists were Communists: that is, they supported the foreign policy objectives of the Soviet Union, sought to ensure favorable public attitudes toward the Soviet Union, and were active in labor organizing and civil rights activities. In a 1944 report summarizing the results of an investigation that had focused on forty-six individuals, an FBI analyst characterized the actions of these targeted subjects as "(1) collecting political information of value to the USSR; (2) infiltrating foreign racial or minority groups for political pressure purposes; (3) infiltrat[ing] U.S. Government bodies or agencies." Their objectives when seeking to infiltrate federal agencies, the analyst concluded, were to "influence foreign policy" and to "secure information of value to the [U.S. Communist] Party. In addition, through their official duties and acquaintances, they are contacted by Party functionaries for the employment of other Communists in Government work."

Hoover submitted no follow-up report to the White House on the COMRAP investigation after May 1943, despite having assured the president that the FBI continued to be interested in and was taking steps to forestall this planned espionage operation. The only reports on Browder, Nelson, and the Soviet officials stationed in the United States sent by the FBI director to the White House described only their political activities (criticisms of U.S. foreign policy, efforts to influence ethnic Americans from the Baltic states, legislative lobbying, and efforts at promoting public sympathy for the Soviet Union). As significantly, at no time did FBI officials recommend that the Justice Department either seek the indictment of any American Communist or effect the recall of any Soviet official.

The same intelligence failure occurred in the case of the September 11, 2001, terrorist operation. Dating from March 1983, FBI agents had broad authority to "anticipate or prevent" terrorism, under guidelines issued by Attorney General William French Smith. Moreover, in response to the series of domestic and international incidents that began with the terrorist truck bombing attacks on the World Trade Center in 1993 and the Albert Murrah Building in 1995 and then intensified with terrorist attacks on an American air base in Saudi Arabia in 1996, on the U.S. embassies in Kenya and Tanzania in 1998, and on the USS *Cole* in 2000, counterterrorism had become an FBI priority. Indeed, the FBI's counterintelligence budget increased from $118 in 1993 to $423 million in 2001, with the number of agents assigned to counterterrorism investigations reaching 1,300.* Special units were also established at FBI headquarters to coordinate FBI investigations of militant Islamic fundamentalists suspected of affiliation with Osama bin Laden's Al Qaeda operation—the Radical Fundamentalist Unit in 1994 and the Usama Bin Ladin Unit in 1999. Furthermore, in late 2000, FBI officials assured the Clinton White House that they had a "handle" on Al Qaeda's operations in the United States.

Despite this intensified effort, FBI officials did not anticipate the September 11 terrorist attack. As in the case of the FBI's COMRAP investigation of 1943–1945 and the FBI's massive investigation of American Communists launched in response to President Roosevelt's August 1936 secret directive, FBI agents once again had focused on individuals identified because of their advocacy of militant political views. For example, in a case subsequently cited as seemingly confirming the cautious conservatism of bureaucrats at FBI headquarters, on July 10, 2001 (two months before the September 11 attack), Agent Kenneth Williams conveyed his suspicions about the "inordinate number of individuals of investigative interest," citing seven or eight who were attending flight schools in Arizona. Williams recommended that FBI headquarters initiate a nationwide program to monitor all Middle Eastern Muslims attending flight schools. Williams's recommendation seems prescient in hindsight even though he cited no example of planned or suspected terrorist activities. His memorandum nonetheless confirms that FBI agents were already monitoring Middle Eastern resident aliens and that the targets of FBI terrorist investigations were Middle Eastern men holding militant fundamentalist views. For example, Williams cited Zakaria Soubra in particular because this British citizen endorsed a worldwide unitary Islamic state. More important, however, Williams had missed Hani Hanjour, another Middle Easterner, who had, over a five-year period, attended a flight school in Tucson and who, on September 11, piloted a commandeered American Airlines jet into the Pentagon. In a second case, a longtime FBI counterterrorism informer residing in San Diego was subsequently found to have been in contact with three of the nineteen

---

* In their 2001 budget request, FBI officials sought an additional $58 million to hire 149 counterintelligence agents, 200 intelligence analysts, and 54 translators. On September 10, 2001, ironically, Attorney General John Ashcroft rejected this budget increase. Following the September 11 attack, however, he endorsed an increase in overall FBI appropriations (from $3,566,275,000 in 2001 to $4,300,000,000 in 2003, with proposed appropriations of $4,600,000,000 in 2004), with FBI personnel increasing from 26,837 in 2001 (a decline from 27,617 in 2000) to 27,856 in 2003.

terrorists—Khalid al-Midhar, Navaf al-Hazmi, and Hani Hanjour—but to have been unaware of their terrorist purposes, in his reports describing al-Midhar and al-Hazmi as trustworthy.

The FBI's failure to have anticipated Soviet espionage in the 1930s and 1940s and its failure to have anticipated the terrorist attack of September 11, 2001, provoked quite different responses. The highly publicized congressional testimony of Communist defectors in 1948 about Soviet espionage activities* precipitated a contentious public debate. Conservative members of Congress (Senator Joseph McCarthy and members of the House Committee on Un-American Activities and the Senate Internal Security Subcommittee) then attributed the Soviets' espionage successes, not to any failure by the FBI, but to the Roosevelt and Truman administrations' "softness toward Communism." These liberal presidents' indifference had permitted Communists and Communist sympathizers to infiltrate the federal bureaucracy and, thereby, influence the formulation and execution of the nation's foreign policy (resulting in the "sell out and betrayal" of Eastern Europe and China). At no time during the late 1940s and the 1950s did Congress evaluate FBI operations—and the quite different reality of an FBI that had not been hamstrung by an indifferent Roosevelt and Truman but that had been provided broad authority and leeway to investigate Soviet officials and American Communists. Soviet espionage successes were due, not to a lack of resources and support, but to the inability of FBI agents to uncover evidence of espionage operations.

The September 11, 2001, terrorist attack precipitated a quite different congressional response. In 2002–2003, the House and Senate Intelligence Committees launched an inquiry into why the FBI (and the CIA and the NSA) had failed to anticipate this devastating terrorist operation. The joint committee's final report, publicly released in July 2003, concluded that the September 11 attack could have been averted had there been better coordination among the U.S. intelligence agencies and had these agencies more aggressively and creatively investigated tantalizing leads. The three intelligence agencies, the authors of this report emphasized (citing specific examples), "too often failed to focus on [available] information and consider and

* The full scope of Soviet espionage activities became known only in the 1990s as the result of the public release of Soviet consular messages that military intelligence officials had intercepted during the 1940s and subsequently deciphered and the limited opening of KGB records to research by American scholars.

appreciate its collective significance in terms of probable terrorist attack," "missed opportunities," failed to "at least try to unravel the plot through surveillance and other investigative work within the United States," and, "finally, to generate a heightened state of alert and thus harden the homeland against attack." The intelligence agencies must better coordinate their activities and adopt a more "creative, aggressive" approach to meet and anticipate the terrorist threat.

These deficiencies underpinned the report's two principal recommendations. First, the joint committee recommended that a cabinet-level position, the director of national intelligence, should be created to serve as the president's "principal advisor on intelligence" and command the "full range of management, budgetary, and personnel responsibilities to make the entire U.S. Intelligence Community operate as a coherent whole." The director of national intelligence should not, however, be allowed to serve as the director of any other U.S. intelligence agency. Second, after pointedly critiquing the FBI's "shortcomings" and proposing changes to strengthen the bureau's "domestic capacity as fully and expeditiously as possible," the joint committee questioned "whether the FBI should continue to perform the [U.S.] domestic intelligence function" and recommended instead that "a new domestic intelligence service should be established in the United States, recognizing the need to enhance national security while fully protecting civil liberties."

The recommended organizational changes and the explicit assumption that better coordination and a more creative and aggressive approach could have averted the September 11 terrorist attack were based on the clairvoyance that comes from hindsight. The cited examples of CIA, NSA, and FBI deficiencies seem convincing given what became known after the attack. More important, despite a passing reference to the need to balance security and civil liberty considerations, the underlying premise of the joint committee's recommendations is the primacy of the goal of achieving absolute security and the feasibility of that goal. However, the history of FBI intelligence operations (notably the COMRAP investigation) confirms the chimerical nature of such a goal. That history also underscores how such an approach serves, not to advance legitimate security interests, but to undermine individual liberties and contribute to a repressive political climate, one that, for example, made possible both the Palmer raids of 1920 and the McCarthyite politics of the 1950s.

The Joint Committee's recommended organizational changes would, if implemented, not only ignore the lessons of the past, but also mark a new departure, one that America's political leaders had never publicly advocated.

There is a precedent for the recommendation that responsibility be centralized in a director of national intelligence, namely, a secret plan temporarily instituted by the Nixon administration in July 1970, the so-called Huston Plan. Convinced that the U.S. intelligence agencies had failed to develop the desired intelligence essential to containing radical anti–Vietnam War and militant civil rights activists, President Nixon appointed a special interagency task force to evaluate current intelligence operations and resources. This task force eventually recommended that the president lift existing restrictions, authorize the use of "clearly illegal" investigative techniques (including wiretaps, bugs, break-ins, mail opening, interception of international messages, and lowering the minimum age of informers to eighteen), and appoint a permanent interagency committee composed of representatives of all the U.S. intelligence agencies (FBI, CIA, NSA) to which a White House official would be assigned with the authority to "coordinate intelligence originating within the committee." In essence, the Huston Plan would have enhanced the ability of the intelligence agencies to obtain advance intelligence about the activities of American citizens unobtainable by legal means and, at the same time, subject the U.S. intelligence community to the close review, and ensure that it operated at the direction, of the White House.

President Nixon did not, however, follow the task force recommendation that he himself issue a secret directive authorizing "clearly illegal" activities and establish a permanent, centralized bureaucracy. Cognizant of the political risk attendant on authorizing "clearly illegal" investigative techniques and of the inevitable politicization of intelligence gathering, Nixon purposefully sought to ensure his own deniability by having White House aide Tom Charles Huston issue the authorization memorandum under his own signature. Ironically, FBI Director Hoover subverted this strategy of deniability when, while briefing Attorney General John Mitchell of his intention to create a written report each time the FBI employed a specific "clearly illegal" investigative technique, he stipulated that this had been done "pursuant to the President's program." Learning of Hoover's intention, Nixon rescinded the Huston Plan.

The establishment of a cabinet-level position of director of national intelligence would repeat this earlier proposed centralization and enable the president's appointee to the position to ensure that the intelligence community would be fully responsive to the political interests of the White House. The possibility of the politicization of intelligence, raised sharply by the debate over whether the Bush White House skewed intelligence about Iraq's links to Al Qaeda and possession of weapons of mass destruction to justify the decision to go to war against Iraq in 2003, recalls the informal relationship between the White House and the FBI that dated from the Herbert Hoover through at least the Nixon administrations.*

At times in response to specific White House requests, and at times on their own initiative, FBI officials briefed the White House on the political and personal activities of radical activists and prominent personalities, activities that FBI agents continued to monitor closely. These reports provided the president with advance intelligence about the plans and strategies, not only of radical activists, but also of mainstream critics. The most egregious example of the uses made of this covert relationship involved a November 1970 Nixon White House request for an FBI report on the suspected homosexuality of a name-redacted Washington-based reporter and a list of homosexuals and "any other stuff" that the FBI had compiled on members of the Washington press corps. This request was prompted by a White House reassessment of a failed "law and order" strategy to defeat incumbent liberal Democrats in the 1970 congressional elections. Deciding to attempt to discredit critical news stories as biased, the Nixon White House proposed as well to raise public doubts about the moral character of Washington reporters. In a similar vein, President Eisenhower's attorney general, William Rogers, and chairman of the Joint Chiefs of Staff, General Nathan Twining, sought in 1958 to circulate derogatory information, earlier developed by the CIA and the FBI, about the syndicated columnist Joseph Alsop's homosexuality. In this case, the Eisenhower administration sought to counter the impact of Alsop's columns criticizing its fiscal conservatism for having contributed to a "missile gap" with the Soviet Union.†

---

* Such reports were sent episodically to the Hoover White House in 1931–1932 but became regular submissions between 1940 and 1973. They more than likely continued after 1973 (if in a scaled-down fashion), but records relating to the FBI–White House relationship after 1973 have not yet been made accessible to independent researchers.

† This 1958 initiative calls to mind the leaking of the identity of the CIA officer Valerie Plame by senior Bush administration officials to the syndicated columnist Robert Novak in July 2003.

The history of past FBI practices raises similar questions about the joint committee's recommendation for a more "creative, aggressive" approach and the possible establishment of a "new intelligence" agency having exclusive responsibilities for domestic intelligence.

Frustrated by a series of Supreme Court rulings that effectively negated the possibility that American Communists could be prosecuted under the Smith Act of 1940 or the McCarran Act of 1950, FBI Director Hoover in August 1956 authorized a special FBI program code-named COINTELPRO–Communist Party. This secret program abandoned criminal law enforcement and, instead, sought to "disrupt, harass, and discredit" the American Communist Party and leading Communist activists through the use of creative and aggressive methods. Formally abandoning a course of law enforcement for a strategy of political containment, these creative measures included sowing dissension within Communist ranks and disseminating to reliable reporters and columnists derogatory political and personal information. Over time, FBI officials extended these tactics, under similarly code-named COINTELPROs, to other radical organizations and their leaders (the Socialist Workers Party, the Ku Klux Klan and other white supremacist organizations, the Black Panthers and other black nationalist organizations, and the Students for a Democratic Society and other New Left organizations). FBI officials concurrently instituted procedures to preclude discovery of these programs as the specific tactics employed violated the privacy and First Amendment rights of the targeted activists and relied on information that either had been illegally obtained or confirmed that agents were closely monitoring noncriminal personal and political activities. The joint committee's recommendation of a "new intelligence" agency having an exclusive counterintelligence role has the earmarks of this CO-INTELPRO—in part because of the assurance of secrecy and in part because such investigations would be divorced from the accountability inherent in law enforcement. In addition, the pressure to ensure results would replicate the COINTELPRO's very establishment—in this case, because the FBI (or an American MI-5) would be pressured not to "miss opportunities," pay "inadequate attention to the potential for a domestic attack," or fail to "identify and monitor effectively the extent of activity by al-Qa'ida and other international terrorist groups operating in the United States."

Should we institute these recommended reorganizations without fully understanding the past history of the FBI—both the consequences of its successful intelligence operations and the consequences of its failures?

Understanding this history not only serves an academic interest in the past, but also offers a critical reference point for assessing recommendations that seem indifferent to the problems for a democratic society posed by the operation of a secret, resourceful agency. This history further highlights that the motivation to achieve absolute security during past periods of intense crisis produced decisions—some public, others secret—that have undermined both civil liberties and accountability without, in the process, safeguarding the nation's security.

The Early Years:
Creation and Proscribed Growth

When drafting the U.S. Constitution, the framers sought to create an effective national government and yet one of limited powers. The Constitution did not specifically define the federal government's powers to tax, conduct foreign relations and negotiate tariffs, enact legislation, and raise and maintain a standing army. The federal government was barred from intruding on the powers of the states, although the boundary between state and federal responsibilities was not clearly defined. Prosecution of crimes against persons and property was not explicitly spelled out as a federal responsibility and was to have been principally (if not exclusively) a state responsibility. Accordingly, when fleshing out the framework of the executive branch, Congress established by law departments of state, war, the navy, and the treasury, to be headed by secretaries who were authorized to appoint the personnel essential to conduct foreign relations, protect the nation from foreign and Indian attack, safeguard the nation's ports and foreign commerce, and collect taxes and disburse appropriated funds. In a companion action, Congress established the office of the attorney general. In contrast to other cabinet officers, the attorney general did not head a department but would represent the federal government in cases before the Supreme Court and advise the president and the cabinet on the constitutionality of legislation enacted by the Congress.

Until the late nineteenth century, the principal role of the federal government was to promote foreign commerce, defend the states from foreign and Indian military attack, negotiate the purchase of adjoining territory (in Florida and beyond the Mississippi River), and encourage economic growth. Presidents negotiated and Congress ratified treaties to ensure markets for American goods or the purchase of adjoining territories. Congress enacted protective tariffs, authorized land and monetary subsidies to fund road and railroad construction and to encourage citizens and recent immigrants to cultivate unused land or engage in mining, and granted to state universities the right to federal land in order to fund the training of engineers and the teaching of scientific agriculture. At the time, neither presidents nor members of Congress envisioned a law enforcement role for the federal government.

By the late nineteenth century, federal responsibilities had changed. The nation's rapid industrialization, the rise of large corporations, the development of a nationwide transportation system, new communication technology that broke down formerly regional barriers, and a sharp increase in immigration led Congress to enact laws regulating business and social activities and restricting immigration. A policy of laissez-faire and of local and state, instead of national, regulation could no longer advance societal interests. Railroad rates were regulated (by the Interstate Commerce Act of 1887), mergers that restrained commerce by promoting monopoly were prohibited (by the Sherman Anti-Trust Act of 1890), Chinese immigrants were barred (by the Chinese Exclusion Act of 1882), and obscene literature and advertisements—including literature promoting birth control and contraceptives—were barred from the postal system (by the so-called Comstock Law of 1873).

Prior to the passage of these laws, Congress enacted legislation in 1870 creating a department of justice. This congressional action had been triggered by the crisis of reconstructing the Union following the defeat of the South in the Civil War and the enactment of the Thirteenth Amendment, abolishing slavery. To protect the rights of the liberated slaves, Congress in the late 1860s enacted a series of civil rights laws the enforcement of which necessitated the creation of a new federal department. Nonetheless, when Congress established the Department of Justice, to be headed by the attorney general, the limited number of federal criminal statutes and the nature of proscribed crimes did not necessitate the appointment of a special division of skilled investigators. The attorney general could have established such a force as Congress in March 1871 appropriated $50,000 for the "detection and prosecution of crimes." Rather than relying on a permanent staff of skilled investigators to develop evidence necessary to secure indictments and convictions, U.S. attorneys themselves interviewed witnesses or subpoenaed and reviewed relevant documents. On the rare occasions when they needed the services of skilled investigators, Justice Department attorneys either contracted with private detective agencies (primarily the Pinkerton Detective Agency) or turned to the Secret Service (a Treasury Department agency created in 1869 to investigate violations of federal pay, bounty, and counterfeiting laws).

The first of these options was foreclosed in 1892, when, responding to the publicized strikebreaking activities of the Pinkerton Detective Agency during the Homestead strike of that year, Congress prohibited government agencies from hiring individuals currently employed in the private sector. Intended to prevent conflicts of interest, this legislative ban barred the Justice Department from contracting for the services of private detectives.

The second option was foreclosed in May 1908, when Congress restricted the expenditure of Treasury Department appropriations for purposes other than enforcing pay, bounty, and counterfeiting laws and protecting the president (the authorized responsibilities of the Secret Service). This appropriation rider was triggered by recent revelations, first, that the Navy Department had used Secret Service agents to spy on the sexual activities of a naval officer on leave and, then, that the Justice Department had employed Secret Service agents during an investigation that led to the conviction of two U.S. congressmen for land fraud.

In 1907 and 1908, moreover, Attorney General Charles Bonaparte had unsuccessfully sought to secure funding for a "small detective force" within the Department of Justice. The House Appropriations Subcommittee twice rebuffed Bonaparte's requests.

Significantly, when justifying decisions either to limit Secret Service appropriations or to reject Bonaparte's requests, members of Congress spoke darkly about the threat to limited government and an independent Congress posed by a "spy system," warning ominously about the dangerous consequences of "a general system of spying and espionage of the people, such as has prevailed in [czarist] Russia, in France under the Empire, and at one time in Ireland," or of executive branch officials "employ[ing] secret-service men to dig up the private scandals of men." New York Congressman George Waldo succinctly summarized these underlying fears when counseling against the creation of "a central secret-service bureau such as there is in Russia today."

When Congress rejected Bonaparte's funding requests, the Justice Department could, nonetheless, still rely on Secret Service investigators. But the restriction on Secret Service appropriations foreclosed that option and precipitated a bold and potentially risky decision by the attorney general. On June 29, 1908, relying on the department's "miscellaneous expense fund," Bonaparte hired ten former Secret Service agents as Justice Department employees. Then, on July 26, 1908, he appointed Stanley Finch to head a new, permanent investigative division of thirty-four agents headquartered within the Department of Justice and stationed in Washington, D.C. At the time, Congress was not in session, having adjourned so that members could return to their districts to campaign for their reelection and to support their party's presidential nominee.

Yet, when establishing a bureau of investigation, Bonaparte in effect contravened the spirit of Congress's recent actions. His decision, however, could not ensure the bureau's permanence. Congress could countermand his order either by restricting his use of contingency funds, by rescinding the "detection" section of the 1871 enabling legislation, or by enacting a legislative charter spelling out the parameters of the newly established bureau's investigative authority. Such a possibility loomed when Congress convened in January 1909 in a lame-duck session (it was not until the mid-1930s that the date of the president's inauguration was moved to January from March).

In testimony before a House appropriations subcommittee that January, Bonaparte (at the time the outgoing attorney general, the recently elected William Howard Taft having as yet not nominated his attorney general) sought to justify his independent action and at the same time allay the concerns articulated by members of Congress when rejecting his initiatives of 1907 and 1908 and when adopting the 1908 appropriation restriction. A departmental detective force, he affirmed, was "absolutely indispensable to the discharge" of the Justice Department's enforcement responsibilities. This force, moreover, would investigate only violations of federal antitrust, postal, and banking laws and criminal acts directed at the federal government. Bonaparte counseled against congressional enactment of legislation defining the scope of bureau investigations. Such micromanagement would undermine sound administration. Instead, the attorney general should be held responsible (and subject to impeachment) if agents strayed beyond their law enforcement responsibilities to monitor the personal or political conduct of American citizens. Bonaparte would not object should Congress limit the department's use of appropriated funds to the "detection and prosecution of crimes against the United States." Congress adopted this limitation, forgoing an opportunity to enact a legislative charter for the recently established Bureau of Investigation. This strict requirement was soon lifted when, in 1910, Congress permitted departmental use of appropriated funds "for such other investigations regarding official matters under the control of the Department of Justice as may be directed by the Attorney General." Bureau agents, however, were barred from making arrests or carrying firearms (highlighting continued fears of a federal police force).

Congress's willingness to grant the attorney general greater discretion in the conduct of bureau investigations was triggered by its expansion of the definition of interstate commerce crimes. This action previewed later congressional responses to the transformation of American society in the twentieth century.

The invention of the automobile, the sharp increase in immigration dating from the 1880s, changes in the ethnoreligious character of immigrants during the first decades of the twentieth century, and an internal population flow from rural to urban America caused many in Congress and in the broader public to question whether local and state police alone could adequately curb crime. This perceived need for a supplemental federal law enforcement role underpinned Congress's willingness to fund a sevenfold increase in bureau appropriations from $329,984 in 1911 to $2,457,104 in 1920, with an attendant seventeenfold increase in the number of bureau agents from 34 in 1908 to 579 in 1920.

These changes in public policy reflected new conceptions of the federal government's role that commanded broad support during the so-called Progressive Era. Motivated by concerns to curb corporate monopolies and the power of corrupt political machines, Americans during the first decades of the twentieth century endorsed a stronger federal regulatory role. These concerns extended to social problems—and specifically the growth of so-called red-light districts in the nation's cities. Concluding that local and state police alone could not address the threat to a moral society posed by the growth of houses of prostitution, Congress in 1910 enacted the White Slave Traffic (or Mann) Act, criminalizing the transporting of young women across state lines "for the purpose of prostitution, or for any other immoral purpose." Local and state police seemed incapable of effectively addressing a perceived problem whereby young rural women attracted to the exciting life of the nation's cities were lured into prostitution. The chief proponent of this legislation, Congressmen James Mann, averred that "most of these girls are enticed away from their homes in the country to large cities. The police power exercised by the State and municipal governments is inadequate to prevent this—particularly when girls are enticed from one State to another."

In contrast to other bureau investigations of interstate commerce crimes, which could be triggered by Justice Department officials in Washington, D.C., because they involved publicized mergers or rate practices, uncovering violators of the Mann Act required the initiative of bureau agents stationed in cities around the nation. Agents could visit known houses of prostitution to interview their owners and employees and seek their cooperation in identifying their clients or the local political and police officials who corruptly provided protection. Mann Act prosecutions, moreover, expanded beyond organized prostitution to cases of private morality, wherein minor women were transported across state lines for sexual liaisons even when no profit motive was involved. Over time, the bureau's Mann Act investigations led bureau officials to seek and maintain sensitive information that had no relation to developing federal criminal cases—records that identified the recipients of political payoffs or the prominent citizens who patronized houses of prostitution. And, if the purpose behind the Mann Act was to curb organized crime, the broader bureau investigations engendered limited opposition because they were responsive to the moralistic fears of the time. The most notorious of these cases involved the African American heavyweight boxing champion Jack Johnson.

Johnson's flamboyant lifestyle and success in the boxing ring challenged the widely held racial prejudices of the time. His open consorting with white women in particular made him the target of interest of local and federal law enforcement agents. Johnson was arrested in October 1912 by the Chicago police on the charge of abducting Lucile Cameron, a nineteen-year-old white woman from Minneapolis. Cameron was, at the time, living with Johnson in a common-law marriage. The police responded to a complaint from Cameron's mother that Johnson had abducted her daughter. But they were unable to sustain the charge. Lucile Cameron refused to corroborate it and, instead, married Johnson a month and a half later. Johnson's exoneration, however, proved to be short-lived. On November 7, 1912, he was indicted by a federal grand jury on the charge of violating the Mann Act, an indictment based on the testimony of another white woman, Belle Schreiber. A former prostitute, Schreiber claimed that Johnson had paid her travel costs from Pittsburgh to Chicago, thereby violating the "immoral purpose" section of the Mann Act. In the ensuing trial, Johnson admitted to knowing Schreiber and paying her travel costs to Chicago but denied paying her for sex. He was, nonetheless, convicted in May 1913, sentenced to one year in prison, and fined $1,000 (aborting his successful boxing career).

This use of the Mann Act to target controversial personalities also led to the indictment of the Ku Klux Klan leader Edward Clarke in March 1923. Clarke was charged and convicted of taking Laurel Marten from Houston to New Orleans in 1921 for sexual purposes. Clarke pled guilty to the charge of violating the Mann Act. Given the puritanical morality espoused by Klan leaders and commanding wide support from the Klan's members, Clarke's conviction served to discredit the Klan's leadership and contributed to its eventual decline in the late 1920s.

Mann Act prosecutions increased steadily until 1917, abated during World War I owing to the priority of espionage investigations, and then rose again during the moralistic 1920s. They declined sharply, however, in the decades after the 1930s, a decline triggered in part by an adverse public reaction to FBI Director Hoover's leadership of vice squad raids in Miami in 1937 and 1940. These raids represented the response of FBI officials to a request from Florida's attorney general for assistance. The attorney general justified his request as occasioned by the seeming indifference of the police and public officials in Miami to the widely publicized operation of houses of prostitution. Hoover's grandstanding when leading these highly publicized raids, which led to the arrest of prominent Miamians, alarmed both liberals and conservatives, who criticized this transgression of states' rights as, in the words of the *New York Daily News* editor and publisher Joseph Patterson, "a convenient instrument to blackmail."

Support for a federal law enforcement role received a further boost in 1919, the by-product of Congress's enactment of the Motor Vehicle Theft (or Dyer) Act. Responding to the surge in automobile sales—and an attendant increase in automobile theft—members of Congress in the Dyer Act expanded the definition of interstate commerce crimes to include cases in which stolen automobiles were transported across state lines. Like the Mann Act, the Dyer Act captured a growing conviction that local and state police could not by themselves address certain crimes and, thus, that there was a need for a supplementary federal role.

Bureau officials were also able to exploit the publicized record of arrests and recovered property in the Dyer Act to strengthen a perception of the bureau's efficiency and cost effectiveness. Indeed, during his congressional testimony of 1922, Bureau Director William Burns specifically cited the value of the stolen motor vehicles recovered by the bureau as "more than our appropriations." FBI Director Hoover repeated this rationale in 1970 when citing the bureau's recovery of 30,599 stolen vehicles the previous year and its record of securing convictions in 3,694 stolen vehicle cases.

World War I and the Origins of Political Surveillance

The crisis of World War I both enhanced and challenged the bureau's stature. When military conflict broke out in Europe in 1914, the Wilson administration initially proclaimed U.S. neutrality and affirmed the right of Americans to trade and travel freely under international law. Endorsing this stand, many German and Irish Americans, pacifists, socialists, and radical trade unionists nonetheless vociferously opposed U.S. involvement and questioned the Wilson administration's neutrality. This dissent abated but did not end when, on April 6, 1917, Congress declared war on the Central Powers of Germany and Austria-Hungary. In the ensuing years—until the November 1919 Senate debate over ratification of the Treaty of Versailles—the administration feared that domestic opposition could undermine its foreign policy goals, whether those were to mobilize the nation to ensure military victory or to contain the spread of the Bolshevik Revolution. For the achievement of these goals required public support for the potentially controversial policies of raising a conscript army, increasing federal spending (from a prewar annual average of $750 million in 1917 to over $18 billion by 1919), and pursuing nonrecognition and limited military intervention to ensure the defeat of the Bolsheviks in the Russian Civil War of 1917–1921. The Wilson administration particularly feared that, given the large immigrant population (especially German and Irish, the latter likely sympathetic to the cause of Irish independence) and the growth of militant anarchist and socialist movements during the prewar years, many American citizens and resident aliens might be open to recruitment to commit espionage and sabotage.

Fears of an internal security threat were not groundless. Prior to 1917, for example, bureau agents had uncovered incidents in which German agents (including German consular officers) sought to sabotage the shipment of military goods from the United States and Canada to Great Britain and France. In addition, between 1915 and 1917, explosive devices were discovered on forty-seven ships bound for England and France, and, on July 30, 1916, and January 11, 1917, suspicious fires resulted in explosions at a munitions dump on Black Tom Island in New York City's harbor and at a munitions firm in Kingsland, New Jersey. The leadership of the Socialist Party and of the radical Industrial Workers of the World (IWW), moreover, attributed wars to the inevitable expansionist needs of capitalist imperialism and claimed that peace required the overthrow of a capitalist economic system.

Prior to U.S. military involvement, Congress acted to contain a possible internal security threat and, in 1916, appropriated funds authorizing the secretary of state to request bureau investigations of foreign-directed activities. The reality of U.S. military involvement heightened congressional concerns and lent support to legislation meant to curb dangerous dissent. In 1917, Congress enacted the Espionage Act, criminalizing the stealing of government secrets with the intent of aiding the nation's enemies, requiring the fingerprinting and registration of resident aliens from enemy nations, and prohibiting oral and written statements that "willfully" or "falsely" "interfere with the operation or success of the military forces of the United States," "promote the success of its enemies," "cause insubordination, disloyalty, mutiny, or refusal of duty" within the armed services, or "willfully obstruct" military recruitment. Congress also enacted the Selective Service Act of 1917, requiring men aged twenty-one to thirty to register to be drafted for military service; the Sedition Act of 1918, forbidding "any" oral or written expression of "disloyal, profane, scurrilous, or abusive language about the U.S. government, Constitution, or armed services" or "any language intended to . . . encourage resistance to the United States, or promote the cause of its enemies"; and the Immigration Act of 1918, authorizing the deportation of resident aliens who were members of anarchist or revolutionary organizations.

Armed with these new federal laws, bureau investigators never focused solely on spies and saboteurs. Of the more than two thousand convictions obtained under the Espionage and Sedition Acts, for example, none involved German or Austrian agents or their recruited American sympathizers. Bureau agents focused, instead, on radical activists, members of the Socialist Party and of the IWW, and even German Lutheran ministers and others critical of the war or the supporters of Irish independence. Those convicted included Charles Schenck, the general secretary of the Socialist Party, for publishing a pamphlet criticizing conscription, and Eugene Debs, the Socialist Party presidential nominee in 1900, 1904, 1908, 1912, and 1920, for a speech he gave in Dayton, Ohio, criticizing the Wilson administration's conduct of the war. In September 1917, bureau agents raided the offices of the IWW, seizing the organization's records, and arresting 165 of its leaders and members. In the ensuing trials, the principal evidence used to obtain convictions involved the IWW's prewar publications condemning corporate influence in the forging of both domestic policy and an imperialist foreign policy. Bureau agents also conducted intimidating interviews of pacifists, of German and Irish Americans, and of others who criticized conscription or the Liberty Bond drives. These activists were urged to desist from their "seditious" views or lectured on proper "Americanism," implying that their continued "disloyal" speech could lead to prosecution. Ironically, one of those convicted for violating the Espionage Act was the producer of a Hollywood movie on the American revolution (*The Spirit of '76*), a film that portrayed the nation's wartime ally, Great Britain, in a negative light.

The bureau's personnel did not increase in tandem with these internal security responsibilities. Both because of budgetary reasons and because these increased investigative responsibilities were believed to be temporary, the number of bureau agents expanded only slightly during the war years, from 570 in 1917 to 630 in 1919. Instead, on March 22, 1917, Bureau Director A. Bruce Bielaski obtained Attorney General Thomas Gregory's approval for a liaison relationship with the American Protective League (APL), a conservative businessmen's organization headquartered in Chicago. APL members were encouraged to forward to their bureau contacts "information concerning the activities of agents of foreign Governments or persons unfriendly to this Government for the protection of private property, etc." In actuality, APL members focused on radical antiwar and labor union activists. In their most controversial action, APL members assisted bureau agents in a September 1918 raid that was intended to enforce the Selective Service Act of 1917 and that resulted in the arrests of thousands of New Yorkers. Because many of those arrested were prominent businessmen who had registered for the draft but simply were not carrying their registration cards, and because APL members had no authority to effect arrests, these highly publicized "slacker" raids provoked critical press and congressional commentary. The bureau's role escaped the brunt of this criticism, which focused on the failure of Justice Department officials to monitor the actions of the APL closely enough.

The bureau's interest in radical activists intensified following the November 1917 Bolshevik Revolution and the revolutionary government's call for worldwide revolution and funding of the Third Internationale. Despite the fact that few American citizens or alien residents belonged to either the

Communist or the Communist Labor Parties (by 1919, both had a com-bined membership of only seventy thousand), bureau officials were equally troubled by the growth of a militant labor union movement during the war years. Responsive to the frustration of many American workers over their limited wage gains during the prosperous war years, and emboldened by the recent upsurge in union membership, labor leaders in 1919 led thirty-six hundred strikes involving over four million workers. Corporate executives, newspaper editors, and many national leaders portrayed this wave of strikes as a forerunner of a violent revolution.

This antiradical climate was further inflamed by a series of publicized bombing attempts. In April 1919, a servant of Senator Thomas Hardwick was killed on opening a mail bomb addressed to the senator. Postal officials soon discovered additional packets containing bombs addressed to various prominent citizens, among them Postmaster General Albert Burleson, Sec-retary of Labor William Wilson, and the millionaires John D. Rockefeller and J. Pierpont Morgan. The culminating event came on June 2, 1919, when a bomb exploded at the front door of Attorney General A. Mitchell Palmer's home, killing the man carrying the bomb. That same night, explo-sions occurred in eight other cities.

Responding to these April bombing incidents, Bureau Director William Flynn that same month ordered "a vigorous and comprehensive" investiga-tion of all anarchists, Communists, and "kindred" agitators. Cognizant that the bureau's authority to investigate radicals would terminate with the for-mal end of the war (the Espionage and Sedition Acts authorized only war-time investigations and further required evidence of intent to assist the nation's enemies), Flynn nonetheless ordered bureau agents to secure evi-dence "which may be of use in prosecutions under the existing statutes or under legislation of that nature which may hereinafter be enacted."

Flynn's order was soon supplemented by Attorney General Palmer's Au-gust 1919 decision creating a special Radical Division (renamed the General Intelligence Division, or GID, in 1920). The GID was empowered to collate all information about radical activities collected by bureau agents, the State Department's consular service, military and naval intelligence, or the local police or forwarded by patriotic citizens. By January 1920, one-third of the bureau's agent force was assigned to monitor radical activities.

The GID soon amassed over 200,000 dossiers detailing the activities of radical activists and organizations, including their role in the 1919 strikes. The targets of this massive investigation were also extended to include five hundred foreign-language newspapers (a move justified as essential in order to keep up with "radical propaganda") and the progressive senator and antiwar critic Robert LaFollette, the settlement house reformer and pacifist Jane Addams, the Irish nationalist Eamon deValera and the pro-Irish *Chicago Tribune* and Hearst newspapers, the militant black nationalist and founder of the Universal Negro Improvement Association Marcus Garvey, members and officers of the National Association for the Advancement of Colored People, and the editors of black newspapers and periodicals whom bureau officials suspected of "exciting the negro element of this country to riot and to the committing of outrages of all sorts."

This antiradical campaign, however, could not be sustained unless Congress enacted peacetime sedition legislation. In the interim, bureau officials decided to share information about alien radicals that agents had developed with the Immigration Bureau. Such information could be used to deport members of organizations proscribed by the attorney general as anarchist or revolutionary under provisions of the 1918 Immigration Act. The first such use occurred on November 7, 1919, when bureau agents raided the offices of the Union of Russian Workers (URW) in New York and eleven other cities. These raids resulted in the arrest of 750. Of these 750, however, only 249 were deported (among them the famed anarchists Emma Goldman and Alexander Berkman). Those 249 left the port of New York on December 21, 1919, on a specially commissioned ship, the *Buford* (publicly dubbed *the Soviet Ark*), to the enthusiastic acclaim of the nation's press. The national law journal *Bench and Bar* commended the deportation proceeding, remarking: "There is only one way to deal with anarchy, and *that is to crush it.*" An even more supportive *Cleveland Plain Dealer* editorialized: "It is hoped and expected that other vessels, larger, more commodious, carrying similar cargoes, will follow in her [the *Buford*'s] wake."

The enthusiastic response to the URW raid encouraged GID Head J. Edgar Hoover and Immigration Bureau Head Anthony Caminetti to implement another bolder and more massive raid. Their coordinated operation was intended to further two different, if complementary, goals—for Caminetti, to expedite Immigration Bureau deportation proceedings and, for Hoover, to create a political climate that would lead Congress to enact peacetime sedition legislation. Their plan required simultaneous raids of branch offices of the Communist and Communist Labor Parties (organizations proscribed by the attorney general as revolutionary) to arrest those alien radicals attending the branch meetings of these organizations and then to deport them under the 1918 immigration statute. Simultaneous raids could ensure that large numbers of individuals would be apprehended, thereby conveying a sense of the seriousness of the revolutionary threat. Success required both using telegraphic warrants that did not specify the individuals to be apprehended and rescinding the rule governing deportation hearings (under the Labor Department's Rule 22, arrested immigrants would have the right to counsel). Capitalizing on the temporary absence of Labor Secretary William Wilson (enforcement of immigration laws was a Labor Department responsibility), Caminetti and Hoover convinced Acting Secretary of Labor John Abercrombie to permit the use of telegraphic warrants and to suspend Rule 22.

Having successfully infiltrated and risen to leadership positions in the Communist and Communist Labor Parties, bureau agents could ensure that the various branches of these parties held simultaneous meetings on January 2, 1920. In raids that night, Bureau of Investigation and Immigration Bureau agents arrested four thousand Communist and Communist Labor Party members, the vast majority of whom were attending branch meetings of these parties in thirty-three cities. An additional two to six thousand were arrested later that night—some apprehended in the vicinity of the meeting places, others at police headquarters, where they had come to inquire about friends or family members who had disappeared.

The so-called Palmer raids initially received widespread positive publicity. Reporters were invited to photograph the arrested radicals (whose unkempt, bearded appearance confirmed the stereotypical image of mad bombers) and to review and photocopy the organizations' publications seized during the raids (seemingly confirming that the arrested radicals were planning a violent revolution). This public relations strategy achieved the desired press coverage, wherein the raids were portrayed, not as deportation proceedings, but as the successful containment of a planned revolution. Indeed, the *New York Times* headlined its article on the raids "Revolution Smashed," and its reporter praised the "clarity, resolute will and fruitful intelligence" of those who had planned the raid. *Bench and Bar* echoed this portrayal, proclaiming: "The need for repression is great, and the time for repression is now." So did Massachusetts Secretary of State Albert Langley, who remarked: "If I had my way, I'd take them out in the yard every morning to shoot them, and the next day would have a trial to see whether they were guilty."

This positive publicity quickly dissipated when cooler heads prevailed. As a result, of the 6,000–10,000 detained, only 3,500 were subject to deportation proceedings (the other detainees having been citizens who either attended the meetings or were swept up during the course of the raids and, either way, should not have been apprehended because they were not liable to deportation). Of these 3,500, only 556 were eventually deported.

Disturbed by the methods employed during the raids, on January 26, 1920, Secretary of Labor Wilson reinstated Rule 22 and prohibited the use of any information that had been obtained from any arrested alien denied the right to counsel during interrogation. In addition, when reviewing the recommendations of hearing boards, Assistant Secretary of Labor Louis Post ruled against deportation unless the 1918 act's standard of "knowing membership" had been met. Wilson's and Post's private concerns were publicly echoed, subjecting the conduct of the raids to critical scrutiny. In May 1920, the liberal National Popular Government League published the findings of twelve distinguished attorneys and legal scholars as *Report upon the Illegal Practices of the United States Department of Justice*. The report's title captures the writers' assessment of the abuses of power underpinning the planning and execution of the raids, and the report itself cited numerous examples of the "continued violation of [the] Constitution and breaking of . . . Laws by the Department of Justice." The authors particularly criticized bureau agents' use of agents provocateurs, lack of legal authority to enforce immigration laws, warrantless arrests, and use of coerced confessions and illegal searches as well as the inhumane conditions under which the arrestees were detained.

Prior to the release of this damning report, Attorney General Palmer publicly condemned Post's actions in overturning deportation rulings, accusing the assistant secretary of labor of coddling dangerous radicals. Palmer's criticisms led members of Congress to initiate hearings to impeach Post. During these hearings, which were conducted by the House Rules Committee, Post rebutted Palmer's criticisms and, in the process, highlighted the abuses employed by bureau agents in their conduct and planning of the raids. The Senate Judiciary Committee revisited this matter in 1921 and, in its final report, sharply condemned Palmer's "deliberate misuse of his office" when abandoning the prosecution of suspected violators of federal statutes to go "into the field of propaganda against radicals." Senator Thomas Walsh chaired these hearings, which lasted from January 19 through March 3, 1921, and pointedly questioned how "one bred in the law could ever have promulgated such an order" to launch the raids. Mercilessly interrogating Palmer and Hoover, both of whom sought to avoid responsibility for the abusive methods employed during the raids, Walsh condemned what he characterized as "the lawless acts of a mob," observing: "There is no warrant in the law for entering a man's house, rifling his drawers, peering into his private papers, and walking off with any document[s] that are his, for any purpose, much less to use as evidence against him."

Unknown at the time to Walsh and to Senate investigators, bureau agents had closely monitored the activities of the legal scholars who had compiled the devastating May 1920 report. Furthermore, Hoover sought to discredit one of the authors, the Harvard Law professor Felix Frankfurter, by questioning his loyalty. Hoover also covertly attempted to assist the efforts of the Harvard overseer Austin Fox to have Harvard trustees dismiss another of the authors, the Harvard Law professor Zechariah Chafee. Hoover had then provided Fox with information to substantiate his claim that Chafee's criticisms were reckless and untrue. Both efforts failed; Hoover had no evidence to support either Frankfurter's alleged disloyalty or Chafee's recklessness. His actions highlight how secrecy permitted both the abuses of the bureau's noncriminal investigations and Bureau officials' subsequent efforts to discredit their respected and responsible critics. Ironically, one by-product of the publicized disclosures of the bureau's abusive conduct in the Palmer raids was that, in 1921, Congress repealed the Sedition Act of 1918.

Abuse of Power, Retrenchment, and Morality

Rebuffed in their attempt to expand the bureau's authority to investigate "seditious" activities in peacetime, bureau officials nonetheless continued in the immediate aftermath of the Palmer raids debacle to monitor radical labor union and civil rights activities. They remained convinced that the Palmer raids had succeeded in effecting "a marked cessation of radical activities in the United States." Accordingly, bureau agents sought to ascertain whether radicals were responsible for precipitating the flurry of strikes and labor organizational activities of the immediate postwar years. Indeed, in October 1920, J. Edgar Hoover broadened the role of the General Intelligence Division (GID) from its original focus on "radical activities in the United States and abroad" to cover "the studying of matters of an international nature, as well as economic and industrial disturbances incident thereto."

Bureau investigations also focused on the more militant civil rights and black nationalist movements that emerged during the interwar years in response to the deterioration of the rights of black Americans following the segregation of the federal bureaucracy in 1913 and of the armed services during World War I. This disaffection underlay the race riots that erupted in twenty-six of the nation's cities during the summer of 1919. Unconvinced that racial prejudice was the cause of black militancy, bureau officials instead concluded that Communist influence was responsible for the encouragement by the National Association for the Advancement of Colored People (NAACP) of black protest and Marcus Garvey's espousal of black nationalism. Bureau investigations of the NAACP and of Garvey's Universal Negro Improvement Association, however, uncovered no evidence of either organization's involvement in espionage or seditious activities. Unable to ensure Garvey's deportation (he was a resident alien), bureau officials in 1923 secured his conviction for mail fraud in his administration of the Black Steamship Line and other business enterprises that he had formed to promote the economic independence of black Americans.

Bureau agents also sought information that could undermine the appeal of the militant white supremacist Ku Klux Klan. Responding to Louisiana

Governor John Parker's request for federal assistance because state authorities were unable to curb the increasingly powerful Klan, bureau officials
were, nonetheless, limited by the fact that Klan violence and vigilante
methods violated no federal law. Unable to secure the conviction of Klan
leaders under the federal civil rights laws of the 1860s, bureau officials instead shifted tactics to effect the conviction of Klan leader Edward Clarke
for violating the Mann Act.

The Klan and Garvey cases highlight the limitations on bureau operations during the interwar years, years marked by the reaffirmation of
states' rights principles and deep suspicions about a dominant federal law
enforcement role. Bureau officials were effectively precluded by this new
politics from recommending prosecution based on the massive files that
bureau agents had accumulated on radical activists. They instead pursued
a different containment strategy, part of which involved seeking to tap
into the strong anti–labor union sentiments held by many in the business
community. In effect intervening in the interwar labor-management conflict, bureau officials willingly shared with business leaders information
that bureau agents had developed about the organizational and strike
strategies of labor activists. In September 1922, moreover, Attorney General Harry Daugherty obtained a sweeping court injunction against the
railroad workers union for promoting a nationwide railroad strike. In response, a bureau investigation was launched, leading to the arrest of over
twelve hundred workers for violating the court's injunction and, thus, to
the breaking of the strike.

Bureau officials also resorted to alternative tactics to utilize the information that bureau agents had developed about radical activists. Learning of a
planned secret national Communist Party convention to be held in Bridg-
man, Michigan, in August 1922, bureau agents raided the meeting, seizing
Party records and capturing some of those in attendance. Because no evidence had been developed that any federal law had been violated, bureau
officials turned over the records seized to the Michigan state police, who
unsuccessfully sought to convict Charles Ruthenberg, the Party secretary,
and William Foster, the Party's liaison to the labor movement, under the
state's anarchist and syndicalist laws. Similar assistance to state authorities in
New York and Arizona did result in the conviction of other Communist
leaders under those states' anarchist and syndicalist statutes. Bureau officials
also shared the information obtained in their monitoring of Communist

activities with the director of the conservative American Defense Society, Richard Whitney, who wrote a series of critical articles for the *Boston Evening Transcript.*

These initiatives proved promising insofar as they conformed to the conceptions held by many American conservatives during the 1920s about labor union and radical activists. Even so, the conservative principles that underpinned the so-called New Era lent support to limited government based on the rule of law. Because bureau officials nonetheless continued to resort to extralegal practices, their actions precipitated a serious crisis that, by 1924, raised anew heightened concerns about the perils of a secret federal police force and about the leadership of Bureau Director William Burns.

The specific catalyst of this crisis was a 1923 Senate investigation launched by Democratic Senators Burton Wheeler and Thomas Walsh into Secretary of the Interior Albert Fall's questionable awarding to the businessmen Edward Doheny and Harry Sinclair of the rights, without competitive bidding, to valuable oil reserves in Teapot Dome, Wyoming, and Elk Hills, California. These reserves had been set aside during World War I for navy use. Suspecting collusion, Wheeler and Walsh succeeded in uncovering a corrupt bargain whereby Fall had received $100,000 from Doheny and Sinclair in exchange for granting these leases. Fall was subsequently convicted and sentenced to one year in prison. In 1924 hearings, the Senate committee shifted its focus to Attorney General Harry Daugherty and to why he had quashed a Justice Department investigation into this deal and, then, why the Justice Department had not investigated other fraudulent sales of war materials.

Prior to the inception of the committee's hearings, Bureau Director Burns had ordered bureau agents to investigate Wheeler's activities in Montana and Walsh's and Wheeler's activities in Washington, D.C. During these investigations, agents tapped Wheeler's and Walsh's phones, opened their mail, and broke into their offices and homes. They even attempted to lure Wheeler into a compromising sexual liaison.

The bureau's investigation led a grand jury in Montana to indict Wheeler for corruption. Wheeler, however, won acquittal. His trial, which began in March 1924, proved embarrassing to the Justice Department as witnesses admitted to committing perjury during their grand jury testimony while defense attorneys were able to establish that the Justice Department had manufactured evidence in an effort to discredit Wheeler—and to leave the definite impression that the purpose in doing so was to undermine the credibility of the investigation that he and Walsh had demanded of the Teapot Dome scandal.

The bureau's monitoring of Wheeler and Walsh commanded wide publicity, with Bureau Director Burns admitting during congressional testimony to a variety of questionable actions taken in the course of the bureau's investigation of Wheeler. The inquiry further established, through the testimony of one of the more flamboyant bureau agents, Gaston Means, that the bureau had monitored other congressional critics of the Harding administration—Senators Robert LaFollette, Thaddeus Caraway, and William Borah and Congressmen Roy Woodruff and Oskar Keller.

These revelations—following the scandals of the 1918 "slacker" raids and the 1920 Palmer raids—highlight how the creation of a secret federal police force could threaten a democratic society. The publicized abuses of power would seem to have confirmed the dire warnings expressed by congressional critics in 1907–1908. However, no attempt was made in 1924 to dissolve the bureau.

By 1924, public policy had come to be based on the necessity of a federal law enforcement role—a necessity confirmed by the passage of the Mann and Dyer Acts and the increases in bureau personnel and appropriations. As important, the conception of responsible governance shaping the politics of the Progressive Era and, then, the more conservative New Era was that corruption and abuses of power were the by-products of the quality of the personnel hired and the efficiency of administrators. Future abuses could be prevented by improving the professionalism of bureau personnel and by a principled attorney general instituting tighter rules.

Accordingly, President Calvin Coolidge (who succeeded to the presidency following Harding's death in August 1923) demanded that Daugherty resign when the attorney general refused to honor a subpoena to testify and produce requested records during the Senate inquiry into Teapot Dome. In one of his first acts, Daugherty's replacement, Harlan Fiske Stone, the dean of Columbia University Law School, fired Burns on May 9, 1924.

The new attorney general sought to restore public confidence in the bureau and to squelch the worsening scandal. Stone conceded "the possibility that a secret police may become a menace to free government and free institutions, because it carries with it the possibility of abuses of power which are not always quickly understood." To prevent this, he imposed strict restrictions on bureau operations, first by dissolving the GID, then by banning wiretapping, and finally by issuing orders confining future bureau investigations to violations of federal laws and barring the sharing of information with business leaders and state authorities. The bureau, Stone emphasized, would not be "concerned with political or other opinions of individuals . . . only with their conduct and then only with such conduct as is forbidden by the laws of the United States." A properly restrained federal investigative force was needed, Stone continued, given the "enormous expansion of Federal legislation, both civil and criminal, in recent years."

To replace the discredited Burns, and to ensure a disciplined and professionalized staff, Stone appointed the then assistant bureau director, J. Edgar Hoover, as acting director on May 10, 1924. This appointment was made permanent in December 1924 as the attorney general had by then concluded that Hoover had demonstrated the required disinterested professionalism. Stone had selected Hoover because of his reputation as a stern taskmaster. He had been willing to consider the youthful Hoover (twenty-nine at the time) despite his involvement in the planning and execution of the Palmer raids and in the surveillance of Senator Wheeler. Hoover's fault was that of a loyal subordinate who followed the orders of his superiors—attributes essential to an efficiently managed bureaucracy. Given the underlying assumption of the New Era that acts of corruption such as those leading to the Teapot Dome scandal stemmed from the independent actions of individuals of low character, Hoover's commitment to strict discipline and unquestionable integrity could effect the needed administrative reforms. The new bureau director immediately initiated a housecleaning of bureau ranks, firing timeservers and part-time employees (many of whom were political appointees and, as in the case of Gaston Means, viewed a bureau appointment as an opportunity for personal enrichment). Stricter hiring standards were instituted consistent with Stone's standard: individuals of "known character and ability, giving preference to men who have some legal training."

The new bureau director had inherited an agency steeped in scandal and commanding little public confidence at a time when a fiscally conservative Congress demanded reduced federal spending. Hoover responded to this political reality and, by 1924, had dismissed sixty-two employees, closed five of the bureau's fifty-three field offices, and returned $300,000 to the U.S. Treasury. Overall force levels between 1924 and 1929 were reduced from 441 agents and 216 support staff to 339 agents and 242 support staff (the slight increase in support staff was intended to ensure stricter supervision), while bureau appropriations of $2,245,000 in 1924 barely increased, standing at $2,250,000 in 1929. The number of field offices was reduced further to twenty-two by 1932. In addition, standards for new agents were raised, and a special training school in the New York office was established.*

Sensitive to prevailing states' rights beliefs, Hoover established in July 1924 the new Investigative Division within the bureau. This division consolidated a bureau-held fingerprint file, acquired in 1923 from the federal prison facility in Leavenworth, Kansas, and fingerprint records compiled by the International Association of Chiefs of Police, until then housed in Chicago. This centralized depository proved particularly useful for local and state police, enabling them to identify criminals who had committed crimes in other locales.† Then, in November 1932, Director Hoover authorized the establishment of the Laboratory Division to assist bureau investigations through the use of the latest technology—microscopes, a collection of automobile tire tracks, and a large gun collection.‡

More important, Hoover instituted new rules to ensure a more disciplined and professional corps of agents. Agents had to meet rigorous dress, deportment, and personal conduct standards. They were subject to "call for duty at all times," required to "give due regard to their personal appearances," and forbidden "to furnish to the press, either directly or indirectly any information." The appointment process was placed beyond the reach of political influence, while judgment of the "quality and quantity" of an agent's performance was to be based on clearly defined rules. Each agent was given a copy of the regularly updated *Manual of Regulations,* which outlined the standards governing the conduct of investigations. The bureau director regularly issued "Bureau Bulletins" to agents describing current rules and procedures and "SAC Letters" to heads of field offices, SACs or special agents in charge, describing new or revised rules. He also established the special Inspection Division to evaluate whether agents complied with rules and met their responsibilities efficiently. Derelict agents were issued letters of reprimand; continued deficiencies resulted in dismissal.

* Training was transferred to the Washington, D.C., field office in 1928 and then to a specially created facility in Quantico, Virginia, in 1972.

† By 1996, what had become the Fingerprint Division had amassed over 200 million fingerprint sets.

‡ The laboratory eventually included handwriting analysts, forensic scientists, specialists in digital imagery and computers, and polygraphers.

Hoover's various reforms did serve to refurbish the bureau's image, particularly since they accorded with the priorities shaping New Era politics — efficiency, rationality, high moral character, and limited government. These priorities were embodied in the Fingerprint Division's role: providing to state and local police an essential administrative service that relied on the latest technology. This limited role comported with states' rights principles: independent and geographically dispersed police agencies benefited at the same time that law enforcement remained a local and state responsibility.

The attempt to tap into the moralistic concerns of the New Era also underpinned Hoover's March 24, 1925, decision to create the Obscene File (to be maintained separately from other bureau records and, eventually, in the FBI Laboratory). The bureau director's purpose was to ensure that "any obscene matter of any nature whatsoever" would be maintained in a centralized depository. All such materials were to be sent to bureau headquarters in sealed envelopes marked OBSCENE.

A separately maintained Obscene File served two purposes. First, it restricted access to obscene or pornographic materials (which included stag films, freehand drawings, novels, strip cartoons, nudist publications, playing cards, and photographs) that "may arouse the curiosity of Bureau employees." Such materials were not to be "shown to other personnel in the office who have no need to observe it." Second, a centralized, permanent collection could ensure that purveyors of pornographic and obscene literature directed at "school children or adults with perverted minds" could be successfully prosecuted, in the process promoting a more positive image of the bureau. In a 1946 directive, Hoover extolled this public relations windfall: "Each obscene literature investigation possesses potential publicity value because of the very nature of the investigation. Every Special Agent in Charge should closely follow obscene matter investigations in order that consideration may be given to obtaining proper publicity in appropriate cases. Where it is contemplated that publicity will result . . . the Special Agent in Charge . . . [must] notify [FBI] headquarters in advance of any contemplated arrest, arraignment, or other development prior to the time any publicity is released." He emphasized that such prosecution could help curb "juvenile delinquency," adding that "local vice and crime is also stimulated through the circulation of pornography and in some instances racial agitation is inflamed."

Bureau officials instituted another practice in 1930, one that further enhanced the bureau's image in the guise of an effort to promote local law enforcement. An annual summary of crime statistics, the *Uniform Crime Reports,* was compiled and publicly released. This quantification of crime trends and the incidence of serious crime proved to be useful to local and state police officials while indirectly highlighting the bureau's important coordinating role and superior professionalism.

The 1920s bureau projected the image of a leaner and more professional agency—and yet a minor player in the law enforcement field. Bureau officials, however, had not abandoned an interest in radical political activities. Bureau agents continued to monitor radical activists and organizations but disguised their sources, reporting that the information that they had collected had been volunteered by patriotic citizens or provided by "confidential informants." Conservative citizens were particularly encouraged to continue volunteering information on the political activities and associations of radical and liberal activists (such as the Communist Party and the American Civil Liberties Union).

Then, with the dramatic change in national politics following the stock market crash of October 1929 and the onset of the Great Depression, the bureau director sought to ensure that President Herbert Hoover was fully informed about the plans of his critics. In October 1931, for example, Hoover responded to the president's request for an investigation of George Menhinick. The editor of a financial newsletter, Menhinick had sharply criticized Hoover's predictions of economic recovery as grandstanding. Bureau agents did investigate Menhinick, while five agents were dispatched to the editor's home in what proved to be a successful attempt at intimidation. The interviewing agents reported back that Menhinick was "scared" and unlikely to "resume the dissemination of any information concerning the banks or other financial institutions." In 1932, bureau agents also infiltrated the so-called Bonus March of the thousands of World War I veterans who had converged on Washington, D.C., to pressure Congress to update to that year, rather than 1945, the date on which they would receive their authorized bonuses. Bureau agents sought information that the beleaguered president, up for reelection, could use to discredit the marchers as criminals or Communists.

These harassment and surveillance actions were, however, exceptional. During the 1920s, the bureau focused primarily on law enforcement, with one exception. It had no authority to investigate violations of the Prohibition statute, a responsibility assigned to the special Prohibition Bureau within the Treasury Department. The unpopularity of this law—flaunted by college students and proprietors of speakeasies—contributed to a culture of lawlessness and created lucrative opportunities for bootleggers. Organized crime gangs moved in to capitalize on this demand, paying off corrupt police officials and municipal leaders in the process. When warring gangs engaged in violence and the local police proved unable to stop them, an alarmed citizenry demanded a more effective policing role. These demands, however, did not automatically ensure an expansion of the bureau's power.

The New Deal and a War on Crime

The stock market crash of October 1929 ushered in the Great Depression, reshaping the politics of the 1930s. The severity of this economic crisis undermined the presidency of the incumbent Republican president, Herbert Hoover. Exploiting Hoover's unpopularity, the Democratic presidential nominee, Franklin Roosevelt, promoted during the course of the 1932 election what he called the New Deal, an expansion of the federal role in order to alleviate suffering and promote economic recovery. This campaign called for bold new initiatives, tapped into public discontent, and led to Roosevelt's overwhelming victory.

The newly elected president moved quickly to steer through Congress a series of laws initiating the New Deal. Roosevelt's New Deal marked a radical departure in national politics, the rejection of long-held laissez-faire principles of limited government in favor of a more activist and interventionist federal role. It also marked a shift away from the states' rights principles governing law enforcement toward acceptance of an enhanced federal role in curbing crime.

The enactment of Prohibition had, ironically, helped create a culture of lawlessness during the 1920s. Americans brazenly flaunted the law, and bootleggers and gangsters serviced the demand for alcoholic beverages. At the same time, the early 1930s were marked by a seemingly unprecedented wave of kidnappings and bank robberies. This perception was popularized by the nation's print media as, for example, between 1920 and 1930 the *New York Times* published forty-three feature stories on bank robberies in Midwestern and Southwestern states (Oklahoma, Arkansas, Indiana, Kansas, and Missouri). Not only were gangsters seemingly able to violate the law with impunity, but local and state police were also seemingly unable to maintain law and order because they were corrupt or lacked the needed resources or skills. An expanded federal policing role—and not simply a federal law enforcement agency acting as a clearinghouse or a coordinator—seemed essential to resolving this perceived crime problem. As one result, between 1932 and 1936, Congress almost doubled bureau appropriations, from $2,978,520 to $5,000,000, and almost doubled bureau personnel, from 821 to 1,580. Bureau agents were no longer obscure detectives; they had become, instead, the revered "G-men" who "always got their man." This popular image of bureau efficiency and professionalism contrasted with that of the overwhelmed state and local police agent, unable to protect the citizenry from brazen and violent criminals.

Two dramatic and highly publicized developments contributed to this new sense of crisis and the creation of an opening for a more powerful FBI. The first involved the kidnapping, on March 1, 1932, of the twenty-month-old son of the famed aviator Charles Lindbergh from the family estate in Hopewell, New Jersey. The kidnapper left a ransom note demanding $50,000. In the ensuing search, volunteers and the New Jersey police were unable to find the infant boy. Fearing the worse, the worried parents accepted the mediation of a retired New York City principal, John Condon, who delivered the ransom money (in marked gold certificates) during a meeting in the Bronx on April 2 in exchange for information on the location of the Lindbergh baby. Condon was told that the baby could be found in a boat near Martha's Vineyard, Massachusetts. The boat was never located, and, on May 12, the baby's body was found in a shallow grave just a few miles from the Lindbergh mansion.

Kidnapping was not, at the time, a federal crime. Nonetheless, President Hoover authorized all federal agencies to cooperate with the New Jersey police. Months passed without any progress. Finally, on October 19, 1933, President Roosevelt ordered the bureau to take charge of the investigation and coordinate the efforts of local and state police and other federal agencies. This initiative brought no immediate result—until, in September 1934, bureau officials received a crucial tip. A New York City gas station attendant had marked down the license plate number of a customer, his suspicions aroused by having been paid with a $10 gold certificate when, the nation having recently abandoned the gold standard, such certificates had gone out of circulation. His action proved crucial: on processing the certificate, a Manhattan bank found it to be one of the marked bills. Informed of the discovery, bureau agents checked with the New York Division of Motor Vehicles and identified the car's owner as Bruno Hauptmann. Arrested on September 20, 1934, Hauptmann was charged and convicted of kidnapping and murdering the Lindbergh baby.

The publicized role of bureau agents in locating and convicting Hauptmann enhanced the bureau's reputation. Hauptmann's discovery had been the result of a series of lucky developments. Nonetheless, the methods employed by bureau agents (publicized during the trial) highlighted their scientific expertise and essential professionalism—a bureau handwriting expert testified during the trial that the ransom note had been written by

Hauptmann, and bureau agents, with the assistance of a Forest Service employee, were able to link Hauptmann to the kidnapping through a handmade wooden ladder found at the scene of the kidnapping.

The second development was the brazen criminal activity of a host of violent gangsters during the early 1930s, activity that received dramatic coverage in the nation's print media. The exploits of these gangsters, assigned colorful nicknames by crime reporters and commentators—"Bonnie and Clyde" (Bonnie Parker and George Clyde Barrow), George "Machine Gun" Kelly, Frank "Jelly" Nash, Lester Gillis "Baby Face" Nelson, Arizona "Ma" Barker, Alvin "Creepy" Karpis, and Charles "Pretty Boy" Floyd—captured the attention of a fascinated public. These violently antisocial gangsters were portrayed as posing unprecedented threats because of their blatant disregard for human life and ability to cross state lines easily and quickly in that relatively recent invention the automobile.*

The foremost of these was "Handsome" John Dillinger, dubbed by bureau officials "Public Enemy Number One." Between May 1933 and July 1934, Dillinger robbed ten banks in five states. On one occasion, he even robbed a police station of guns and ammunition and, on another, brazenly escaped from a Crown Point, Indiana, jail after having been photographed at the time of his incarceration with the local sheriff, Lillian Holley, and prosecutor, Robert Estill. Dillinger added insult to injury by sending a photograph of himself holding the wooden gun that he had used in his escape to an Indianapolis newspaper.

Bank robbery, like kidnapping, was not, at the time, a federal offense, although Dillinger's exploits seemed to confirm the inadequacy, if not the incompetence, of the local and state police. Bureau officials nonetheless tapped into the loss of faith thus engendered by moving quickly to apprehend Dillinger, not for robbing banks, but for having violated the Dyer Act by crossing state lines in stolen automobiles in the course of his bank robbery spree.

Bureau officials were, at first, publicly embarrassed by their own failure to capture Dillinger in a raid in Little Bohemia, a resort town in northern Wisconsin, having received a tip that he was vacationing there. This embarrassment was soon offset by a second, more successful effort. Alerted, on July 21, 1934, by Anna Sage (a female companion of Dillinger's

* The sense of crisis that these gangsters generated seems remarkable by postwar standards in that they operates alone or in small gangs, not in the vast organized crime syndicates that we know today.

who volunteered the information in return for reward money and bureau intercession to prevent her deportation) that Dillinger planned to attend the screening of a movie at the Chicago Biograph that evening, bureau agents devised a plan that ultimately proved successful: establishing a stake-out and killing him as he left the theater.

The Dillinger and Lindbergh cases provided the catalyst for a radical change in federal policy. As early as 1933, Attorney General Homer Cummings had proposed that Congress enact what he called the Twelve Point Crime Program to expand federal law enforcement powers. Congress did not, at first, honor this request, in part because it gave priority to addressing the economic crisis, and in part because it was unwilling to abandon states' rights principles. Events conspired, however, to change congressmen's minds.

The bureau's successes in apprehending Hauptmann and Dillinger followed on other equally publicized cases seemingly confirming how limiting the bureau's powers denied the nation the resources necessary to curbing a serious crime problem. The most electrifying of these cases occurred in the Kansas City, Missouri, railroad station on June 17, 1933, when four criminal associates of Frank Nash's engaged in a gun battle with the state police and bureau agents escorting Nash to the federal penitentiary in Leavenworth, Kansas. Two bureau agents were killed (as was Nash himself), highlighting both the indifference to life of hardened criminals and how prevailing restrictions hamstrung bureau agents, preventing them from addressing this threat. The agents' deaths proved crucial in leading Congress to enact legislation empowering bureau agents to carry guns.

Five highly publicized ransom kidnappings conducted between June 15, 1933, and January 19, 1934, and involving prominent businessmen, by contrast, highlighted the prowess and professionalism of bureau personnel, who succeeded in capturing notorious criminals where the local and state police had failed. In the case of the kidnapped oilman Charles Urschel, bureau agents were, on the basis of their diligent research of weather records and airplane schedules, able to locate the hideout of Urschel's kidnapper, George "Machine Gun" Kelly. In the process, they acquired the popular nickname "G-men" when, at the time of his capture on September 26, 1933, a frightened Kelly reportedly pled: "Don't shoot, G-men."

The G-man image was concurrently popularized by the growing film industry, which had its own, commercial interest in capitalizing on the public's fascination with notorious gangsters. In a series of movies released in the mid-1930s (six in 1935 alone) under such titles as *G-Men, Public Enemy*

Number One, and *Show Them No Mercy,* Hollywood graphically portrayed the cruel brutality of gangsters and the cool professionalism and dedication of bureau agents. In the ensuing years, FBI officials worked closely with Hollywood producers to convey a carefully crafted image of the FBI as a highly disciplined, ethical, and professional organization.

This image was also widely disseminated in popular magazines (*Colliers, Popular Science, Redbook, American Magazine*), cartoon strips ("War on Crime," "Secret Agent X-9"), and radio shows ("Radio Crimebusters," "Gangbusters"). Alert to the value of publicity, FBI Director Hoover extolled the bureau's successes in his book *Persons in Hiding* (1938) and in a series of articles in popular magazines (some ghostwritten by Courtney Ryley Cooper). He succeeded in personalizing the problem of the gangsters' brutality and conveying the sense of a moral confrontation between good and evil, a confrontation to be won only by skilled, highly trained, and disciplined professionals.

Astute bureaucrat that he was, Hoover was not content to rely on his own media access to shape the public's understanding. Instead, beginning in the mid-1930s, he launched a continuing and well-managed public relations campaign, one led by FBI Assistant Director Louis Nichols. As head of the Crime Records Division, Nichols was able to exploit his control over FBI records to promote favorable press coverage through carefully orchestrated leaks of information.

This public relations campaign succeeded because, by the mid 1930s, the public had accepted the need for an enhanced federal role. The original champion of this change was President Roosevelt. In his January 3, 1934, State of the Union address to Congress, the popular president identified crime as a serious threat to "our security" and one that required the "strong arm of [the federal] Government" to combat it. Roosevelt demanded that Congress enact the Twelve Point Crime Program that Attorney General Homer Cummings had proposed in July 1933 to expand federal jurisdiction to include kidnapping, extortion, and bank robbery. "The safety of our country," Cummings had warned, was threatened by the "organized forces of crime" operating "across State lines." Because of the seriousness of this crime threat, an increased federal role was imperative: "The police of the great cities were hopelessly corrupt. The rural system of crime control which was lodged in the sheriff and the constable was unsuited to modern conditions. If the elements of an offense were not all committed in a single State, such criminals might sometime escape prosecution altogether."

By the 1930s, a majority of Americans had concluded that crime was a national and not simply a local problem, convinced by the fact of organized gangs crossing state lines to commit crimes and, in the process, escaping apprehension by police hamstrung by regional boundaries. Responding to Roosevelt's and Cummings's lobbying efforts, Congress endorsed a new view of federal-state relations aptly summarized in a *Philadelphia Record* editorial: only "a central agency can supervise our national battle against organized crime." Congress did not, however, approve Cummings's Twelve Point Crime Program in its entirety. Only six of his twelve recommendations were enacted. Still, kidnapping became a federal crime when the victim was transported across state lines or when the perpetrator's ransom demands were communicated telephonically or through the mail; federal jurisdiction was extended to interstate racketeering, transporting stolen property across state lines, bank robberies, and extortion; it became a federal crime for a witness or felon to cross state lines to avoid facing prosecution or having to testify. It also became a federal crime to kill an agent. The new perception of the G-man as cool professional also led Congress to empower agents to carry firearms, execute warrants, and make arrests.

Consistent with this new image and these expanded responsibilities was the renaming in 1935 of the refurbished Bureau of Investigation the Federal Bureau of Investigation, a title capturing the agency's role as the nation's principal law enforcement agency. FBI officials further promoted this conception of the agency's primacy when establishing in July 1935 the FBI Police Training School, administered by the FBI's Training Division (which also conducted and coordinated training for FBI in-service and new agent personnel). The school was renamed the FBI National Police Academy in 1936 and then the FBI National Academy in 1945.* The purpose of the academy's eleven-week curriculum was to train carefully selected police officers and sheriffs from around the country in the latest scientific techniques and law enforcement methods. Graduation from the academy was a coveted honor, and those attending rendered often invaluable assistance to FBI agents after returning to their original assignments.

* First located in federal barracks at the Marine Corps base in Quantico, Virginia, the Academy moved in 1972 to a specially constructed facility that allowed FBI officials to increase the number of attendees from one hundred to one thousand annually.

The Origins of FBI Intelligence, the Crisis of World War II

The Great Depression had created a political climate that spawned an upsurge of radical political movements. The seeming collapse of capitalism and the loss of public confidence in established institutions provided the catalyst of the dramatic growth of American fascist and Communist movements. These movements also drew inspiration—and direct support—from Nazi Germany and the Soviet Union. Because of their allegiance to these expansionist governments, they were regarded by the Roosevelt administration, and many liberals and conservatives, as, not indigenous, but "fifth column" movements, movements that, through stealth and betrayal, intended to promote the foreign policy goals and interests of Nazi Germany and the Soviet Union.

Owing to the primacy of the economic crisis and widespread public discontent with the status quo, the Roosevelt administration at first focused on promoting economic recovery and alleviating social hardship. Roosevelt did not initially endorse the alarmist proposals of his more hard-line advisers. Urged by his military advisers at a May 1934 cabinet meeting to take vigorous action to curb the influence of fascist and Communist movements, the president requested, instead, a limited investigation to ascertain whether the racialist and "anti-American" activities of American fascists had "any possible connection with official representatives of the German government in the United States."

Still convinced that vigorous action was necessary, Secretary of War George Dern approached Attorney General Homer Cummings in January 1936, citing the so-called Rumrich case (discussed later in this chapter) as a "definite indication" of foreign espionage, and declaring that "some [domestic] organizations would probably attempt to cripple our war effort through sabotage." Dern's point was that a civilian counterespionage service should be established to "prevent foreign espionage in the United States and to collect information." Federal officials would, in the event that the United States went to war, thereby be prepared to detain "any person intending to cripple our war effort by means of espionage or sabotage."

Dern's recommendation did receive attention, buttressed as it was by reports (sent to the White House by the FBI and naval and military intelligence) about the purported links between American fascists and Communists and Nazi Germany and the Soviet Union. In 1935, FBI agents had uncovered a German espionage ring that had been operating in New York City since 1927. Still other reports claimed that right-wing business leaders and the conservative radio priest Charles Coughlin had financed a planned anti–New Deal military coup to be led by General Smedley Butler and launched from Mexico, that the Soviet embassy official Constantine Oumansky was orchestrating the activities of American Communists, and that the Comintern in Moscow had ordered all American Communists to vote for Roosevelt in the 1936 presidential election because the Republican nominee, Alf Landon, was opposed to "class warfare."

Roosevelt, however, did not approve Dern's recommendation of a special counterespionage service and, instead, met with FBI Director J. Edgar Hoover on August 24, 1936, to solicit his views on "the question of subversive activities in the United States, particularly Fascism and Communism." Hoover briefed the president on "recent developments in the Communist activities," specifically that Communists sought to gain "control" of the International Longshoremen's Union, the United Mine Workers Union, and the Newspaper Guild and that "by doing so they would be able at any time to paralyze the country" by stopping "all shipping in and out" through the International Longshoremen's Union, by stopping "the operation of industry" through the United Mine Workers Union, and by stopping "the publication of newspapers" through the Newspaper Guild. The FBI director further warned the president about Communist subversive activities "within Governmental service . . . particularly in some of the Departments and in the National Labor Relations Board."

An alarmed Roosevelt then asked how he might obtain "a broad picture of the general [fascist and Communist] movement and its activities as may affect the economic and political life of the country as a whole." Hoover responded by citing a 1916 appropriation statute that, at the request of the State Department, the FBI could be authorized to "conduct such other investigations [beyond crimes against the United States] regarding official matters under the control of the Department of Justice and the Department of State as may be directed by the attorney general."

Roosevelt arranged a meeting the next day with Hoover and Secretary of State Cordell Hull. Reminding Hull of this 1916 statute, Roosevelt emphasized that because the Communist and fascist movements "were international in scope and that Communism particularly was directed from Moscow . . . the State Department would have a right to request an inquiry to be made." Hull concurred. To ensure confidentiality, the secretary of state agreed not to make this request in writing. The meeting concluded with Roosevelt directing Hoover to brief Attorney General Cummings about this matter and to coordinate this investigation with the Military Intelligence Division (MID) and the Office of Naval Intelligence (ONI).

Acting quickly and decisively, on September 5, 1936, Hoover ordered all FBI field offices to "obtain from all possible sources information concerning subversive activities conducted in the United States by Communists, Fascisti, and representatives or advocates of other organizations or groups advocating the overthrow or replacement of the Government of the United States." Hoover's directive ushered in a broad-based "intelligence" program. FBI agents were ordered to monitor the maritime industry; "Governmental affairs"; the steel, coal, newspaper, clothing, garment, and fur industries; "general strike activities"; the armed services; educational institutions; and "general activities—Communist and Affiliated Organizations, Fascist, Anti-Fascist movements, and activities in Organized Labor organizations."

This order captured a new mind-set—one that marked a far-reaching departure from past FBI operations—outlined in Hoover's distinction between *investigative* and *intelligence* activities. An investigation was to be "conducted when there is a specific violation of a Criminal Statute involved, always presuppose an overt act and is proceeded upon with the very definite intention of developing facts and information that will enable prosecution under legislation." In contrast, "an entirely different premise" underpinned intelligence activities: "Much of the activity indulged in by Communists and subversive elements does not, in the original stage, involve an overt act or violation of a specific statute. These subversive groups direct their attention to the dissemination of propaganda and to the boring from within process, much of which is not a violation of a Federal Statute at the time it is indulged in, but which may become a very definite violation of the law in the event of a declaration of war or of the declaration of a national emergency."

Hoover's reference to "the dissemination of propaganda" and "boring from within" ensured that FBI intelligence investigations would focus on radical activists because of their involvement in labor union, civil rights, lobbying, and even journalistic activities or their opposition to the president's foreign policy decisions or the FBI's surveillance activities. Because such investigations were not predicated on a law enforcement standard, the methods that FBI agents employed and the information that they subsequently obtained were not subject to the potentially embarrassing disclosures inherent in court cases. Court proceedings would normally be covered by the press, and defense attorneys could submit discovery motions that could reveal either the FBI's resort to illegal investigative techniques or its interest in noncriminal personal and political activities.

Ironically, from the very start FBI intelligence investigations exceeded the president's very limited purpose that the FBI provide him a "broad picture" that would allow him to determine whether the American fascist and Communist movements were subject to foreign direction. In an action that previewed the future relationship between the FBI director and his ostensible superior, the attorney general, Hoover had initiated this program on his own, without having briefed and obtained the required approval of the attorney general. Only belatedly, on September 10, 1936, did he inform Cummings of his meeting with Roosevelt and Hull (and even then misleadingly dated this meeting as having occurred on September 1). Sharing the president's desire for secrecy, Cummings verbally directed Hoover to proceed and to coordinate this investigation with the State Department, MID, and ONI.

The crisis of World War II, following the German invasion of Poland in September 1939, provided additional impetus to the FBI's expansion and independence. Sharing the view that American fascists and Communists sympathized with Nazi Germany and the Soviet Union and might act to subvert the national interest, Congress in 1939–1940 enacted a series of laws that expanded the FBI's law enforcement authority. The Hatch Act of 1939 barred from federal employment any member of "any political party [notably, the Communist Party and the German American Bund] which advocated" the violent overthrow of the government. That same year Congress amended the Foreign Agents Registration Act of 1938 to require any individual "who, within the United States, acts at the order, request, or under the direction of a foreign principal" to register as a foreign agent with the Justice Department. Then, in 1940, Congress enacted the Alien Registration (or Smith) Act, which required the fingerprinting of all resident aliens and forbid anyone from "knowingly or willfully" advocating or in any way abetting or teaching "the duty, necessity, desirability or propriety of violently overthrowing" the government or printing, writing, or disseminating such a doctrine or organizing such groups.

In addition, Congress went beyond President Roosevelt's 1939 request to increase FBI appropriations to "handle counterintelligence activities." Roosevelt had recommended a $150,000 increase, but Congress approved the higher amount of $300,000—influenced by Hoover's alarmist testimony of May 1939 before a House appropriations subcommittee citing the dramatic increase in spy cases from an annual average of 35 prior to 1938 to 634 in 1938 and a projected 772 in 1939.

The crisis of World War II further altered the FBI's role in the American intelligence community, providing an opportunity for FBI officials to ensure that all domestic intelligence operations would be centralized within the FBI.

Because the formal authority for President Roosevelt's 1936 request derived from the 1916 statute empowering the secretary of state to request Justice Department assistance, ongoing FBI intelligence investigations could be triggered only by an explicit State Department request. FBI officials became concerned about this requirement when, in 1939, State Department officials insisted on a controlling voice to coordinate such investigations. To neutralize the State Department's role, FBI Director Hoover in March 1939 urged Attorney General Frank Murphy to approve a plan to ensure that the FBI—and not the State Department—would directly control FBI investigations "intended to ascertain the identity of persons engaged in espionage, counter-espionage, and sabotage of a nature not within the specific provisions of prevailing statutes." Under current policy, Hoover explained, the State Department's "specific authorization" was required, and Assistant Secretary of State George Messersmith had instituted a cumbersome system that might result in State Department control over all federal intelligence activities. Attorney General Murphy immediately obtained President Roosevelt's agreement to issue another secret directive on June 26, 1939. Roosevelt's directive dissolved the State Department's interdepartmental committee and ordered that only the FBI, MID, and ONI "control and handle" investigations relating to "all espionage, counterespionage, and related matters." In the future, all other agencies were to forward to the FBI "any data, information, or material" that they might obtain "bearing directly or indirectly on espionage, counterespionage, or sabotage."

FBI officials soon parlayed their trumping of the State Department into an exclusive FBI monopoly. After 1919, and through 1939, MID and ONI agents had continued to monitor pacifist and other groups critical of an expansionist foreign policy as well as radical labor leaders who could disrupt military production. Military and naval intelligence officials also closely monitored "subversive activities that undermine the loyalty and efficiency" of army and navy personnel and civilians employed in military construction and maintenance. Because of their scope, MID's and ONI's investigations intruded on what FBI officials considered their responsibilities.

To resolve this potential conflict, in June 1940 (and then again in February 1942), FBI officials successfully concluded delimitation agreements with MID and ONI under which the FBI would have exclusive responsibility to "handle all cases involving allegations of espionage, sabotage and related matters as pertained to persons in the United States." The FBI would also coordinate all information developed by any agency "relating to subversive activities," would chair an interdepartmental committee on intelligence, would ascertain "the location, leadership, strength and organization of all citizen groups designed to combat 'Fifth Column' activities," and would monitor the "activities and developments of Un-American groups whose activities are aimed to frustrate or interfere with the national defense program." The sole exception concerned individuals who were directly employed by the Navy and War Departments "who attempt to frustrate plans for national defense." Under this arrangement, the FBI would share all information it had developed and maintain regular liaison with MID and ONI whenever FBI officials concluded that such information might be of interest to these agencies. And, finally, ONI and MID officials agreed that the FBI would retain exclusive authority to investigate "all cases in those categories [espionage, sabotage] directed from foreign countries . . . in which State, War or Navy Departments specifically request investigations of a designated group or set of circumstances."

Consistent with this enhanced stature were the foreign intelligence and counterintelligence operations conducted by FBI officials in Central and South America. Alarmed by German efforts to exploit anti-Yankee sentiments there, President Roosevelt in June 1940 authorized Hoover to create a special FBI division, the Special Intelligence Service (SIS), to neutralize German influence in the Western Hemisphere. Then, when in 1942 the president created the Office of Strategic Services as the nation's first worldwide intelligence agency and directed it to "plan and operate such special services as may be directed by the United States Joint Chiefs of Staff," his order excluded this spy agency from operating in SIS's bailiwick in the Western Hemisphere.

Roosevelt's willingness to rely exclusively on the FBI for domestic intelligence operations (and his decision to authorize an FBI foreign intelligence role in the Western Hemisphere) stemmed from FBI agents' discovery in 1935 of a German spy ring that had been operating in New York City since 1927. German intelligence operatives had recruited this group of eighteen pro-Nazis (both German Americans and German resident aliens) to infiltrate defense plants (particularly those involved in airplane and ship production) and the U.S. military to obtain information about military technology and plans as well as ship movements in the port of New York. This information was then relayed to Germany through couriers, who were either employed in the shipping industry or used false passports.

In February 1938, New York City policemen assisted FBI agents in arresting Guenther Gustav Rumrich for conspiring to commit espionage. Further inquiries led to the discovery of other recruited spies—including Erich Glaser, Johanna Hoffman, Ignaz Griebl, and Otto Voss. In interviews with FBI agents, and during his trial in 1939, Rumrich described how German operatives used couriers to relay sensitive military information to Germany, including codes, ciphers, military technology, and plans for the military defense of the East Coast and the Panama Canal. Yet not all members of the so-called Rumrich spy ring were apprehended and convicted—fourteen (including Griebl) were able to avoid arrest by fleeing to Germany.

The Rumrich investigation previewed the course of action that FBI officials would employ to contain the domestic fascist threat, a course of action that relied on prosecution and not simply preventive intelligence gathering.

For example, relying on the broad conspiracy provisions of the 1940 Smith Act, twenty-six American fascists (notably Gerald Winrod, Elizabeth Dilling, and Gerald L. K. Smith) were indicted in June 1942 for conspiring to overthrow the government. During their trial, however, U.S. attorneys were unable to prove the conspiracy charge. Securing a second indictment in 1944 (expanded to thirty individuals, including Lawrence Dennis), Justice Department attorneys eventually moved to dismiss the case when the raucous trial was aborted by the death of the presiding judge. Justice Department attorneys suffered a further defeat in 1945 when the Supreme Court overturned the convictions of leaders of the German American Bund for having counseled resistance to the wartime Selective Service Act. Justice Department attorneys lost another case in 1940, having that January arrested seventeen members of the pro-German Christian Front on the charge of stealing arms and ammunition from a National Guard armory as part of a "vast plot" to overthrow the government and establish a profascist dictatorship. During the trial, defense attorneys challenged the truthfulness of the FBI's key informer, Denis Healy, and the ideological character of the FBI's evidence.

Not all efforts to prosecute American fascists were unsuccessful. In fact, the FBI profited from the highly publicized arrest and trial of members of the so-called Duquesne-Sebold spy ring. William Sebold was a naturalized citizen of German descent who, on a trip to Germany to visit his family in 1939, had been pressured by German intelligence officers to serve as a spy. Immediately on his return to the United States, however, Sebold briefed State Department officials about the nature of his assignment. Referred to the FBI, Sebold agreed to serve as a double agent and played a key role in an elaborate scheme devised to identify others who had been recruited as German spies. With the FBI's assistance, Sebold established a shortwave radio station in Centerpoint, Long Island, to transmit to Germany the information given to him by the recruited German operatives. FBI agents screened the information transmitted to minimize the damage done, but, in order to deceive the Germans, they did allow most information submitted to be transmitted. After conducting this operation for sixteen months, FBI officials shut it down in June 1941, having by then identified thirty-three recruits who had given Sebold messages for transmission to Germany. Nineteen pled guilty, while fourteen (including Duquesne, the ringleader in New York) denied the charges. All those fourteen were convicted on December 12, 1941.

The FBI's most highly publicized success, however, involved the arrest and prosecution of eight saboteurs who had been recruited by German intelligence. Their mission was to sabotage American transportation and industrial facilities along the East Coast, an aluminum plant in Tennessee, and locks on the Ohio River. Transported by German submarines, the saboteurs landed in two teams of four, one in the town of Amagansett on Long Island on June 13, 1942, the other in Jacksonville, Florida, on June 17. Apprehended before they could implement their mission, the eight were tried and convicted in a special military court (six being German citizens).

While this case seemingly highlighted the FBI's efficiency and professionalism—one newspaper headline proclaimed, "FBI Captures 8 German Agents Landed by Subs"—the breakthrough was more the consequence of simple good luck. On landing in Long Island, one of the teams was observed by a Coast Guardsman, John Cullen, who was patrolling the beach. Cullen was unconvinced by the claim that the four were fishermen, his suspicions having been aroused by their speaking in German and their attempting to bribe him. Concerned for his safety, Cullen accepted the bribe but immediately reported the incident to his superiors. The next morning, a Coast Guard team scoured the beach area, discovering buried uniforms and equipment, and immediately reported the discovery to the FBI.

In the interim, the four had traveled to New York City, where they separated. Whether concerned that they had been discovered or having second thoughts, one of the four, George Dasch, reported the plot to the FBI, revealing as well that a second team had landed in Florida. Dasch also provided FBI agents with a list of the possible contacts for the members of the two teams as well as the cover names of the other saboteurs. This information led to the arrest of the three other members of the Long Island team on June 20, the arrest of two members of the Florida team in New York on June 23, and, finally, the arrest of the other two members of the Florida team in Chicago on June 25.

FBI investigations during World War II were not confined to developing evidence to prosecute violators of espionage and sabotage statutes. Exploiting the crisis of World War II and presidential concerns about an insidious subversive threat, FBI officials acted to change how FBI investigations were conducted, the subjects of FBI interest, and the extralegal practices employed to contain a perceived subversive threat.

The outbreak of war in Europe in September 1939 raised the prospect of the recurrence of the vigilante-type activities that had been widespread during World War I. These concerns underpinned FBI Director Hoover's September 1939 briefing of Attorney General Frank Murphy on the plans of the New York City police to monitor subversive activities. Hoover urged Murphy to curb this police initiative. On Murphy's recommendation, President Roosevelt, on September 6, 1939, issued a directive authorizing the FBI to "take charge of investigative work in matters relating to espionage, sabotage, and violations of the neutrality regulations." "All police officers, sheriffs, and other law enforcement officers," Roosevelt ordered, should forward "promptly" to the FBI any information they acquired relating to "espionage, sabotage, subversive activities, and related matters." Roosevelt extended this requirement on January 8, 1943, directing "all patriotic organizations and individuals" to report to the FBI all information relating to "espionage and related matters." The 1939 and 1943 directives seemingly only reaffirmed the FBI's coordinating role, as was the case with interstate prostitution and theft cases. In this instance, however, Roosevelt's orders assured the FBI a vast network of police and citizen informers.

A 1940 American Legion plan whereby legionnaires would monitor suspicious activities in defense plants and their local communities generally only furthered the ability of FBI officials to monitor "subversive activities," again for the seemingly innocent purpose of curbing vigilante-type activities. After a November 1940 briefing by FBI officials, Attorney General Robert Jackson sidetracked this plan and, instead, authorized a special American Legion Contact Program whereby FBI agents would recruit legionnaires and direct their monitoring activities. FBI officials exploited this opportunity and ordered FBI agents to recruit legionnaires to monitor "groups or settlements of persons of foreign extraction or possible un-American sympathies." They were to identify "the leaders of these groups, the locations of their meeting places, the identities and scope of operation of their social clubs, societies, language schools, etc.; whether persons are sent into communities to spread propaganda, to raise funds for various purposes, or for the purpose of agitating such foreign extraction groups." By the end of World War II, over forty thousand legionnaires had been recruited as FBI informers. The breadth of the FBI's guidelines for these informers, moreover, ensured that massive amounts of information would be collected, not only about potential saboteurs, but also about the planned political activities of radical activists. FBI officials also established the Plant Informant program to guard against espionage and sabotage in American defense industries. These investigations were again wide-ranging—and also extended to those active in labor organizational and strike activities.

In a further effort to anticipate espionage and sabotage, following the outbreak of hostilities in Europe in September 1939, FBI Director Hoover devised a program directed at "individuals, groups and organizations engaged in . . . subversive activities or espionage activities, or any activity that was possibly detrimental to the internal security of the United States." Under this program, code-named Custodial Detention, FBI agents were to identify all "persons of German, Italian, and Communist sympathies," whether citizens or resident aliens, and any others whose "interest may be directed primarily to the interest of some other nation than the United States." On the basis of the reports thus generated, FBI officials would determine which individuals "whose presence at liberty" at the time of U.S. involvement in war "would be dangerous to the public peace and safety of the United States Government." Such persons were then to be listed in a Custodial Detention index.

FBI agents were encouraged to adopt broad standards when recommending which individuals to list as dangerous, specifically, that individuals should be "watched carefully . . . because their previous activities indicate the possibility but not the probability" that they could harm the national interest. The controlling standard was to be, not actual conduct, but anticipated conduct. That individuals' names appeared on the list did not, however, mean that they could be detained because the program lacked statutory authority. At first, then, the FBI director emphasized the need for confidentiality, advising agents the next year that, if they were questioned about the purpose of their investigations, they should cite the 1938 Foreign Agents Registration Act, the statute requiring individuals to register as agents of a foreign power.

While Hoover hoped to minimize the risk of discovery, his action when creating the Custodial Detention index in 1939 served no legitimate purpose; the information developed by FBI agents was for the most part insufficient to trigger Foreign Agents or Alien Registration Act cases. To resolve this problem, Hoover in June 1940 belatedly sought Attorney General Jackson's approval to compile "a suspect list of individuals whose arrest might be considered necessary in the event the United States becomes involved in war." Jackson was convinced and approved the Custodial Detention program, which was to be implemented following a declaration of war and foreign agents listed in the Custodial Detention index arrested (under provisions of a 1798 alien detention statute). The Attorney General also established a special Justice Department committee and directed it to determine whether listed citizens could be prosecuted under the Alien Registration Act "or some other appropriate statute." And he furthermore agreed that Justice Department attorneys would not initiate any case that might publicly compromise either the FBI's "counter-espionage" activities or its confidential sources (informers or wiretaps) "without the prior approval of the Bureau."

Following U.S. military involvement in World War II in December 1941, Attorney General Francis Biddle (Jackson's successor) authorized the detention of the listed dangerous German and Italian aliens. (Japanese aliens and Japanese Americans were detained under President Roosevelt's February 1942 order.) Biddle, however, did not authorize the detention of "Communist" aliens (by then the Soviet Union was a wartime ally), nor did he consider prosecuting those U.S. citizens listed in the FBI's Custodial Detention index. In July 1943, moreover, Biddle ordered Hoover to discontinue the Custodial Detention program, having concluded that this "classification system is inherently unreliable." In all cases wherein individuals had been listed in the index, Biddle stipulated, the files should include a stamp that such a listing was unreliable and, thus, canceled. "There is no statutory authorization or other present justification" for such a list of citizens, the attorney general emphasized, adding that the Justice Department's "proper function" was to investigate persons "who may have violated the law" and that this purpose "is not aided by classifying persons as to dangerousness."

Hoover's response to Biddle's order highlights how the secrecy inherent in FBI intelligence operations had the unanticipated consequence of undermining the ability of attorneys general to oversee the FBI. In a highly confidential directive sent to senior FBI officials in August 1943, the FBI director technically complied with Biddle's order to terminate the Custodial Detention program. He then stipulated: "Henceforth, the cards known as Custodial Detention cards will be known as Security Index." FBI agents were to continue "to investigate dangerous and potentially dangerous" citizens and resident aliens for listing in this Security Index. To preclude discovery of his insubordination, Hoover emphasized that the renamed index was to be "strictly confidential and should at no time be mentioned or alluded to in investigative reports or discussed with agencies or individuals outside the Bureau," with the exception of MID and ONI officials, and "then only on a strictly confidential basis."

The crisis of World War II provided further impetus to the expansion of the FBI's investigative authority. The FBI could already, under the Hatch Act, investigate any federal employee currently a member of "subversive organizations" (see above). Now, following military involvement, the Civil Service Commission issued a regulation barring the employment of any individual about whom there was "a reasonable doubt as to his loyalty to the Government of the United States." This broad standard provided the FBI with the authority to investigate the political activities of both incumbent and applicant employees. And, because the scope of the resulting FBI investigations into political activities became known to officials of the various federal agencies and departments who received FBI reports on suspected subversives, this practice was leaked to the press and became the subject of a critical article published in *The Nation*. To allay concerns about the quality of information in the FBI reports (both rumors and hard evidence), Attorney General Biddle in April 1942 created a special interdepartmental committee to assist federal agency and department heads in evaluating FBI reports. The committee's recommendations were not binding, and adverse, dismissal rulings were to be based on evidence of membership in either the Communist Party or the German American Bund or the personal advocacy of revolution. Biddle also required agency and department heads to institute procedures for hearings to enable accused individuals to defend their loyalty and to ensure that a dismissal decision was based on evidence and not uncorroborated suspicion.

Nonetheless, the sense of crisis that had triggered FBI intelligence investigations, the centralization of internal security investigations in the FBI, and the inception of a host of liaison programs also led the president and the FBI director to reassess FBI methods. Spies and saboteurs, well trained and operating with stealth, could not be apprehended or their planned operations aborted by legal means—physical surveillance, intimidating interviews of suspects, infiltration by FBI agents or recruited informers, the recruitment of defectors as double agents. Only intrusive investigative techniques—wiretaps, bugs, break-ins, mail opening—could ensure that those planning to conduct espionage or sabotage could be apprehended and their plans prevented. Such techniques were, however, illegal, and their use, if discovered by defense attorneys through pretrial motions, would lead to the dismissal of any case built on them and, thus, hinder the prosecution of spies and saboteurs.

Wiretapping had been banned since the 1934 Communications Act, which regulated the communications industry (radio, telephone, telegraph) and contained a provision explicitly banning the "interception and divulgence" of communications "transmitted by wire." Because the language of the statute and the hearings leading to its passage focused on the actions of corporations and private individuals, Justice Department officials privately concluded that its ban did not apply to federal agents conducting a criminal investigation. This reasoning was, however, rejected by the Supreme Court in rulings of 1937 and 1939 in *Nardone v. United States.* The Court held first (in 1937) that the ban against wiretapping covered federal agents and then (in 1939) that any indictment based on an illegal wiretap was tainted and required the dismissal of the case.

The Court's second *Nardone* ruling came at a time when President Roosevelt was deliberating on how the government could best address an anticipated internal security problem—and specifically assessing the value of wiretaps in uncovering the plans of suspected spies. On May 21, 1940, Roosevelt issued a secret directive authorizing FBI wiretaps during "national defense" investigations. The president privately reasoned that the Court's rulings governed only criminal cases—and then only when intercepted information would be "divulged" to effect prosecution. This limitation did not apply when the purpose was not prosecutorial, but to obtain advance intelligence. Accordingly, the president authorized the FBI wiretapping of persons "suspected of subversive activities against the United States, including suspected spies." To ensure that FBI wiretapping would be confined to national defense cases, Roosevelt required that the attorney general approve of each wiretap in advance, "after investigation of the need in each case," and that FBI wiretapping be confined "to a minimum" and "limit[ed] ... insofar as possible to aliens."

Roosevelt's secret directive did not legalize wiretapping, and, in consequence, the wiretapping of suspected spies would still preclude prosecution under the espionage statutes. More important, the president's private assessment of the Court's ruling and his interest in ensuring that this practice remain secret placed his attorney general in a delicate position. Jackson responded by adopting a procedure to minimize discovery of FBI wiretapping, informing Hoover during a follow-up meeting that he intended to "have no detailed record concerning the cases in which wiretapping would be utilized." The only record of FBI wiretapping would be maintained in Hoover's "immediate office, listing the time, places, and cases in which this procedure is utilized."

Jackson's decision not to keep separate records of his approval of FBI wiretapping requests subverted his ability and that of his successors to monitor FBI wiretapping practices. His failure also to have issued guidelines governing the length of national defense wiretaps or to have required that approved wiretaps be reauthorized after a certain, specified time period had the unanticipated consequence of encouraging FBI officials to continue such wiretaps long after failing to uncover any evidence of a national defense threat and even to install wiretaps without the attorney general's advance approval.*

Motivated to minimize the risk that their illegal actions would be discovered, FBI officials on their own authorized still other illegal investigative techniques. In 1940, for example, they instituted the code-named Z-Coverage

---

* Extant records maintained in FBI Assistant Director D. Milton Ladd's secret office file document that FBI officials on their own authorized at least seventeen wiretaps during the World War II period.

mail-opening program, which at first targeted only Axis and Soviet embassies in Washington, D.C., but was soon extended to their consulates in New York City and the embassies of Axis-aligned governments (Spain, Portugal, Vichy France). Following the Japanese attack on Pearl Harbor, FBI and military intelligence officials also effected an arrangement with officials of the international telegraph companies (Western Union, RCA, and ITT) under which FBI and military intelligence officials would be allowed to copy all telegraph messages of identified Axis and Axis-aligned governments and of the Soviet Union.

In addition, beginning in 1940, FBI officials authorized break-ins either to install bugs or to photograph the records of suspected "subversive" individuals and organizations. By 1942, the FBI director had concluded that the regular use of this "clearly illegal" but "invaluable" investigative technique was necessary "in combating subversive activities of a clandestine nature aimed at undermining and destroying our nation." Unwilling to "obtain any legal sanction" (i.e., to seek either the attorney general's or the president's authorization), Hoover instead required FBI agents to obtain his prior authorization under a special "Do Not File" procedure and outlined the safeguards to be employed to preclude discovery. Hoover's purpose was to ensure that FBI agents did not conduct break-ins indiscriminately and recklessly.

Dating from 1940, FBI agents "discreetly" and extensively employed wiretaps, bugs, break-ins, mail covers, and mail intercepts during intelligence investigations. The targets of FBI break-ins included the Soviet Government Purchasing Commission, the American Youth Congress, the American Peace Mobilization, and the Washington Committee for Democratic Action. The targets of FBI wiretaps included the German, Italian, Japanese, and Soviet embassies in Washington, D.C., the headquarters of the U.S. Communist Party in New York City and other pro-Communist organizations, and the offices of six profascist organizations. Also wiretapped were hundreds of radical political and labor union activists and organizations. Among those whom the FBI either tapped or bugged were the radical attorney Carol King, the National Association for the Advancement of Colored People (NAACP), the (World War II) March on Washington Movement, the Gandhi Society for Human Rights, the Congress of Industrial Organizations Council, the National Maritime Union, the United Automobile Workers Union, and the United Mine Workers Union.

The scope of FBI break-in, wiretapping, and bugging practices underscores one inadvertent consequence of President Roosevelt's authorization of FBI intelligence investigations. The president might have intended that the FBI ascertain whether domestic activists and organizations were controlled or directed by Nazi Germany and the Soviet Union. But his interest in secrecy and his broad authorization enabled FBI officials to monitor individuals and organizations involved only in efforts to influence public policy and popular culture.

Ironically, one of the many targets of FBI intelligence investigations were prominent German writers (Bertolt Brecht, Thomas Mann, Lion Feuchtwanger, Heinrich Mann, Ruth Berlau, Anna Seghers, Berthold Viertel, Billy Wilder, Hanns Eisler) who had fled Nazi Germany and obtained asylum in the United States. As political refugees, they sought to influence the direction that U.S. policy toward postwar Germany would take—in this instance, toward the institution of democratic political reforms and a socialist economic system. Their activities in forming groups such as the Free Germany Committee and the Council for a Democratic Germany triggered an intensive FBI investigation that relied on the extensive use of wiretaps, bugs, break-ins, mail covers, and mail opening.

This belief that radical activists could influence public opinion triggered an even more massive FBI investigation of the motion picture industry, under the code-named COMPIC program. Launched in 1942, this investigation of Communist influence continued until 1956, when FBI officials concluded that such influence in Hollywood was "practically nonexistent at the present time."

FBI agents had since the mid-1930s closely monitored the role of Communists in the formation of unions and strike activities in the film industry. Their focus shifted in 1942 when Hoover ordered the FBI's Los Angeles field office to ascertain Communist influence in the making of films. The FBI director demanded an intensified investigation following the release in 1943 of a number of pro-Soviet (*Mission to Moscow*) and antifascist (*For Whom the Bell Tolls, Hangmen Also Die*) films. Ironically, these films comported with U.S. foreign policy interests—given the wartime alliance with the Soviet Union against Nazi Germany. Furthermore, this FBI investigation targeted individuals employed in the private sector who were producing films and were in no position to sabotage defense plants or steal classified information.

Hoover's purpose in this case (as in that of the German refugees) stemmed from his concern that Communists could influence popular culture. FBI agents succeeded in identifying those Communists who were employed in various capacities in the film industry, having broken into the Los Angeles section of the Communist Party. After photocopying the Party's membership records, FBI agents then linked the identified Communist producers, directors, writers, actors, and stagehands with specific films. During the course of this investigation, FBI agents wiretapped Hollywood employees (John Lawson, Waldo Scott, Hubert Biberman, David Robison) and the labor and political activists with whom the identified Hollywood Communists were in contact (Elizabeth Leach, Marguerite Anderson, C. B. Baldwin). Their reports on this intensive investigation not unexpectedly emphasized that the films with which the identified Communists were involved "contained Communist propaganda" and that the Hollywood Communists "exploited the apparent patriotic position of the [Communist] party to recruit new members, and control fellow travelers, and sympathizers," succeeded in "forc[ing] the making of motion pictures which glorify the Soviet Union and create sympathy for the Communist cause," or pressured producers to make "motion pictures delineating the Negro race in most favorable terms as part of the general line of the Communist Party."

The FBI's COMPIC investigation underscores how FBI officials defined the internal security threat in their wartime intelligence investigations. This myopic concern over Communist influence in American society had an effect on even legitimate FBI national security investigations—an effect seen particularly clearly in the highly sensitive COMRAP (Comintern Apparatus) investigation, launched in 1943.

From a wiretap of Communist Party headquarters, FBI agents had intercepted a conversation between the Communist Party chief, Earl Browder, and the Communist activist Steve Nelson in which Browder alerted Nelson about a forthcoming (but unspecified) sensitive operation. FBI agents thereupon bugged Nelson's residence in Oakland, California, eventually monitoring his April 1943 meeting with Vassili Zubilin, the third secretary of the Soviet embassy in Washington. At this meeting, Zubilin gave Nelson a "large sum of money" for the "purpose of placing Communist party members and agents in industries engaged in secret war production in the United States so that information could be obtained for transmittal to the Soviet Union." FBI officials concurrently learned of the identities of other Soviet agents, a disaffected Soviet employee having in August 1943 sent an anonymous letter to the FBI director naming Soviet officials then stationed in the United States who were involved in espionage: among others, the Soviet embassy personnel Vassili Zubilin, his wife, Elizabeta, and

Vassili Dolgov; the Soviet consular officials Pavel Klarin (New York) and Gregory Kheifets (San Francisco); the Amtorg* employees Semen Semenov and Leonid Kvasnikov; and the employees of the Soviet Government Purchasing Commission Andrei Schevchenko and Serghei Lukianov.

Thus, when launching the COMRAP investigation, FBI officials could focus on specific Soviet officials and their principal American Communist recruiter. The resultant investigation lasted two years, with FBI agents beginning by physically and electronically monitoring the identified Soviet agents and Nelson (their movements and contacts) and then monitoring those with whom they came into contact (and, in turn, following them, wiretapping them, monitoring their mail, and, in some cases, bugging their meetings and breaking into their residences to photocopy their papers).

This intensive investigation did not lead to the uncovering of a single instance of wartime Soviet and Communist espionage—beyond the initial Zubilin-Nelson meeting. FBI reports summarizing the results of this investigation confirm that FBI agents had established only that American Communists were Communists—that is, that the targeted Communists were actively involved in recruiting new members for the Communist Party; sought to "influence the people and Government of the United States toward acceptance of Soviet foreign policy"; distributed "pro-Russian propaganda" through the media and Communist front groups; "collect[ed] political information of value to the USSR"; and infiltrated federal agencies "to influence foreign policy," to "secure information of value for the [Communist] Party," and to promote "the employment of other Communists in Government work."

The failure of FBI agents to uncover any instance of Soviet espionage did not mean that Soviet agents were unable to recruit American Communists to spy on their behalf. During the World War II period, American Communists employed in various wartime federal agencies were recruited to provide Soviet agents classified information about such things as the wartime atomic bomb project at Los Alamos, U.S. wartime military production, and the Roosevelt administration's planned foreign policy toward the Soviet Union.

What went wrong? For one thing, Soviet officials who were the targets of the FBI's COMRAP investigation were aware that FBI agents were monitoring them. In their reports to their superiors in Moscow acknowledging the

---

* Amtorg was a Soviet trading company based in New York City.

monitoring they conveyed no concern that their activities had been uncovered and also disclosed the methods that they employed to preclude discovery—their precautions to ensure that recruited Americans were "quite developed" and familiar with "conspiracy"; their suspicions that their phones were tapped; their contacts "only with special reliable undercover" Communist Party members who "are not suspected" of involvement in intelligence work; their use of automobiles to arrange secret meetings (to negate FBI physical surveillance); their suspension of planned meetings or recruitment whenever suspecting that they were being monitored by the FBI; and their practice of never using the "real surnames of recruits" and destroying all their notes after transmitting coded messages, rendering possible break-ins useless).

Also, ideological blinders led FBI agents to focus on the wrong Communists—prominent Communist Party officials (Nelson, Browder, Alexander Bittelman, Louise Bransten, Boris Morros, Haakon Chevalier). In the process, they missed those Communists who had been recruited or had volunteered to engage in espionage and who had either severed their public links with the Communist Party (Nathan Silvermaster, Victor Perlo) or were low-level functionaries and, therefore, could not be discovered through monitoring national Communist Party meetings (Judith Coplon, Julius Rosenberg, David Greenglass, Theodore Hall).

FBI agents even missed an opportunity to uncover Nathan Silvermaster's role as the leader of one of two wartime Soviet espionage rings composed of individuals employed in sensitive wartime agencies in Washington. Silvermaster was already the subject of a Hatch Act investigation. In December 1944, FBI agents uncovered his meeting with Louise Bransten, one of the subjects of the COMRAP investigation. This discovery did not, however, lead FBI agents to monitor him under the COMRAP program. And, while FBI agents did not then seek to ascertain whether Silvermaster had been recruited as a spy, Soviet officials had for over a year been troubled by the centralized character of the Silvermaster spy ring. They feared that Silvermaster's insistence on controlling all contacts with the wartime employees whom he had recruited and his reliance on the courier Elizabeth Bentley to transmit this information to them in New York could lead to the operation's being compromised. Silvermaster had been able to resist Soviet demands to decentralize this operation "into smaller units" to ensure "greater secrecy" until April 1945. But, in that month, in part because they feared Silvermaster's dismissal (knowing that he was under investigation),

Silvermaster's Soviet handlers instituted a new system whereby whatever information Silvermaster's Washington recruits provided would thereafter be transported to New York "only in film and in several batches" by several couriers (and *not* by Silvermaster or Bentley), who would take "turns making the trip to Washington."

The COMRAP and COMPIC investigations also highlight how FBI intelligence investigations undermined the accountability central to a democratic society. Secrecy ensured that FBI officials were never subject to the kind of critical scrutiny that could have uncovered their failure to apprehend Soviet agents involved in espionage and their focus on political and professional activities having no relation to espionage or sabotage, a focus that had a potentially chilling effect on First Amendment and legitimate commercial rights (including who should be employed in the film industry and what kinds of movies should be produced).

FBI intelligence activities also contributed to fundamental changes in the role of the presidency. The catalyst to this development stemmed from President Roosevelt's political concerns following the outbreak of war in Europe in September 1939. Frustrated by the difficulty first of convincing Congress to repeal the Neutrality Acts of 1935–1937 and then of developing a consensus in support of a more activist foreign policy to avert an Axis victory, Roosevelt turned to the FBI for information about the plans and background of his anti-interventionist critics.

In May 1940, for example, the president forwarded to Hoover the names of individuals who had written or telegraphed to protest his nonneutral foreign policy. "It was the President's idea," Stephen Early, Roosevelt's press secretary, wrote the FBI director on Roosevelt's behalf, that the FBI "might" record the "names and addresses of the senders." Hoover welcomed this opportunity and immediately forwarded to the White House reports detailing whatever derogatory information FBI agents had already accumulated about the identified critics. In those cases where an individual was not the subject of an FBI file, a special FBI inquiry was initiated and the results duly reported to the White House. These FBI reports detailed these individuals' associations with suspected fascist or Communist groups and their political activities (specifically, their positions on foreign and domestic policy, civil rights, and strikes by labor unions). And, even though these reports confirmed that the FBI was monitoring political activities that violated no federal statute, the Roosevelt White House raised no objection and, instead, expressed appreciation and invited future such submissions—with Roosevelt ordering the White House aide Edwin Watson "to prepare a nice letter to Edgar Hoover thanking him for all the reports on investigations he has made and tell him I appreciate the fine job he is doing."

From 1939 and throughout the war years, Hoover dutifully reported on the plans and tactics of the administration's critics—including Senators Burton Wheeler and Gerald Nye—and of the organizations opposed to the president's domestic and foreign policies (the America First Committee, the Christian Front, the NAACP, the Polish American Congress, the Communist Party). The FBI also monitored and reported on both profascist publications and editors and reporters of mainstream conservative newspapers. In the latter case, the FBI director closely monitored the editorial commentary and news reporting of the president's long-term adversaries in the conservative press—notably, the *Chicago Tribune* publisher Robert McCormick and reporters Chesly Manly and Stanley Johnson, the *Washington Times-Herald* publisher Eleanor Patterson and gossip columnist Inga Arvad, and the *New York Daily News* publisher Joseph Patterson and reporter John O'Donnell. And, when Attorney General Biddle hesitated to prosecute the administration's media critics, Hoover alerted Early, emphasizing that "until some of the Attorney General's instructions had been changed [FBI] agents could not operate," having been "blocked by the Attorney General time and time again." Briefed on Biddle's unwillingness to follow the president's "desires," Roosevelt met with the attorney general to discuss the matter of "seditious publications in the United States—the clear and present danger." A chastised Biddle did initiate prosecution of profascist publications but was unable to secure indictments of the president's far more effective critics in the conservative mainstream media.

By 1945, the FBI had emerged as the unacknowledged intelligence arm of the White House. FBI reports might not have shaped the course of national politics. The president's encouragement nonetheless emboldened FBI officials to collect, and then maintain, massive amounts of noncriminal but derogatory personal and political information. That resource proved crucial to the FBI's evolution during the Cold War period into a more powerful and autonomous agency.

The Early Cold War Years: Anticipating and Curbing Subversion

The end of World War II in 1945 did not usher in an era of peace or a retrenchment from the nation's international role. The United States almost immediately became involved in a nonmilitary confrontation with the Soviet Union, the so-called Cold War. Although the United States and the Soviet Union never engaged in direct military conflict, U.S. policy was based on the premise that the Soviet Union was a hostile adversary. The Soviet threat, however, was not perceived to be merely that of a great power that, because of its military strength, industrial production, and technological prowess, could threaten U.S. interests. U.S. policymakers instead viewed Soviet leaders as subversive adversaries orchestrating worldwide revolution. Safeguarding U.S. security accordingly required a strategy to anticipate the attempts of Soviet leaders to achieve world domination, not just through military strength (including the use of nuclear weapons), but also by stealthily exploiting the socioeconomic discontent that made revolutionary change attractive to many anticolonial leaders and radical activists in postwar liberated Europe and in Third World countries. Communist (i.e., Soviet) expansion could be contained through, on the one hand, a major military buildup and foreign aid programs and, on the other, a vigilant countersubversive policy. Successfully maintaining the latter necessitated anticipating attempts of American Communists and Communist sympathizers to steal military and diplomatic secrets or to undermine national unity and promote policies that advanced Soviet interests.

These internal security concerns catalyzed the FBI's explosive growth during the postwar years. Owing to communism's subversive character, more creative and aggressive tactics were needed—and, at times, FBI agents would have to violate federal laws, privacy rights, and civil liberties. Secret executive directives granted the FBI broad authority to use illegal investigative techniques to anticipate espionage. The underlying purpose was, not to prosecute spies or saboteurs, but to prevent their presence at large during possible "war and national emergencies" or deny them employment in sensitive federal agencies.

Beginning in 1940, FBI agents had installed wiretaps and bugs during intelligence investigations of a host of profascist and pro-Communist activists and organizations. The more sinister crisis of the Cold War conflict emboldened FBI officials to exploit the deference of Attorneys General Tom Clark, J. Howard McGrath, James McGranery, and Herbert Brownell to expand their authority to use these techniques beyond even the broad national defense rationale authorized by President Roosevelt's 1940 directive. In fact FBI agents had wiretapped in cases not covered by Roosevelt's directive, rendering FBI officials vulnerable should these uses become known. To resolve this problem, FBI Director Hoover attempted to capitalize on Cold War fears of the Communist "subversive" threat. In July 1946, he drafted a letter that Attorney General Tom Clark signed and sent to President Truman. Ostensibly seeking Truman's reaffirmation of the 1940 Roosevelt directive, this letter implied that Roosevelt's purpose extended to "subversive" investigations and then proposed a minor expansion to include such use in cases "vitally affecting domestic security or when human life is in jeopardy." Unknown to Truman, who had accepted the characterization of Roosevelt's purpose at face value, the Hoover-drafted letter quoted from the final authorization paragraph of the 1940 directive but dropped its last qualifying sentence: "You are requested furthermore to limit these investigations so conducted to a minimum and to limit them insofar as possible to aliens." By dropping this sentence and proposing only to reaffirm Roosevelt's policy "in the present troubled period in international affairs, accompanied as it is by an increase in subversive activities, here at home," Hoover craftily obtained Truman's authorization to wiretap domestic organizations and citizens. This effort succeeded for the additional reason that the expansion was to be achieved, not by the president issuing his own directive, but by the president signing and returning the Hoover-drafted letter to Clark.

The duplicity of this tactic in time posed problems for FBI officials as the by-product of a controversy triggered by evidence of illegal FBI wiretapping that came to light during the trial, on espionage charges, of Judith Coplon (discussed later in this chapter). To deflect criticism and convey the impression that the FBI's wiretapping practices had been conducted under a policy instituted by the revered Roosevelt, Justice Department officials in January 1950 proposed that Truman publicly release the text of Roosevelt's 1940 directive but not his own 1946 letter. For the first time, White House aides reviewed and then contrasted the texts of the 1940 directive and the letter that Truman had signed, in the process discovering the subterfuge. Truman momentarily considered rescinding his 1946 directive, but opted not to do so. In the highly charged anti-Communist politics of the early 1950s, the president could not risk an action that could be construed as restricting FBI authority and would at the same time underscore his carelessness in allowing himself to have been blindsided.

Coplon was convicted, but, because the evidence against her was obtained through an illegal wiretap, the conviction was overturned on appeal. The court's ruling required FBI officials to seek the attorney general's policy guidance whether to continue current wiretapping practices. At this time, Hoover for the first time briefed the attorney general about the FBI's use of bugs to obtain "intelligence information highly pertinent to the defense and welfare of the country." Such bugging practices raised Fourth Amendment questions because, normally, the installation of a bugging device required that an office or a residence be broken into. When responding to Hoover's briefing, Attorney General J. Howard McGrath reaffirmed current wiretapping procedures. In the case of bugs installed by means of trespass, however, McGrath stipulated: "I cannot authorize the installation of a microphone *involving a trespass* under existing law."

McGrath did not, however, directly ban such practices. He had, nonetheless, created a written record of his conclusion that such installations were illegal. In consequence, the sole effect of his reply was that FBI officials scaled back, but did not terminate, such practices.

With the election of the more sympathetic Eisenhower, FBI officials were encouraged to revisit this matter. The specific occasion was the ruling in *Irvine v. California,* in which the Supreme Court expressed abhorrence over the installation of a bug in a bedroom during a criminal investigation. In response, in March 1954, FBI officials proposed that Attorney General Herbert Brownell adopt the same procedure governing wiretaps for FBI bugging installations during national security investigations—prior approval by the attorney general on a case-by-case basis. Brownell concurred that bugs were an invaluable technique in uncovering the activities of "espionage agents, possible saboteurs, and subversive persons." Yet, because he was uneasy about directly authorizing a violation of the Fourth Amendment, he concluded that he "would be in a much better position to defend the Bureau in the event there should be a technical trespass if he had not heretofore approved it." Instead, in May 1954, the attorney general issued a broadly worded secret directive empowering FBI officials to install microphones by trespass during national security investigations without having to notify him and obtain his advance approval in each case.

Brownell's willingness to defer to the FBI effectively subverted the ability of Justice Department officials either to oversee FBI microphone installations or to limit their duration. This deference invited FBI officials to decide on their own to expand the scope and targets of such uses. Indeed, within days of Brownell's issuance of this secret directive, FBI officials decided to use bugs as well during "important" crime cases on the understanding that such uses "will only be approved by high Bureau officials."

The secret directives authorizing FBI wiretapping and bugging underscore how legal and constitutional limitations no longer governed administration policy toward the FBI—and how containing the Communist internal security threat no longer required that Justice Department officials first seek legislation that would authorize FBI programs and procedures.*

Thus, when planning for the contingency that the United States and the Soviet Union might in the immediate future go to war, Truman administration officials willingly acceded to a far-reaching FBI proposal. In March 1946, FBI Director Hoover recommended that Attorney General Tom Clark "determine what legislation is available or should be sought" to institute a program to detain all identified "members of the Communist Party and any others" who "might be dangerous" in the event that the United States broke diplomatic relations or went to war with the Soviet Union. Hoover identified these "others" as including those holding "important positions" in the organized labor and civil rights movements, in education, in churches, and in the media "who have shown sympathy for Communist objectives and policies." Instituting such a detention program, Hoover observed, would require "statutory backing." Hoover did not then advise Clark that, since 1943 (and in violation of Attorney General Biddle's order), the FBI had already instituted the Security Index listing program.

The attorney general concurred on the need for a preventive detention program but was unwilling to seek congressional authorization for it, fearing that this "would only bring on a loud and acrimonious discussion." After lengthy FBI–Justice Department discussions, the attorney general on August 3, 1948, authorized FBI officials to identify and list such dangerous

---

* The Roosevelt, Truman, and Eisenhower administrations had unsuccessfully lobbied Congress to legalize national security wiretapping in 1941, 1951, 1953, and 1955. Their failures did not influence their policies on such uses.

individuals. Rather than seeking legislative authorization, Clark proposed the preparation of a draft resolution that would be introduced in the crisis atmosphere following the outbreak of war to obtain ex post facto congressional authorization. To ensure future support for such an initiative, he launched a campaign to educate the public that "Communism is dangerous."

In September 1950, acting independently of the Truman administration and the FBI, Congress enacted legislation authorizing a preventive detention program. The standards for listing and then detaining individuals under the so-called McCarran Act were, however, less stringent than were those of the ongoing Security Index program. Unwilling to conform to Congress's mandate, FBI and Justice Department officials at first lobbied Congress to amend the McCarran Act to correspond to the Security Index. When this effort failed, Attorney General McGrath decided to ignore the congressional standards and reaffirmed that the FBI's listing and detention standards would continue to be based on Attorney General Clark's 1948 authorization.

The Security Index program never became operational even after U.S. involvement in the Korean War in June 1950. The intent to anticipate subversive activities, moreover, underlay a companion initiative that the Truman administration instituted, once again by executive order.

On March 22, 1947, President Truman authorized the Federal Employee Loyalty Program, meant to ensure that all federal employees would "be of complete and unswerving loyalty to the United States." Incumbent and applicant employees would thereafter be subject to a thorough investigation of their past and current activities and beliefs. They would be denied employment or fired if, "on all evidence, reasonable grounds exist for the belief that the person involved is disloyal to the Government of the United States." (This standard was changed in 1951 to "if there is reasonable doubt as to their loyalty to the Government of the United States.") The established loyalty program also ensured the confidentiality of the FBI files on which a denial of clearance or a dismissal decision was based. During an appeal of an adverse ruling, employees (and their attorneys) would be denied access to the reports or the identities of the FBI's sources. In effect, Truman's loyalty program authorized a radical increase in FBI investigations since it could not be known which citizens might in the future seek federal employment. More important, the confidentiality requirement permitted FBI officials to use information obtained illegally (e.g., through wiretaps) in loyalty dismissal proceedings—information that could not have been used for prosecutive purposes—and to certify, without the right of an independent evaluation, the reliability of their sources.

Armed with expanded powers to monitor subversives, FBI officials targeted radical activists and organizations critical of administration foreign policy and their own internal security initiatives. The subjects of their investigations included even artists, writers, college professors, and reporters, anyone who "might influence others against the national interest or are likely to furnish financial aid to subversive elements."

FBI agents had for decades been closely monitoring the American Communist movement, beginning with the Bolshevik Revolution of 1917. This monitoring did not cease when, in 1924, Attorney General Stone banned political surveillance investigations. After 1936 and intensifying during the World War II and Cold War periods, investigations of American Communists and suspected Communist sympathizers became the dominant FBI priority, and, as one by-product, the FBI had by 1950 emerged as a powerful and effectively autonomous agency.

Ironically, this expansion was not the result of FBI agents having successfully apprehended Soviet spies and their American recruits. For the most part, FBI agents were unable to develop admissible evidence documenting Soviet espionage activities. Even the small number of convictions that were obtained in the highly publicized internal security cases of the early Cold War years were less the result of FBI investigative discoveries than of the fortuitous defections of Elizabeth Bentley and Whittaker Chambers, the keen observations of an analyst in the Office of Strategic Services (OSS), and the code-breaking abilities of military intelligence analysts.

Elizabeth Bentley had joined the Communist Party in the 1930s. During World War II, using as cover her employment with the Soviet export company Amtorg, she was recruited by her lover, Jacob Golos, to act as a courier for two Washington-based Soviet espionage rings headed by Nathan Silvermaster and Victor Perlo. Bentley traveled frequently to Washington, D.C., to pick up microfilmed documents or reports provided by Communists employed in various wartime agencies and the Treasury Department. Golos's death in 1944 and then the April 1945 decision of Soviet intelligence officials to drop Bentley as a courier led her in November 1945 to contact the FBI. In a series of interviews, she described in detail this wartime espionage operation and identified by name over a hundred federal employees who had provided her (directly or through Silvermaster and Perlo) with government records that she had then delivered to Soviet agents in New York. That month, and continuing until March 1946, FBI Director Hoover sent a flurry of reports to President Truman and other high-level administration officials reporting Bentley's allegations.

An immediate FBI investigation was launched to corroborate Bentley's account, including having her recontact her Soviet handler. As their purpose was to identify the participants in a wartime (and possibly continuing) espionage operation, FBI officials authorized FBI agents to employ various illegal investigative techniques—wiretaps, break-ins, mail covers, and mail intercepts. Such actions could foreclose prosecution but reflected the priority of shutting down an ongoing espionage operation.

This intensive FBI investigation failed to uncover evidence that the identified federal employees were participants in a Soviet espionage operation. Soviet officials had already learned about Bentley's defection to the FBI from another of their recruits, Harold "Kim" Philby, a British intelligence officer assigned to Washington who maintained a liaison relationship with the U.S. intelligence community. This operation was immediately shut down, with Soviet officials ordering their contacts in New York and Washington to "cease immediately their connection with all persons known to Bentley in our work," to review and then destroy all unnecessary files and notes in their offices, and to "warn other agents about Bentley's betrayal." The recruited American sources were specifically instructed that, in the event they were interviewed by the FBI, they should "deny their secret connection" with Bentley, claiming that her charges were a "lie," but not deny "simply being acquainted with her" since FBI agents might have monitored their meetings.

These tactics negated the hopes of FBI officials to exploit Bentley's defection to uncover evidence of a past and possibly ongoing Soviet espionage operation. In an October 1946 report to the White House, FBI officials lamely attributed their failure to have corroborated Bentley's charges to the "time element." Because Bentley's espionage operation dated "back several years" and became known only in November 1945, FBI officials emphasized that "the reader [of this FBI report] must consider the difficulty of actually proving these activities by investigation at this later date." FBI agents had been able to establish only that the individuals named by Bentley knew each other personally and professionally and were in frequent contact at either public meetings or private social events. Through a break-in at Silvermaster's residence, FBI agents had discovered photographic equipment in his basement but not evidence that this equipment had been used to microfilm pilfered documents.

This failure led FBI Supervisor Edward Morgan in January 1947 to recommend that FBI officials not seek any indictments. "We have no evidence for which 'intent or reason to believe' can be proved or reasonably inferred," Morgan observed. "At this point, the evidence very definitely is insufficient to sustain a successful prosecution under the espionage statutes."

Morgan's counsel was ignored, ironically by senior Justice Department officials. Convening a grand jury in September 1947, Justice Department officials hoped to use the threat of a perjury indictment to "crack" one of the named conspirators (considered a "weak sister"), who would then testify against the others. This strategy failed. All those called to testify either took the Fifth Amendment or denied Bentley's allegations and also offered a more benign account of their relationships with other federal employees as personal and professional.

Despite this failure, FBI agents continued in their efforts to corroborate Bentley. In 1954, for example, they attempted to exploit recently enacted legislation granting immunity to those testifying before a grand jury (negating a Fifth Amendment claim). Edward Fitzgerald, one of those named by Bentley, was subpoenaed but "refused to talk" when questioned by the specially convened grand jury. His refusal led to his being sentenced to five months in prison. FBI officials finally conceded their failure in 1970 when recommending that the wiretap records developed during the course of this massive investigation be destroyed. They then admitted privately that, despite having analyzed this case "over and over again" since 1945, they had never been able to "obtain information to substantiate and corroborate the allegations of BENTLEY."

Of those named by Bentley, William Remington was the only person to be prosecuted. This seems perplexing since Bentley had not identified Remington as a member of either the Silvermaster or the Perlo spy rings. In her original account to the FBI, and in 1948 congressional testimony, Bentley had contended that Remington had only paid her Communist Party dues and once provided her secret information on aircraft production in the belief that this information was to be given to the Communist Party chief, Earl Browder.

Remington's vulnerability was not, however, the result of the FBI's discoveries. Following the failure of the federal grand jury to indict any of those named by Bentley, the reporter Frederick Woltman wrote a series of articles in the *New York World Telegram* hyping the allegations of the "Red Spy Queen." The resultant publicity triggered two congressional inquiries during which Bentley's charges and the responses of those she named were aired. All those named publicly by Bentley took the Fifth Amendment when testifying while professing their innocence in public—except Remington. Then an employee of the Commerce Department, Remington admitted to having known Bentley during the war years. Denying her charge that he had paid her Communist Party dues, he claimed to have known her as a freelance reporter for a leftist publication and admitted having given her nonsensitive information, claiming that his intent was to allay suspicions among radicals that the United States was not vigorously prosecuting the war against the Axis Powers.

Remington was, however, indicted in 1950—as a result of the actions of John Brunini, at the time the foreman of a federal grand jury in New York. In January 1950, while the grand jury was not in session, Brunini met with Bentley and urged her to write a book about her experiences as a Soviet espionage agent. Then, acting as her literary agent, Brunini helped negotiate a book contract for her with the New York publishing house Devin-Adair under which he served as her ghostwriter and collaborator. Indeed, as the historian Kathryn Olmsted concluded on the basis of her research in Brunini's private papers, his "sweaty stylized" prose helped project the "false drama" of Bentley's book *Out of Bondage.*

Brunini's covert friendship with Bentley and his financial interest in her reputation ultimately determined Remington's fate. In May 1950, under Brunini's leadership, the grand jury subpoenaed Bentley's attorney and Remington's estranged wife. After lengthy and persistent questioning by U.S. Attorney Tom Donegan and Brunini, Anne Remington, who had originally expressed her desire not to testify against her husband (on whom she depended for financial support), protested: "I'm hungry, I would like to get something to eat. I haven't eaten since a long time ago. . . . I would like to postpone the hearing. . . . I want to consult my lawyers and see how deep I am getting in." When Donegan persisted and pointedly asked her whether William Remington had paid Communist Party dues, Brunini interjected by warning her: "A witness before a Grand Jury hasn't the privilege to refuse to answer a question. When we get a witness who is contemptuous, who refuses to answer questions, we can take them before a Judge." Repeating Donegan's question, Brunini threatened her: "You have no privilege to refuse to answer the question." A frightened and tired Anne Remington relented, admitting that her husband had, in fact, paid Communist Party dues.

Anne Remington's testimony proved crucial to her husband's perjury indictment (he had denied having been a member of the Communist Party but not having been a Soviet spy). Remington was convicted, but a federal appeals court ordered a retrial on the grounds, first, that the presiding judge's instructions to the jury on what constituted Communist Party membership were "too vague and indefinite" and, more important, that Remington's attorneys were denied access to Anne Remington's grand jury testimony.

Rather than retry Remington, Justice Department attorneys secured a new indictment for his perjurious testimony during his trial. This strategy reflected Justice Department attorneys' recognition of the vulnerability of their case since the records of Anne Remington's grand jury testimony would call into question Brunini's actions as foreman. Remington's attorneys would undoubtedly have called Brunini as a witness to question him about his relationship with Bentley and his zealousness. Indeed, not only had Brunini falsely advised Anne Remington that she had no privilege (which she had as Remington's wife), but the grand jury records would have exposed, first, his questionable role in ensuring Remington's indictment and, then, his self-interest as Bentley's collaborator. Justice Department officials had been aware of this problem since October 1950 (before the onset of Remington's first trial). At the time, Brunini suspected that Remington's attorneys might have uncovered his relationship with Bentley and had advised U.S. Attorney Donegan that he had helped Bentley find a publisher for her book and had served as her unpaid collaborator. He inquired whether he should accept a collaborator's fee offered by Bentley and her publisher. Briefed by Donegan about this problematic relationship, Justice Department officials at first considered reconvening another grand jury, fearing that, otherwise, Remington's attorneys would be able to make a strong case challenging their client's indictment. They decided to proceed, taking the risk that Remington's attorneys would not learn about the Brunini-Bentley relationship.

Remington's indictment, and Bentley's exoneration, stemmed from the actions of a partisan grand jury foreman—and the complicity of Justice Department officials in covering up this questionable relationship. Ironically, the Justice Department's secret decision to grant FBI officials broad discretion to employ wiretaps to corroborate Bentley's allegations and then to ensure Remington's conviction backfired on the Truman administration. The public understanding prevalent by 1951 was of an administration indifferent to the Communist threat (witness Remington's Loyalty Review Board clearance), in striking contrast to the actions of a congressional committee committed to exposing the Communist threat.

The same scenario was repeated in a more widely publicized case, one that had even more profound consequences for the public's understanding of the respective roles of the Truman administration and the FBI. This case involved the charges of another former Communist, Whittaker Chambers.

Chambers had joined the Communist Party in the mid-1920s, serving as a paid functionary until the mid-1930s, when he went underground. Assigned to Washington, D.C., Chambers until his defection in 1937–1938 recruited various federal employees (in the State and Treasury Departments and at the Aberdeen Proving Grounds) to provide him with classified information (some of which was photographed) for transmittal to the Soviet Union.

The FBI informer Ludwig Lore first alerted FBI agents to Chambers's espionage activities in May–August 1941. Lore had then told them that Chambers was a former Soviet agent who was reluctant to "reveal the true story" of Soviet intelligence operations. During the 1930s, Lore recounted, Chambers had been "in contact" with three secretaries (two employed in the State Department and the third in the Commerce Department) who had provided him with "all necessary [Commerce Department] statistical data" and with "the extra copies" of State Department correspondence that they had typed and had supervised approximately seventy Soviet espionage operatives. On the basis of this tip, Chambers was interviewed. He did name twenty individuals (including Alger Hiss) who, he claimed, had been members of a Communist "underground" group whose purpose was to influence government policy. However, despite the contradictions between Lore's sinister and Chambers's relatively benign accounts, FBI agents did not succeed in breaking Chambers and obtaining an admission that he had acted as a courier for a Soviet espionage ring.

Hiss's loyalty became a pressing concern for FBI officials only in late 1945 as the result of the defection of Igor Gouzenko, a Soviet consular official stationed in Ottawa, Canada. On defecting, Gouzenko had disclosed to Canadian security officials his direct knowledge of Soviet espionage operations in Canada, operations that involved the recruitment of Canadian Communists. Gouzenko further claimed that one of his Soviet superiors had told him that the Soviet Union had "more agents in the United States" and that one of them was "an assistant to [Secretary of State Edward] Stettinius."

Briefed on this matter, FBI Director Hoover surmised that the individual in question was Alger Hiss. FBI officials immediately launched an intensive investigation, which lasted through 1946 and included wiretapping Hiss's phone, monitoring his contacts, and opening his mail. The investigation failed, however, to uncover any evidence that Hiss was currently or had in the past engaged in espionage.

Hoover nonetheless urged that, rather than instituting loyalty dismissal proceedings, Secretary of State James Byrnes (Stettinius's successor) force Hiss's resignation by leaking unsubstantiated allegations about him to leading members of Congress. Claiming to be too busy "to contact anyone on the Hill," Byrnes instead confronted Hiss personally. Hiss denied the charge and repeated this denial to the FBI. Thwarted in the strategy of thus sidelining Hiss, Hoover's only option was to develop evidence sufficient to sustain a Hatch Act dismissal—which would require proving Hiss's membership in the Communist Party or "any organization with subversive tendencies."

FBI Agent Thomas Spencer thereupon interviewed Chambers, quizzing him about his earlier charges that Hiss had been a member of a Communist cell during the mid-1930s. Chambers responded by describing Hiss as being "favorably impressed with the Communist movement" but indicated that he had "no documentation or other proof" to substantiate Hiss's membership. When Spencer persisted, asking Chambers again whether he had any "documentary evidence or any independent recollection that HISS was a dues paying member of the Communist Party," Chambers repeated his denial. If he did have this information, Chambers emphasized, he would be "more than glad" to supply it to the bureau.

Chambers had finessed Spencer's question to avoid admitting his own role in Soviet espionage and possession of documents that would confirm Hiss's espionage activities during the 1930s. Chambers did eventually produce this evidence, in a dramatic development that highlights both the politics governing FBI officials' actions and the limitations of the FBI's investigative capabilities.

Chambers's relationship with Hiss emerged as a major political issue in the summer of 1948, at the outset of the presidential campaign. Subpoenaed by the House Committee on Un-American Activities (HUAC), Chambers in August publicly identified Hiss as a member of a Communist cell during the 1930s. He still did not describe the purpose of this cell as espionage, indicating instead that it was intended to promote Communist infiltration of the New Deal bureaucracy. Hiss immediately insisted on the right to testify before HUAC and denied under oath either having been a member of a Communist cell or having known anyone "by the name of" Whittaker Chambers.

Hiss's seemingly firm but qualified denial placed the committee on the defensive. The committee member Congressman Richard Nixon proposed that HUAC adopt a strategy that would not require proving Hiss's Communist Party membership but, instead, focus on whether Chambers and Hiss had known each other during the 1930s. This strategy worked primarily because of the congressman's privileged access to information developed by the FBI. Working indirectly through the Catholic priest John Cronin, FBI officials provided Nixon with "the results of the Bureau's investigation into Hiss." Whenever the "FBI turned up" such information, Cronin telephoned Nixon's private line—something he did "frequently between August and December 1948"—to supply "the F.B.I. tidbits."

HUAC members had established an "informal" relationship with the FBI, one that dated at least to May 1947—but on the strict condition that FBI officials' covert assistance not become known. Indeed, as the former HUAC member Karl Mundt described this relationship: "Most of our [HUAC's] work with the F.B.I. had to be on a personal basis, rather than an official basis." Nixon, by contrast, forged an even closer relationship with the FBI in 1948, having "worked very close with the Bureau and with [FBI Assistant Director Louis] Nichols during the past year [1948] on [the Hiss-Chambers] matter."

The timing and nature of Chambers's HUAC testimony necessitated some response from President Truman, particularly since that testimony occurred at a time when he had called Congress back into special session to embarrass the Republican congressional leadership into enacting the broad reform agenda promised in planks adopted at the Republican National Convention earlier that summer. Questioned at a press conference that month, Truman dismissed the hearings as a "red herring" intended to divert public attention from the "reactionary" record of the Republican-led Eightieth Congress. It seems puzzling that Truman did not at the time reserve judgment until the hearings had run their course. But his dismissive comment—which came back to haunt him—reflected his unwarranted assumption about the thoroughness of FBI investigations. After all, the FBI had been unable to confirm Gouzenko's statement, had failed to corroborate Bentley's more dramatic charges, and had elicited from Chambers only the contention that Hiss and several others were involved in a conspiracy to promote Communist influence in the federal bureaucracy—a stale charge championed by HUAC members since the committee's creation in 1938.

Hiss immediately challenged Chambers to repeat the charges that he had made before HUAC publicly so that he could bring a libel suit. Chambers did so later that month during a "Meet the Press" interview—although again affirming that Hiss's purpose was, not espionage, but the promotion of Communist influence in government. Chambers also repeated this account during October testimony before a grand jury convened to consider indictments of suspected participants in Soviet espionage. Asked by a grand juror whether he "could give one name of any body who in your opinion was positively guilty of espionage against the United States," Chambers equivocated, responding: "Let me think a moment and I will try to answer that. I don't think so and I would like to have an opportunity to answer you more definitely. Let me think it over overnight." On resuming testimony the next day, having been granted the reprieve, Chambers asked whether the juror meant by *espionage* "the turning over of records or confidential documents." The juror responded: "Or information—oral information." Chambers then unqualifiedly stated: "Or oral information. I do not believe I do know such a name."

In an abrupt turn of events, when responding to questions from Hiss's attorneys during a pretrial deposition involving Hiss's libel suit, Chambers turned over on November 17, 1948, four memoranda in Hiss's handwriting and sixty-five typewritten pages of copied State Department documents—dated 1938. And, in an even more startling development, on December 3, 1948, Chambers took two HUAC investigators to a pumpkin patch on his farm and retrieved from a hollowed-out pumpkin microfilm copies of other State Department documents also dated 1938.

Two days before the pumpkin-patch episode, on December 1, 1948, Congressman Nixon had learned from Nicholas Vazzana, an investigator hired by Chambers's lawyers to aid them in the Hiss libel suit, that Chambers had recently turned over to Hiss's attorneys documents that could "break the case." That night, Nixon and HUAC Counsel Robert Stripling traveled to Chambers's home in Westminster, Maryland. Chambers then admitted to having turned over "key documents" and added that he still had "other documents and materials." Returning to Washington, Nixon telephoned FBI Assistant Director Louis Nichols in the middle of the night to advise him of this development "so that the FBI would not be caught off base." Nixon added that HUAC "intended to handl[e] the matter" by holding hearings later that month and to do so in such a manner "that there would be no criticism of the FBI." Nixon then asked that the FBI "do nothing about this information" and specifically not "tell the Attorney General that we [FBI] were told of this information as the Attorney General undoubtedly would try to make it impossible for the Committee to get the documents . . . [and further that] the Bureau not look themselves." FBI officials honored Nixon's brazen request.

Chambers's production of these records in November–December posed two serious problems for FBI officials and Nixon. First, because, under FBI interrogation, Chambers had consistently characterized the purpose of the Communist underground as promoting Communist influence in the New Deal bureaucracy, not espionage, and consistently denied possessing any documentary evidence relating to Hiss, it raised questions about his credibility and highlighted the deficiencies in FBI interrogation techniques. Second, it meant that he would almost certainly be indicted for perjury, his October denial before the grand jury amounting to the obstruction of an inquiry whose central purpose was to uncover evidence of Soviet espionage activities.

Congressman Nixon finessed this latter problem. On December 8, he convened hearings to publicize the committee's acquisition of the microfilmed State Department documents. Emphasizing the committee's breakthrough in uncovering a Soviet espionage ring (and turning the tables on Truman as the partisan who had wrongly attempted to discredit HUAC), Nixon characterized Chambers's revised account as "technical perjury." Should Chambers be indicted, Nixon warned, this would undermine any case against those who had collaborated with him in this espionage conspiracy insofar as the principal witness would be a convicted perjurer.

Nixon, moreover, adopted a bolder strategy, utilizing his physical control over the microfilmed documents to pressure the grand jury to indict Hiss. On December 13, U.S. attorneys subpoenaed the congressman's testimony before the grand jury. Their purpose was to pressure him to turn over the original microfilm that remained in HUAC's possession so that its authenticity could be corroborated. Nixon refused to do so, claiming that this would require a vote by the full House of Representatives (at the time not in session). He agreed to allow FBI agents to examine and establish the authenticity of the microfilm and, in the event that the Justice Department needed the original microfilm during a criminal prosecution, further allowed that "certainly it would be made available at that time for this purpose."

Nixon quickly exploited his appearance to lecture the grand jurors on their responsibility. He emphasized the need to cross-examine Hiss "relentlessly" and at the same time questioned the Justice Department's handling of the matter. Nixon was "confiden[t]" that the grand jurors would reach "the decision that will be in the best interest of the country," but only if the "Justice Department does a proper job in presenting all the facts . . . and does a proper job in relentlessly and ruthlessly cross-examining all that are involved." Nixon concluded with an explicit threat: should no indictment be returned, HUAC "intended to go ahead with our investigation."

Nixon's intervention had the desired result: on December 15, Hiss was indicted on two counts of perjury. Of course it also represented an unwarranted politicization of the proceedings, a pressuring of the grand jurors to indict against the weight of the evidence, something that the mandated secrecy of grand jury operations had been designed to prevent.

Recently released grand jury records relating to Hiss's indictment further underscore the FBI's limitations. On the one hand, FBI agents provided expert testimony that linked Hiss to the typewritten documents that Chambers had produced in November. FBI experts confirmed that these documents had been typed on the same typewriter used by Priscilla Hiss to type other correspondence during the 1930s. On the other hand, FBI agents sought to corroborate Chambers's claim that he had obtained the microfilmed documents from Hiss. In his revised December testimony, Chambers described in detail this espionage operation, claiming that he met Hiss regularly to receive State Department documents and, further, that most of the documents that he received from Hiss (and his other sources) were then filmed by a Communist associate, whom he knew as "Felix." To corroborate this account, FBI agents tried to identify Chambers's "Felix" and seemingly had done so, producing Samuel Pelovitz as a witness.

A former Communist, Pelovitz had for a time lived on Callow Avenue in Baltimore, the address and city cited by Chambers as the filming center for the ring's espionage operation. Subpoenaed to testify before the grand jury, Pelovitz unqualifiedly denied having known Chambers. More important, he denied having any photographic skills and, further, claimed to have lived in New York City in 1936–1937 (when, according to Chambers, the espionage operation took place). Following Pelovitz's testimony, Chambers was brought before the grand jury, at which time he positively identified Pelovitz as "Felix." Because Pelovitz's claim to have lived in New York City during 1936–1937 and to have no photographic skills could be easily confirmed, the blindsided Justice Department attorneys (who had counted on the FBI's efficiency) reassessed their strategy in having Chambers confirm that Pelovitz was Chambers's "Felix." Thus, they brought Chambers back before the grand jury again to revise his earlier identification. Pelovitz was not Felix, Chambers now testified, and then explained his revised account as based on a closer examination of Pelovitz's build and facial structure, observing that Pelovitz "is Jewish and Felix was not Jewish."

FBI officials escaped critical scrutiny of their ineffectiveness, whether that involved their original identification of Pelovitz as Felix* or their inability to have broken Chambers when interviewing him in 1941 and 1946. Their earlier failure in part stemmed from the ideological blinders that governed FBI investigations, the underlying belief that the principal goal of American Communists (and Communist sympathizers) had been seeking to influence government policy and public opinion.

The FBI intelligence failures, moreover, were repeated in the cases of other suspected Soviet espionage operations confirmed after the fact by sources other than the FBI's own agents and informers. In these cases, the FBI's actions either had the effect of foreclosing the possibility of conviction or generated evidence insufficient to secure indictments.

One such case involved the editor and individuals associated with the radical journal of Far Eastern affairs *Amerasia.* In January 1945, Kenneth Wells, an OSS analyst, was struck by the publication in the January 26, 1945, issue of the journal of an almost verbatim account of a classified report that he had written on U.S. policy toward Thailand. Wells called this to the attention of his superiors, and, on March 11, 1945, OSS operatives broke into the journal's New York office, discovering hundreds of classified OSS, State Department, and Office of Naval Intelligence (ONI) documents. They immediately reported this discovery to the FBI.

FBI agents then themselves broke into the *Amerasia* office. They did so in order to find a way in which to identify which individuals (in OSS, State, ONI) would have had access to the particular pilfered documents and, hence, to identify the sources of the leaks. In addition, FBI agents wiretapped and bugged the *Amerasia* office and the residence of its editor,

---

* After Hiss's indictment, FBI agents were able to identify Chambers's Felix, Felix Inslerman. Inslerman, however, took the Fifth Amendment rather than deny or corroborate Chambers's account. Accordingly, during Hiss's trials, an FBI agent testified that one of the cameras that Inslerman possessed, a Leica, was the same make as that used to film State Department documents.

Philip Jaffe, broke into the residences of the associate editor, Kate Mitchell, and the freelance writer Mark Gayn, and broke into and bugged the residence of the State Department employee Emmanuel Larsen. That they resorted to these illegal methods meant that FBI officials were willing to risk being unable to prosecute suspects either under espionage statutes or for unauthorized possession of classified documents—and, thus, that their main purpose was, in fact, shutting down the leaks, not gathering the kind of evidence necessary to mount a successful prosecution. Consequently, having in June 1945 sought indictments against those individuals identified by the FBI as receiving or supplying the leaked information, Justice Department attorneys were faced with cases that would be very difficult to prosecute.

At the time, junior Justice Department attorneys had advised against prosecution, emphasizing that the FBI had failed to uncover "the necessary legal evidence" to convict the identified suspects. Their concern centered on the FBI's illegal uses of wiretaps, bugs, and break-ins to identify the participants in this leaking operation, the results of which "cannot be used in evidence." Senior Justice Department officials overruled them, opting for what turned out to be a risky and counterproductive strategy of attempting to finesse the evidentiary problem. Assistant to the Attorney General James McInerney proposed that FBI agents arrest Jaffe and Mitchell at the *Amerasia* office and Larsen and Gayn at their homes "in order that agents could conduct a [lawful] search" of their premises at the time of arrest—knowing of the presence of the pilfered documents from earlier FBI break-ins. The discovery of this evidence, McInerney added, could be useful in securing admissions from those arrested, observing that, in 80 percent of all criminal cases, suspects made "damaging admissions" when confronted by "incriminating documents."

McInerney's strategy was effected on June 6, 1945, with the arrests of Jaffe, Mitchell, Gayn, and Larsen (as well as of the ONI officer Andrew Roth and the State Department official John Service). On August 10, 1945, however, a grand jury indicted only Jaffe, Larsen, and Roth—and only on the charge of conspiring to remove or unauthorized possession of classified documents (not that of espionage, no evidence having been uncovered that the arrestees intended to deliver these documents to a foreign power).

Justice Department officials were ultimately unable to convict neither Jaffe, Larsen, nor Roth as McInerney's crafty strategy had backfired. Struck by how quickly FBI agents located the State Department documents after arresting him, Larsen suspected that they had earlier broken into his apartment. Confronting his janitor, he learned that his suspicion was warranted. His attorney then moved to have his indictment quashed. At the time, Justice Department attorneys were involved in negotiations with Jaffe. Fearing that Jaffe would learn of Larsen's motion and similarly seek to ascertain whether FBI agents had also broken into the *Amerasia* office, they offered him a plea bargain—a fine but no imprisonment.

The FBI's illegal practices had precluded prosecution of the *Amerasia* defendants. Another, but far more dramatic, case also highlights the limitations of the bureau's intelligence efforts. This case dominated national politics in the 1950s, was dubbed by FBI Director Hoover in a *Reader's Digest* article *the crime of the century,* and involved the arrest of two committed Communist activists, Julius and Ethel Rosenberg, for their role in a Soviet-directed conspiracy to steal the "secret of the atomic bomb."

The FBI limitations in this instance involved agents' failure to uncover Julius Rosenberg's recruitment of his brother-in-law David Greenglass (who, in 1944–1945, was employed at the Los Alamos laboratory) to pilfer information about the atomic bomb project. This discovery was the work of military intelligence. U.S. military intelligence began in 1940 intercepting Soviet consular messages transmitted telegraphically from Washington, D.C., and New York to Moscow. Because these messages were transmitted in code, military intelligence officials in 1943 established a special unit—codenamed the Venona Project—to attempt to decipher them. Analysts made their first breakthrough in 1946 and, by 1949, had succeeded in deciphering a large number of the coded messages—a success that led, in early 1950, to the uncovering of the Rosenberg-Greenglass atomic bomb conspiracy.

The sensitivity of the Venona Project meant, however, that the source of the discovery could not be disclosed, intelligence officials hoping to learn about other Soviet intelligence operations, both during World War II and later.* Although unable to rely directly on the Venona evidence, FBI officials did use this information indirectly when interrogating Greenglass (and also Harry Gold, Greenglass's courier, and Max Elitcher, an associate of Julius Rosenberg's). FBI agents succeeded in obtaining Greenglass's,

* The Venona Project proved to be of no value for uncovering Soviet intelligence operations after 1948, Soviet officials having learned in that year, from their mole Harold "Kim" Philby and another recruit, William Weisband, employed at the time in military intelligence, of the U.S. cryptanalysts' success in deciphering their consular messages and acted to correct the coding mistake that made possible military intelligence's breakthrough.

Gold's, and Elitcher's admission to having been participants in this conspiracy and their agreement to testify against Julius and Ethel Rosenberg. The only evidence that was introduced during the Rosenbergs' trial that FBI agents had developed independently was essentially circumstantial—corroborating Greenglass's testimony that Julius Rosenberg had purchased a console in 1944 (to film the stolen documents) and that Gold had stayed overnight in Albuquerque in June 1945 when (as a courier for the Rosenberg operation) he had retrieved information from Greenglass.

The Rosenbergs' and Greenglass's conviction became a major news story in the 1950s and enhanced the FBI's reputation as an efficient counterespionage agency. What was not known at the time was that FBI agents had failed to corroborate a second case of atomic espionage also uncovered by the work of the Venona Project, this one involving two Communist friends, Theodore Hall and Saville Sax.

Hall had graduated from Harvard College at eighteen, earned a Ph.D. in physics from the University of Chicago, and obtained employment at the Los Alamos project in 1944–1945 conducting research in the thermonuclear process of nuclear implosion. Visiting New York on leave in 1944, Hall was urged by Sax to report his knowledge of the atomic bomb project to Soviet officials. Hall agreed, writing an initial report that Sax delivered to the Soviet consulate in New York. Soviet officials thereupon trained Sax in espionage techniques, and Sax subsequently traveled to New Mexico in 1945 to act as a courier for Hall's further reports. Hall's original report had identified the "key personnel" participating in the Los Alamos project—among them "all the outstanding physicists of the U.S., England, Italy and Germany (immigrants)"—and revealed that the cost of the project ran into the billions of dollars and that the project relied on four cyclotrons. This and subsequent reports were welcomed by Soviet physicists, their "great interest" relayed to New York by their Soviet supervisors. In contrast to Greenglass, a military inductee with only a high school education, lacking any theoretical training, and assigned to Los Alamos as a low-level technician, Hall was a prized recruit.

Alerted by the Venona intercepts, FBI officials in 1950 launched an intensive investigation of Hall and Sax. FBI agents culled the records of the FBI's surveillance of American Communists in New York during the 1940s (where Hall and Sax resided), sought additional information from military intelligence (the agency had the primary responsibility for security investigations at Los Alamos), and closely monitored Hall's and Sax's activities in

1950–1951 (including breaking into their residences and photocopying their mail). This intensive investigation, however, uncovered no evidence that either Hall or Sax had been or continued to be involved in espionage.* FBI agents uncovered only their past and current involvement in radical politics, civil rights, and labor union activities.

Stymied by their own investigative failures, FBI officials hoped to salvage an espionage case by breaking either Hall or Sax through vigorous interrogation. In separate interviews conducted in March 1951, FBI agents pointedly questioned whether the two had engaged in espionage activities in 1944 and 1945 (not revealing, of course, that the source of their suspicions was the Venona Project). For example, Sax was asked why he had visited the Soviet consulate in New York in 1944 and the purpose of his trips to Albuquerque in 1945. Both brazenly denied any involvement in espionage, while Sax explained his visit to the Soviet consulate as occasioned by his family's interest in providing financial assistance to relatives in the Soviet Union (citing his mother's public involvement in Russian war relief work) and his trips to New Mexico as intended to pursue his interest in an undergraduate degree in anthropology.

The failure of FBI agents to break either Hall or Sax led FBI officials to close the investigation in 1952, having concluded that "all outstanding leads have been exhausted." In a stark admission of their own investigative limitations, FBI officials privately conceded that the "only indication" that they had of Hall's and Sax's atomic espionage activities came from the Venona Project and that such information could not "be disseminated outside the Bureau."

FBI officials also failed to ensure the conviction of another American Communist who had been recruited in 1944–1945 to spy on behalf of the Soviet Union, Judith Coplon. As in the Rosenberg/Greenglass and Hall/Sax cases, Coplon's recruitment and espionage activities were uncovered in December 1948 through the Venona Project. In contrast to the others, however, Coplon was at the time a Justice Department employee who might have continued to provide information to Soviet intelligence about current FBI investigative targets and procedures. In an effort to identify her Soviet contacts and possibly other coconspirators, FBI agents monitored her

---

* Having been denied a security clearance in 1946 owing to his political activities, Hall was thereafter denied access to classified information (during both his graduate and his postgraduate work at the University of Chicago).

movements and wiretapped her office and home phones and the phone of her parents in New York (with whom she visited frequently). This surveillance led to the discovery of her meeting in January 1949 with Valentin Gubitchev, a Soviet citizen employed on the United Nations staff. Rather than effect her dismissal under the Federal Employee Loyalty Program, Justice Department officials decided to launch a sting operation to obtain evidence to prosecute her for espionage. Purposefully granted access to a specially created FBI report "that contained enough truth to make it [the report] seem important and enough false information to make it imperative for Coplon to grab it and quickly deliver it to her Soviet contact," Coplon took the bait. Following her to New York City, FBI agents arrested her on March 4, 1949, as she was attempting to deliver twenty-eight FBI reports to Gubitchev.

This apparently successful sting operation quickly unraveled, to the great embarrassment of FBI officials. During Coplon's first trial in Washington, D.C., her attorney, Archibald Palmer, moved to have the twenty-eight FBI reports found in her handbag at the time of her arrest introduced as evidence. He argued that Coplon could not be tried for unauthorized possession of classified documents without the defense having the right to evaluate the sensitivity of the documents in open court. When Judge Albert Reeves ruled in Palmer's favor, FBI Director Hoover urged Attorney General Clark to drop the case. Producing the documents, Hoover warned Clark, raised a "broader issue of the future of the Bureau," adding that he would prefer to "see the Coplon case go by default if other legal steps are not available for the protection of the security of our files and the rights of individuals [identified in the FBI reports] not formally charged with any crime."

Clark rejected Hoover's plea, having decided to make an example of Coplon in order to deter future leaks or espionage. When released, however, the FBI reports did not damage legitimate FBI security operations or the reputations of innocent Americans. They did, however, confirm that the FBI had massively monitored political activities—the subjects of these FBI reports included an individual working on a master's thesis on the New Deal in New Zealand, a supporter of Henry Wallace's Progressive Party presidential campaign in 1948, critics of HUAC, Bureau of Standards Director Edward Condon, the White House aide David Niles, and the Hollywood actors Edward G. Robinson and Frederick March. The reports further confirmed the extent of FBI wiretapping—fifteen of the twenty-eight containing information so obtained. On the basis of the latter disclosure, Palmer requested a pretrial hearing to ascertain whether his client's phone had been tapped. Judge Reeves, however, acceded to U.S. Attorney John Kelly Jr.'s dismissal of this motion as merely a "fishing expedition."

During Coplon's second trial in New York, her attorney again raised the wiretapping issue. This time the presiding judge, Sylvester Ryan, ordered a pretrial hearing that led to the disclosure that the FBI had wiretapped Coplon's phone, both before and after her arrest (potentially intercepting privileged conversations with her attorneys), that the FBI agent who had originally testified that he had no knowledge whether Coplon was wire-tapped had, in fact, routinely received reports based on these tapes, and, further, that FBI officials had ordered the destruction of these wiretap records "in view of the imminence of her [Coplon's] trial." Because of these revelations, Coplon's conviction was reversed, with the judge ordering a re-trial. Justice Department officials never retried the case, however, although delaying until 1967 before formally dropping prosecution.

Were these cases, then, representative of FBI counterintelligence abil-ities, confirming as they do FBI failures either to have anticipated espionage or to have developed admissible evidence and, thus, ensure successful pros-ecution? Continued restrictions on access to relevant FBI records preclude any understanding of their representative or atypical nature. Regardless, these were the major cases brought during the early Cold War years, cases that were instrumental* in enhancing the FBI's reputation and also in pro-moting a McCarthyite politics. More important, the secrecy that at the time shrouded FBI operations from public and congressional scrutiny enabled FBI officials to escape disclosure of the limitations of FBI counterespionage operations and also of the role that they themselves played in promoting a McCarthyite politics.

* Excepting Hall's, which was not known at the time.

Promoting McCarthyism—
and Morality (Again)

It was not happenstance that during the Cold War years conservative congressmen successfully accused the Roosevelt and Truman administrations of direct or indirect responsibility for Soviet espionage successes and international influence. Since the 1930s, they had attempted to exploit the "Communists-in-government" theme to discredit the Roosevelt New Deal. Such charges, however, commanded limited support and were for the most part seen as partisan in purpose. By 1950, however, they had been refined to focus on those holding sensitive positions in the State Department and, thus, commanded greater credence in the security-obsessed climate of the early Cold War years. Still, strikingly absent from this debate was any assessment of the FBI's counterespionage failings. Had an independent inquiry been conducted, it would have confirmed that both Roosevelt and Truman had provided FBI officials broad authority to investigate American Communists and Soviet officials stationed in the United States. Furthermore, both presidents had authorized the FBI to conduct intelligence investigations and use wiretaps and had instituted far-reaching loyalty programs to preclude the hiring or effect the dismissal of subversive federal employees. Rather than hamstring the FBI, both presidents purposefully avoided either monitoring how their broad authorizations were used or inquiring as to why FBI officials had failed to anticipate Soviet espionage. Recently released FBI records, moreover, confirm that, while FBI agents missed Soviet espionage activities, they had collected massive amounts of information confirming that American Communists were subservient to the Kremlin and were actively seeking to influence public policy and the political culture. Such information might have no value for counterintelligence purposes or for promoting prosecution—because it failed to confirm either a violation of a federal statute or a planned espionage operation. This essentially political information, however, acquired a different value during the Cold War years. Having accumulated (and continued to accumulate) such information, FBI officials were emboldened to embark on a course of political containment.

FBI officials had always believed that Communists posed a serious subversive threat but also that the general public was either indifferent to or unaware of this threat. Accordingly, in February 1946, they launched an "educational campaign" so that "in the event of an emergency we will have an informed public opinion." This campaign relied on the release through "available channels"—for example, certifiably reliable reporters, columnists, editors, and members of Congress—of "educational material" demonstrating the "basically Russian nature" of the U.S. Communist Party. This material was released on the strict condition that the recipients would not disclose their own covert assistance. The resultant propaganda campaign could heighten public awareness of the Communist threat and expose the "support which the Party receives from 'liberal' sources and its connections in the labor unions."

The educational campaign launched in February 1946 previewed a host of initiatives undertaken during the 1940s and 1950s. Heretofore cautious, FBI officials were emboldened to move aggressively given the positive results of a onetime May 1947 request from House Committee on Un-American Activities (HUAC) Chairman J. Parnell Thomas and HUAC Counsel Robert Stripling.

Thomas and Stripling had traveled to Hollywood that month to conduct a preliminary investigation of Communist influence in the motion picture industry. They hoped to be able to develop sufficient information so that, on their return to Washington in June, they could convince the full committee to authorize public hearings on the dangers of Communist influence in Hollywood.

On their arrival in Los Angeles, however, Thomas and Stripling became frustrated over their inability to develop the needed evidence. They then decided to contact Richard Hood, the head (special agent in charge, or SAC) of the FBI's Los Angeles field office, to request a meeting. Hood immediately briefed FBI Director Hoover about this request. As he had in the past and as recently as March 1947, Hoover opposed having the FBI publicly involved with the controversial HUAC. He explicitly instructed the Los Angeles SAC to inform Thomas that he, Hood, "could not appear before the Committee in open session" but would be willing to point out any Hollywood personalities who had been publicly identified as Communists.

When meeting Hood, however, Thomas and Stripling did not raise the matter of his public appearance. Instead, they emphasized their difficulties in developing information about Communist influence and asked

Hood to check FBI files for "any data that might be of assistance to them concerning" nine named individuals and any "background and other definite data that could be of assistance." He did not want to do anything, Thomas assured Hood, that "might embarrass our [FBI] Sources of Information or interfere with our investigations."

Relieved that Thomas and Stripling had no intention of seeking the FBI's public involvement, Hoover agreed to provide "*every* assistance to this Committee." FBI officials dutifully prepared a detailed report, "Re: Communist Activities in Washington," summarizing whatever information FBI agents had compiled on each of the named nine (including their Communist "membership book number") as well as the "names of known Communists who have some basis for knowledge of Communist activities, the known Communist front groups, and officers whom the Committee might investigate." In addition, FBI officials identified nine "non-Communist" "cooperative and friendly witnesses" whom Thomas and Stripling could interview (including Ronald Reagan, Robert Montgomery, Leila Rogers, and Jack Warner). Hoover nonetheless proffered this assistance on the condition that Thomas and Stripling would not use this information in "any way [that could] embarrass the Bureau" and that "under no circumstances will the FBI source of this information be disclosed."

The FBI's helpful, if covert, assistance enabled Thomas to secure the full committee's approval to hold public hearings on Communist influence in Hollywood, hearings originally scheduled for September 1947. The very limitations that had led the HUAC chair to seek FBI assistance in May, however, led him to seek a personal meeting with the FBI director on June 24.

Thomas began this meeting by pledging to "work even closer" with the FBI in the future. He specifically extolled the usefulness of FBI files because they contained "vast knowledge of subversive activities" that could provide "leads and information of value to the Committee" and promised to ensure that any assistance provided by the FBI to the committee would remain confidential. On the basis of this assurance and the further assurance that the "Bureau would not be publicly drawn into the investigation nor be called to appear in any capacity," Hoover agreed that FBI officials would be "as helpful to the Committee as we could." Briefing his senior aides on his decision, the FBI director explained his rationale: "I do think it is long overdue for the Communist infiltration in Hollywood to be exposed, and as there is no medium at present through which the Bureau can bring that about on its own motion I think it entirely proper and desirable that we assist the Committee in Congress that is intent upon bringing to light the true facts in the situation."

In the ensuing months and until HUAC held public hearings in October 1947, FBI officials fed the HUAC chair detailed accounts of the Communist affiliations of fifty-one Hollywood personalities. The FBI's assistance included information about these individuals' affiliations with so-called Communist front groups and photostats of their Communist membership cards—which FBI agents had obtained through a series of break-ins. This assistance proved to be crucial. During public hearings in October, committee members questioned each of ten subpoenaed witnesses about their Communist affiliations. All refused to answer on First Amendment grounds, and the committee chair announced his intention of having them cited for contempt of Congress. HUAC counsel was then called to describe in detail each of these witnesses' affiliations with Communist front groups and to introduce into the record photocopies of their Communist Party membership cards. An elated Thomas telephoned FBI Assistant Director Nichols at the conclusion of the hearings to ask him to convey his "heartfelt appreciation" to Hoover because the FBI director was "more than any other person . . . responsible for [the] Committee not being put out of business."

The FBI's assistance to HUAC in 1947 was not a one-shot initiative. FBI officials provided, as we have seen, similar assistance to Congressman Nixon during HUAC's 1948 hearings in the Hiss-Chambers affair. Thereafter, FBI assistance to the committee varied, influenced sometimes by FBI Director Hoover's petty ragings against the committee's taking credit for exposing the Communist menace and other times by the tendency of HUAC members and staff to compromise the committee's covert relationship with the FBI. Assistance would be provided for a time, then severed when committee members failed to honor the "proper relationship" with the FBI, only to be resumed again following renewed assurances of confidentiality. By 1956, FBI officials had become so exasperated with the committee's recklessness and continued violation of the confidentiality pledge that they established strict conditions for future assistance. FBI Assistant Director Nichols (and then his successor, Cartha DeLoach) would work only with HUAC's chief counsel and would only provide the names and addresses of and background information on prospective witnesses; the names of financial contributors to the Communist Party; advice on "friendly" witnesses or experts whom the committee might consult; and editing assistance to correct errors in committee reports.

FBI officials replicated this covert assistance to HUAC in the case of the nation's most controversial anti-Communist, Senator Joseph McCarthy, following McCarthy's dramatic emergence as the symbol of Cold War anti-communism. In a series of public speeches beginning on February 9, 1950, and culminating in a February 20, 1950, speech on the Senate floor, McCarthy claimed to have evidence of "known Communists in the State Department." Confident that McCarthy could not document his indictment that the Truman administration was "soft toward Communism," Senate Democrats in March authorized a special inquiry, chaired by Senator Millard Tydings, into the eighty-one cases that McCarthy had cited in his February 20 Senate speech. And, because McCarthy had no independent expertise and had not anticipated a critical inquiry into his claimed evidence, his highly publicized charges were potentially vulnerable to being refuted as exaggerated and irresponsible. Even the Republican Senate minority leader, Robert Taft (who subsequently urged McCarthy to "keep talking and if one case doesn't work out, proceed with another one"), had privately characterized the senator's February 20 speech as a "perfectly reckless performance."

McCarthy, however, was able to sustain the initiative. Having inadvertently become the target of Democratic efforts to discredit the Republican-led attack on the Truman administration's "softness toward Communism," he benefited from the assistance of a bevy of conservative reporters and congressional aides who had long researched the Communists-in-government issue. In addition, McCarthy sought FBI assistance. FBI officials willingly responded, first by advising him to hire the former FBI agent Don Surine as an investigator. More important, FBI officials made every effort to assist the senator. As former FBI Assistant Director William Sullivan later recounted, Hoover had ordered FBI personnel to give "McCarthy all we had, but all we had were fragments, nothing could prove his allegations." Although agreeable to assisting McCarthy, the wily FBI director understood the political perils of this action—as McCarthy's target was the incumbent Truman administration and his efforts were part of a broader Republican assault on the Democratic administrations of Roosevelt and Truman. Thus, FBI officials carefully camouflaged their assistance. They never provided the senator copies of FBI reports. Instead, they culled information from FBI files and typed it in blind memoranda (to be discussed in the next chapter).

On the receipt of these memoranda, Surine inserted "the information appearing in the Bureau report in the form of a summary of information appearing in the CSC [Civil Service Commission] files, thus making it appear that his office had secured a CSC file rather than a Bureau file."

McCarthy had been reviled since 1950 as an irresponsible and partisan demagogue (the syndicated cartoonist Herb Block coined the term *McCarthyism* when depicting the senator emerging from the sewers of Washington, D.C., carrying a broad brush in one hand and a bucket of tar in the other). McCarthy personified the virulent anti-Communist politics that stifled political debate during the Cold War years. His tactics proved to be invaluable for Republican operatives and contributed to Republican successes in the 1952 presidential and congressional elections. Emboldened by these successes and his elevation to chair of the Senate Government Operations Committee in 1953 (the Republicans having won majority control of the Senate), McCarthy sought more direct FBI assistance. As committee chair, the senator would command a forum to launch highly publicized hearings. Yet, if these hearings were to succeed, McCarthy would, henceforth, need credible evidence about the Communist menace—for his charges would carry the committee's imprimatur and would be subject to the critical scrutiny of Democratic members of the committee and their staff.

Thus, when preparing to assume the chairmanship of the Senate Government Operations Committee, McCarthy contacted Guy Hottel, the head (SAC) of the FBI's Washington, D.C., field office, in late November 1952. The senator asked Hottel to convey to Hoover that he "anticipated closer cooperation and more extended use of the FBI and its facilities following the beginning of the new Congress" and, thus, wanted to confer with Hoover "in the not too distant future relative to his obtaining suggestions for potential investigators" to be hired by the committee. McCarthy met with Hoover on December 1, 1952, and again on January 12, 1953, at which time he solicited the FBI director's recommendations of "a number of competent investigators that he might consider for appointment to the staff." Hoover should also, McCarthy emphasized, "contact him whenever [he, Hoover] saw any activity of any member of his [McCarthy's] staff . . . which [he, Hoover] did not feel was in the best interest of administration," adding that he himself would "contact" the FBI "from time to time." A sympathetic FBI director ordered his aides to develop the requested list of possible investigators and to provide input into McCarthy's plans for the committee. More than willing to promote the committee's political agenda,

Hoover also had FBI Assistant Director Nichols serve as a "close liaison" to McCarthy, with the assigned task of honoring the various "name check" requests (i.e., requests for a search for all information in FBI files on a named individual) of the committee counsels Roy Cohn and Don Surine.

FBI assistance to McCarthy continued until July 1953, when, because of the senator's impolitic decision to hire Francis Carr as committee counsel, Hoover ordered a halt. McCarthy had sought Hoover's clearance for the Carr appointment insofar as Carr was a current FBI supervisor. Informed that the FBI director had reservations, Jean Kerr (the senator's administrative assistant) met with Hoover, at which time he informed her that he would neither approve nor disapprove this appointment, adding that it was Carr's decision. Hoover then pinpointed the consequences should McCarthy appoint a current FBI employee "engaged upon work dealing with subversive activities." Such an appointment "would, no doubt," he observed, "be seized upon by critics of the Senator and of the FBI as a deliberate effort to effect a 'pipe line' into the FBI and that it would be necessary for the Bureau to be far more circumspect in all of its dealings with the McCarthy Committee should Mr. Carr be appointed." Because Kerr did not brief him about Hoover's reservations, McCarthy appointed Carr. Hoover immediately severed all FBI assistance to the senator, as recorded in FBI files: "Since then [July 1953] no information has been furnished to this Committee."

The FBI's relationship with HUAC and McCarthy was also replicated in the case of the Senate Internal Security Subcommittee (SISS), another congressional committee in the forefront of the attempt to publicize the Communist menace. In contrast to the informal relationship that FBI officials had maintained with HUAC and McCarthy, their liaison role with SISS was in March 1951 formally approved by Attorney General J. Howard McGrath, who delegated to Hoover "complete responsibility" to do "whatever the Director felt should be done." Hoover had already decided to cooperate with SISS Chair Pat McCarran on "a personal basis" and, thus, leapt at this opportunity to honor SISS requests for "information," having been assured by his staff of McCarran's "very high personal regard" as well as his offer that, should the FBI require "any help on the Hill," he should be contacted to "take care of any matter." Under this arrangement, SISS counsel would submit SISS's name check requests to FBI Assistant Director Nichols, who would then provide the requested reports as well as "suggestive leads and/or information to be used in questioning witnesses." McCarran personally assured Hoover that no one would learn "exactly what cooperation was extended by the FBI" and that he intended "to use the Committee to not only strengthen internal security for the good of the United States but to help the Bureau in every possible manner."

This covert liaison program lasted until 1954, when, after discussions with Attorney General Herbert Brownell, FBI officials terminated the assistance. The catalyst was, ironically, an overtly partisan attempt of Brownell's to discredit Harry Truman, the former Democratic president.

During the 1952 presidential election, Brownell had served as Eisenhower's campaign manager, orchestrating a campaign that implied that the Truman administration had hamstrung FBI investigations into the Communist menace and that an Eisenhower administration would change this. On assuming office, administration officials released statistics on the number of people who had been dismissed as security risks by the newly elected administration. Brownell repeated this general theme of the Truman administration's indifference to FBI reports detailing Communist influence during a speech to a businessmen's group in Chicago in December 1953, taking the opportunity to contrast the Democratic administration's indifference with the new Republican administration's vigilance. As an example, he cited Truman's failure in 1946 to have acted on FBI reports questioning the loyalty of Harry Dexter White that Hoover had sent to the White House after Truman had nominated White as executive director of the International Monetary Fund. Truman soon responded by accusing Brownell of McCarthyism and then claiming that he had not withdrawn White's nomination in order not to compromise an ongoing FBI investigation (one based on the Communist defector Elizabeth Bentley's charges). To rebut Truman, Brownell arranged joint testimony by himself and Hoover before SISS. Hoover's testimony infuriated many Democrats, including conservative Southern Democrats, who sharply criticized the FBI director for unnecessarily interceding in a partisan dispute and for having politicized the FBI.

Brownell's speech and the SISS hearing followed shortly after a second publicized incident that seemed to offer further evidence of a politicized FBI. In a speech before a men's social club in Utah, Republican Senator Karl Mundt commented in passing that FBI officials had regularly leaked information to congressional committees investigating Communist activities. Democratic Senator J. William Fulbright learned of Mundt's remarks and denounced this practice—although Hoover and FBI officials falsely denied having done anything of the sort.

Fearing the consequences of the Mundt and Brownell incidents for the FBI's image as an apolitical law enforcement agency, FBI officials reassessed the SISS secret liaison program—at a time when they were already concerned about the volume of SISS requests. In July 1954, Hoover and Brownell agreed that the FBI would no longer honor SISS requests.

By 1954, FBI officials had succeeded in both promoting a McCarthyite politics and disguising their own crucial assistance to congressional McCarthyites. This was not, however, the sole instance in which FBI officials worked surreptitiously to influence public opinion. A companion initiative capitalized on the homophobia of the time to sustain fears about the threat posed by the continued employment of homosexuals in government. Many believed that, should homosexuals obtain federal employment, they could be blackmailed into committing espionage.

This theme underlay another Republican assault on the Truman administration initiated in early 1950. At the very time that Senator McCarthy was accusing the Truman administration of "softness toward Communism," New York Governor Thomas Dewey, Republican National Committee Chairman Guy Gabrielson, and Senators McCarthy, Mundt, and Kenneth Wherry charged that there was a companion internal security threat: namely, that homosexuals "have infiltrated our Government in recent years." As in the accusations of McCarthy's eighty-one cases, the Senate authorized another investigation, to be led by Senator Clyde Hoey. This investigation was conducted in secret, however, given the delicacy of exploring the sexual orientation of suspected individuals. In its final report released in December 1950, the so-called Hoey Committee concluded that the employment of homosexuals did threaten the nation's security. Their "lack of emotional stability" and the "weakness of their moral fiber" made them "easy prey to blackmailers." "Each complaint of sexual perversion" must be investigated, the committee emphasized, to ensure that "perverts can be put out of Government and kept out."

To address this perceived problem, FBI Director Hoover on June 20, 1951, instituted the code-named Sex Deviate program.* Under this program, FBI officials would furnish to specified executive, legislative, and judicial branch officials all "information concerning allegations" of homosexuality involving "present and past employees."

* The FBI had, however, been compiling files on homosexuals since 1937.

At the time of its inception, the purpose of the Sex Deviate program had been simply to purge suspected homosexuals from federal agencies, congressional committees, and the federal courts. By 1954, however, FBI officials had begun disseminating information on suspected homosexuals "in appropriate instances where the best interests of the Bureau is [*sic*] served" to other "proper" officials and to "institutions of higher learning or law enforcement agencies." The scope and purpose of the expanded program cannot, however, presently be established because, in 1977, FBI officials destroyed all relevant records. Four examples of FBI practices involving alleged homosexuals hint at the perversity and abuse informing the FBI's monitoring of and maintenance of information on suspected homosexuals.

The first, and most perverse, involved the FBI's discovery in 1965 that the Hollywood actor Rock Hudson was homosexual. FBI officials immediately passed this information along to the Johnson White House. It is unclear why since Hudson did not then hold and was not being considered for a sensitive government position. Regardless, they were deeply concerned that Hudson might play an FBI agent in a movie.

The second example involved Adlai Stevenson, the Illinois governor and Democratic presidential nominee. On the basis of the unsupported allegation of Gene Melchiore (a Bradley University basketball player arrested that year for fixing games), FBI officials in April 1952 listed Stevenson in the FBI's Sex Deviate index card file, recording that he was homosexual, was well-known as "Adeline," and, because of this, "would not run for President." Stevenson's national prominence, however, led Hoover to maintain this Sex Deviate index card in a folder under Stevenson's name in his secret office file—which explains why the card escaped the massive record destruction of 1977. The Stevenson folder further confirms the extent to which FBI officials sought to verify and their various attempts to exploit this malicious allegation.

For example, in August 1952, Milt Hill, a former national correspondent for Federated Publications who had been commissioned to write the official Republican biography of the Democratic presidential nominee, contacted FBI Assistant Director Nichols. Hill's purpose was to seek confirmation of derogatory information that he had come across about Stevenson, including "scuttlebutt" that the Democratic presidential nominee had been arrested in New York City "on a morals charge, put up bond, and elected to forfeit." While this allegation was never printed, rumors of Stevenson's alleged homosexuality were circulated widely during the 1952 presidential campaign, including by SAC Hottel.* Moreover, Hoover cited this unsupported allegation in summary reports on Stevenson sent first, in 1961, to the Kennedy White House and then, in 1964 and 1965, to the Johnson White House.† Because the FBI was unable to confirm this misinformation, Kennedy submitted Stevenson's name for confirmation as the U.S. ambassador to the United Nations, and Johnson retained Stevenson's services.

The third case involved the syndicated columnist Joseph Alsop. During a visit to the Soviet Union in February 1957, Alsop was arrested in his Moscow hotel room during a homosexual tryst, the victim of a KGB trap. KGB officials unsuccessfully sought to use the threat of prosecution to get Alsop to "help them a little if they were to help him" avoid arrest and ensure "absolute security." The syndicated columnist succeeded, however, in escaping Moscow in a ruse orchestrated by the U.S. ambassador. On his arrival in Paris, Alsop met with a CIA officer and briefed him on this incident and his "incurable homosexuality." Alsop did so to protect himself from any future Soviet blackmail attempt, and he specifically asked that his admission be brought to the "attention" of CIA Director Allen Dulles and FBI Director Hoover and "be kept out of the general file and placed in a special file."

Dulles and Hoover were both briefed on this matter, and Hoover opened a special folder in his secret office file to maintain this and follow-up reports. Dulles duly informed the secretary of state, his brother, about the Alsop "incident"; Hoover informed Attorney General Brownell and the White House aide Sherman Adams. Hoover's reports cited in addition to the Moscow incident two other instances of Alsop's homosexuality that FBI agents had already recorded.

Initially, these reports had no effect beyond ensuring that senior Eisenhower administration officials were aware of the Moscow incident. In 1959,

* Hottel's indiscreet rumormongering came to the attention of the Stevenson campaign. Senior FBI officials moved quickly to contain the damage by having Hottel sign a carefully worded affidavit denying that he personally made this charge at the Mayflower Hotel (where the source claimed to have overheard others reporting Hottel's remark) and that he had no access to or awareness of FBI "files" (the records were all held in Hoover's office and not in FBI files).

† Prompting the October 1964 Johnson briefing was the morals arrest of the White House aide Walter Jenkins that month by the Washington metropolitan police. In an attempt to contain any adverse fallout, President Johnson requested FBI reports on all members of the Republican presidential nominee Barry Goldwater's Senate staff.

however, the derogatory information about Alsop commanded greater attention, an interest triggered by the series of columns that Alsop had written that year criticizing the Eisenhower administration's fiscal conservatism on the grounds that it had contributed to a "missile gap" between the United States and the Soviet Union. The administration's unwillingness to increase defense spending, Alsop darkly warned, amounted to "playing Russian roulette with the whole course of human history."

Alsop's columns both infuriated and worried Attorney General William Rogers, who promptly asked Hoover to "get together what we [i.e., the FBI] have on Alsop" for his use in briefing Secretary of Defense Neil McElroy. Rogers advised Hoover that he further intended to share this information with President Eisenhower, Under Secretary of State Christian Herter, the White House aide Wilton Persons, and Secretary of the Cabinet Robert Gray and that he would not "take the responsibility for such information not going further."

Apparently, Rogers (if not McElroy) had in turn briefed Air Force General Nathan Twining, the chairman of the Joint Chiefs of Staff, about "the Alsop matter." Wondering "how Alsop could be trusted," Twining contacted Rogers to convey his concern that, while Alsop might be confident that "there would be no disclosure by this government," he must know that "he was vulnerable to blackmail by the Russians." "There might be an obligation," Twining continued, "to let some of the publishers [i.e., the newspapers carrying Alsop's column] know of this incident."

FBI officials were not responsible for the attempts of Eisenhower administration officials to discredit their influential media critic. Nonetheless, their ability to obtain and disseminate such information highlights the predictable consequences of secretive intelligence operations. This is underscored by the fourth case.

Convinced that liberal Democratic senators in what were traditionally Republican states were vulnerable in their bid for reelection in 1970, President Nixon had helped Republican operatives orchestrate a nationally coordinated "law and order" strategy to discredit the Democratic incumbents. The strategy failed; the incumbent Democrats won reelection. And, in its postelection assessment, the Nixon White House attributed this failure to critical reporting by the national media. The White House opted to raise doubts about the Washington press corps's liberal bias in a campaign spearheaded by Vice President Spiro Agnew. President Nixon sought to supplement this effort and had his principal aide, H. R. Haldeman, seek

FBI assistance. Telephoning the FBI director on behalf of the president on November 25, 1970, Haldeman asked Hoover to confirm the homosexuality of a certain reporter (whose name the FBI has redacted) and to provide a "run down on the homosexuals known and suspected in the Washington press corps" as well as "any other stuff" the FBI might have compiled on reporters. The president thought, Haldeman continued, that Hoover "would have pretty much of it on hand so there would be no specific investigation." Nixon assumed correctly. Two days later, the requested report was hand delivered to the White House—confirming, not only that the FBI already collected information on homosexuals, but also that FBI officials had devised an efficient system to retrieve such information about reporters.

As the "any other stuff" request confirms, FBI agents had also been compiling information about the sexual affairs of prominent Americans. Beginning no later than the mid-1940s, Hoover maintained in his secret office file whatever information FBI agents had accumulated about prominent citizens—members of Congress, a vice president (Henry Wallace), a first lady (Eleanor Roosevelt), White House aides, cabinet officers—allegations of homosexuality, adultery, and consorting with prostitutes both confirmed and uncorroborated. FBI officials soon refined and rationalized this informal system to ensure their ready access to derogatory personal and political information about all members of Congress. Abandoning an earlier ad hoc and random system, they demanded in the mid-1950s that FBI agents in field offices and at headquarters compile discreetly any derogatory information on congressional candidates. Such reports were to include all known instances of their "subversive activities" and "immoral conduct," to be incorporated in "summary memoranda" on all candidates.

FBI officials were just as interested in the sexual indiscretions of elected members of Congress. FBI agents were specifically encouraged to report and record any such discoveries and to do so discreetly. During an interview with the so-called Pike Committee in 1975, a former FBI agent described this practice. Puzzled over why such information was being collected, the agent claimed to have consulted his boss, FBI Assistant Director Cartha De-Loach. He then recounted DeLoach's response: "The other night we picked up a situation where the Senator was seen drunk, in a hit-and-run accident, and some good-looking broad was with him. He [DeLoach] said, 'We got the information, reported it in a memorandum' and DeLoach—and this is an exact quote—he said 'By noon of the next day the good Senator was aware that we had the information and we never had any trouble with him on appropriations since.'"

FBI officials' interest in sexual liaisons was not confined to those of members of Congress. It was also not determined solely by a bureaucratic interest in ensuring support for FBI appropriations. It also reflected a realization of the value of such information as leverage—exemplified by Hoover's personal interest in reports about Presidents Dwight Eisenhower's and John Kennedy's sexual activities. And it was, moreover, voyeuristic.

It might seem surprising that Hoover and senior FBI officials would be interested in confirming Dwight Eisenhower's alleged sexual indiscretions given the FBI director's and the president's shared political interests and the latitude that the Eisenhower administration accorded FBI operations. Regardless, FBI officials readily welcomed and then sought to verify even the most spurious and gossipy of allegations. For example, in 1954, an FBI wiretap of an organized crime figure, John Vitale, intercepted his conversation with a criminal associate in Detroit. Vitale was looking for a good attorney, one who had influence. The associate recommended Henry Hyde, a trial attorney employed by the General Service Administration, and attributed Hyde's influence to his attractive wife and the fact that President Eisenhower "has been trying to get into her pants." Vitale's associate added that Hyde was "getting more powerful all the time" and "is scheduled to get a judgeship." FBI Director Hoover was immediately briefed on this intercepted conversation and ordered an investigation. Because the FBI has withheld in its entirety the ten-page memorandum summarizing the results of this investigation, we cannot learn what FBI agents were able to confirm and what action was then taken on their findings.

This practice was repeated in 1955 when FBI Assistant Director Louis Nichols received a tip from Senator McCarthy's aide Don Surine. At the time, McCarthy and Eisenhower were bitter adversaries, and Surine had a political interest in discrediting the president. McCarthy's aide astutely set up the FBI. In May 1955, he advised Nichols "in confidence" of "scuttlebutt" about Eisenhower's wartime affair with a military aide, Kay Summersby. Four months later, Surine recontacted Nichols to report that Summersby "has been staying at the [Washington] Shoreham Hotel for the last 30 to 45 days under an assumed name."

Hoover was immediately briefed about this rumor. Rather than dismissing the report on the basis of its source, the FBI director ordered: "See if we can discreetly get the name." An intensive effort was made to verify this allegation. On the one hand, Nichols "discreetly contacted" Surine to learn the name of his "confidential source," without revealing the "interest of the FBI in matter." On the other hand, FBI agents made a "discreet check through contacts at Shoreham" but discovered that "no individual is registered there under the name of Kay Morgan [Summersby's married name], Mrs. Raymond H. Morgan, or Kay McCarthy (maiden name). Other variances [of names] were checked with negative results." FBI agents in New York followed up through two "pretext" phone conversations with Summersby/Morgan at her home. They were unable to learn anything "which would indicate whether she had recently been in Washington or not." Briefing Hoover on these disappointing findings, Hoover's aides emphasized that all their checks into this matter had been "made with complete secrecy and it is felt that no interest has been aroused on the part of outsiders concerning this matter."

In contrast to Eisenhower, John Kennedy was widely rumored to be a womanizer. Not surprisingly, then, FBI agents closely monitored allegations of Kennedy's alleged sexual activities and relationships. They duly reported such allegations to Hoover, who maintained their reports in his secret office file—whether the reports were based on hard evidence or simply malicious gossip.

In December 1941, an intensive FBI investigation had been launched of Inga Arvad, a gossip columnist for the *Washington Times-Herald* who had been maliciously accused of being a German spy. Although no evidence was uncovered of her alleged espionage activities, FBI agents did discover her sexual relationship with the then naval ensign John Kennedy. Alerted through a wiretap that Arvad planned to spend two weekends visiting Kennedy, then stationed in Charleston, South Carolina, FBI agents bugged her hotel room, recording her and Kennedy's involvement "in sexual intercourse on several occasions" over two weekend visits in February 1942. In this case, the original target of FBI surveillance was an employee of the arch-conservative *Washington Times-Herald* (a bitter critic of President Roosevelt's New Deal and of his interventionist foreign policy). Because of this, FBI Assistant Director Nichols personally maintained the records of the Arvad investigation in his secret office file. He had done so to preclude discovery of the fact that FBI agents were monitoring Arvad, fearing that, should this surveillance be uncovered, the "Times-Herald would be quick to expose the FBI." The Arvad file was retained in Nichols's (and then his successor, DeLoach's) office until July 13, 1960 (the day that Kennedy won the Democratic presidential nomination), when it was transferred to Hoover's secret office file.

Although Hoover did not physically possess the Arvad file until July 1960, he had before that date maintained a folder on Senator Kennedy and subsequently created a second folder captioned *President Kennedy.* Included in these folders were, among others, reports that Kennedy was "shacking up" with Judith Campbell; had been "compromised" with a woman in Las Vegas; had been a participant in sex parties with prostitutes in Palm Springs, Las Vegas, and New York City; had been involved with two mulatto prostitutes in New York; had a sexual affair with Pamela Turnure (his wife's press secretary); had been involved with the prostitutes Ellen Rometsch and Marie Novotny (the latter reportedly "traveling on pre-election rounds with the presidential candidate"); had been married to Malcolm Durie and had subsequently obtained a secret annulment from the Vatican; and had been engaged to Alicia Purdom but, because she was "a Polish Jewish refugee," had at his father's insistence broken off the relationship.

Hoover's decision to transfer the Arvad file to his own office and his maintenance of reports alleging Kennedy's sexual indiscretions have been cited as examples of his blackmail tactics. Hoover, however, never directly confronted either Eisenhower or Kennedy with his discoveries—not even in the Arvad and Campbell cases, where FBI agents had developed hard evidence. To have done so would have exposed Hoover, and the FBI, to the serious charge of having monitored the private life of the president and could have triggered an investigation that would have confirmed that FBI agents extensively monitored the private activities of many Americans, both prominent and obscure. Consistent with their practice of leaking information to Congress, FBI officials acted purposefully to preclude discovery of their monitoring of sexual activities. Indeed, FBI Director Hoover revealed his discovery of derogatory information only when his actions could not be questioned.

Hoover's subtle methods are illustrated by two examples. In the first, the FBI director met with President Kennedy in March 1962 to report that FBI agents had learned that Judith Campbell had frequently (on November 7, 10, 13, and 14, 1961, and February 14, 1962) telephoned the president's press secretary, Eunice Lincoln. Hoover then informed the president about Campbell's questionable relationship with the mob boss Sam Giancana—information obtained through an FBI wiretap of Giancana (who was also having an affair with Campbell). Because this wiretap had been approved and involved an investigation of an organized crime boss, Hoover could safely convey this discovery without his action being called into question. Significantly, Hoover did not at the time inform the president that FBI agents had reported to him (and that he personally retained such reports) that Kennedy was "shacking up" with Campbell. In the second example, Hoover informed Attorney General Robert Kennedy of rumors being circulated about the president's "first" marriage to Malcolm Durie. Claiming that his purpose was simply to alert the attorney general that the rumor was being circulated, Hoover did not advise him that FBI agents had, in fact, "discreetly" sought to confirm it.

Press release detailing Mann Act arrests. (Courtesy National Archives.)

Emma Goldman, arrested and deported in 1919. (Courtesy National Archives.)

J. Edgar Hoover, appointed Director of Bureau, 1924.
(Courtesy National Archives.)

Bruno Richard Hauptmann,
convicted of kidnapping baby son
of Charles Lindbergh.
(Courtesy National Archives.)

WANTED

JOHN HERBERT DILLINGER

On June 23, 1934, HOMER S. CUMMINGS, Attorney General of the United States, under the authority vested in him by an Act of Congress approved June 6, 1934, offered a reward of

$10,000.00

for the capture of John Herbert Dillinger or a reward of

$5,000.00

for information leading to the arrest of John Herbert Dillinger.

DESCRIPTION

Age, 32 years; Height, 5 feet 7-1/8 inches; Weight, 153 pounds; Build, medium; Hair, medium chestnut; Eyes, grey; Complexion, medium; Occupation, machinist; Marks and scars, 1/2 inch scar back left hand, scar middle upper lip, brown mole between eyebrows.

All claims to any of the aforesaid rewards and all questions and disputes that may arise as among claimants to the foregoing rewards shall be passed upon by the Attorney General and his decisions shall be final and conclusive. The right is reserved to divide and allocate portions of any of said rewards as between several claimants. No part of the aforesaid rewards shall be paid to any official or employee of the Department of Justice.

If you are in possession of any information concerning the whereabouts of John Herbert Dillinger, communicate immediately by telephone or telegraph collect to the nearest office of the Division of Investigation, United States Department of Justice, the local addresses of which are set forth on the reverse side of this notice.

JOHN EDGAR HOOVER, DIRECTOR,
DIVISION OF INVESTIGATION,
UNITED STATES DEPARTMENT OF JUSTICE,
WASHINGTON, D. C.

June 25, 1934

Wanted poster for gangster John Dillinger. (Courtesy FBI.)

FBI laboratory, 1932. (Courtesy National Archives.)

FBI director Hoover fingerprinting Vice-President John Nance Garner.
(Courtesy National Archives.)

Guenther Rumrich, German spy.
(Courtesy National Archives.)

J. Edgar Hoover (left) and Clyde Tolson vacationing in Atlantic City, 1941.
(Courtesy National Archives.)

PHOTOGRAGH OF FREDERICK DUQUESNE
TAKEN JULY 1, 1940, BY FBI AGENTS.

PHOTOGRAPH OF FREDERICK DUQUESNE IN
EARLIER DAYS FOUND IN HIS POSSESSION
WHEN HE WAS ARRESTED JUNE 28, 1941.

FREDERICK DUQUESNE AND WILLIAM SEBOLD,
TAKEN BY FBI AGENTS MAY 29, 1940.

FREDERICK DUQUESNE, TAKEN MAY 29, 1940,
BY FBI AGENTS.

FBI surveillance photos of suspected spy Frederick Duquesne.
(Courtesy National Archives.)

Senator Joseph McCarthy (far left), Clyde Tolson (left), unidentified person, and Hoover vacationing in La Jolla, California, 1953. (Courtesy National Archives.)

President John F. Kennedy (left), Hoover, and Robert F. Kennedy. (Courtesy National Archives.)

President Lyndon B. Johnson and Hoover admiring Johnson's beagles. (Courtesy National Archives.)

Hoover and President Richard M. Nixon. (Courtesy National Archives.)

Secrecy and Power— the Undermining of Accountability

The way in which the FBI actually operated during the 1940s and 1950s differed radically from the way in which it was viewed at the time—as an apolitical, professional, and disciplined law enforcement agency that respected privacy and First Amendment rights and safeguarded the confidentiality of its files. The radical disparity between myth and reality raises serious questions for a democratic political system based on the rule of law, limited and defined powers, and accountability. How could a federal law enforcement agency violate with impunity the Fourth Amendment as well as laws banning wiretapping and mail opening? How could FBI officials brazenly affirm the confidentiality of FBI files when, in fact, they selectively released their contents to ideologically sympathetic journalists and members of Congress? How could FBI agents monitor the political activities and personal conduct of American citizens and resident aliens who had violated no federal law? More strikingly, how could FBI agents monitor the personal conduct of members of Congress and of the media? Finally, how could FBI officials monitor the personal activities of presidents and, further, how could they preclude discovery of their practice of sharing information that advanced the partisan interests of a president's political adversaries?

In theory, FBI officials should not have been able to do what they, in fact, did. As the investigative division of the Department of Justice, the FBI was authorized only to investigate violations of federal laws. Congress retained the power to enact laws expanding FBI responsibilities, for example, by criminalizing bank robbery, organized prostitution, espionage, and terrorism. Conversely, Congress always had the power to limit FBI operations, whether by prohibiting wiretapping (or regulating its uses) or by outlining through legislative charter the parameters of the FBI's authority. Congress too had the power to oversee FBI operations, by holding hearings to evaluate either their effectiveness or lawfulness, and it also had the power to subpoena FBI records. The courts posed another potential check, specifically when honoring defense attorneys' discovery motions. Such public proceedings could expose FBI agents' resort to illegal investigative techniques and could, thus, serve to deter such practices or to prompt the enactment of laws precluding future abuses. And, because the FBI director was subordinate to the attorney general, who in turn was the appointee of the president, FBI officials should not have been able to avoid discovery of practices that promoted the partisan interests of the president's political adversaries. The attorney general furthermore had the responsibility of ensuring that FBI officials complied with (and did not violate) the law and were not purposefully involved in curtailing the activities of those individuals and organizations whose political objectives they found abhorrent.

Contributing both to the FBI's departure from its authorized role and to its ability to escape accountability was the secrecy inherent in intelligence investigations and the deferential treatment accorded the bureau by presidents and attorneys general concerned to minimize discovery of FBI surveillance tactics. Also, insofar as intelligence investigations were not intended to result in prosecution, they escaped the oversight that would have been inevitable during judicial proceedings. Yet the undermining of accountability was not the by-product simply of the shift in the FBI's role after 1936 from collecting evidence to effect prosecution to attempting to anticipate threats to the nation's security by focusing on the individuals and organizations whom FBI officials suspected might commit espionage or engage in subversive activities. The key reason that FBI officials were able to neutralize presidential, congressional, and judicial oversight and to deny, without risk of discovery, doing what in fact they were doing was a series of procedures that they instituted during the 1940s and 1950s to ensure secrecy.

Beginning in 1940, FBI officials had informally authorized FBI agents to install bugs through break-ins. They did, of course, recognize the political perils of this unconstitutional practice, particularly since the nation was not at war and a debate raged within Congress and in the broader public over President Roosevelt's nonneutral foreign policy. And many conservatives did, in fact, express a deep concern that the administration might use the FBI to silence dissent, some even viewing FBI Director Hoover as a witting henchman of the despised Roosevelt. The passage in 1934 of the legislative ban against wiretapping nicely captured this underlying suspicion of Big Brother.

FBI Director Hoover was particularly attuned to this hostile climate and the deep suspicions about federal surveillance powers. Committed to employing any technique that would enable the FBI to anticipate subversive activities in the heightened security atmosphere following U.S. military involvement in World War II, Hoover intended to have FBI agents employ bugs and conduct break-ins more extensively. To avert discovery of these practices, he instituted special rules to govern when FBI agents could conduct break-ins, whether to install bugs or to photograph records. Privately conceding that break-ins were "clearly illegal" and, thus, that neither he nor senior FBI officials could seek the attorney general's explicit authorization to conduct them, Hoover in 1942 required heads of FBI field offices (SACs, or special agents in charge) to obtain either his or a designated FBI assistant director's advance approval before authorizing a break-in. His purpose was to ensure both that agents would not resort to this practice capriciously and that they would take care to avoid discovery. SACs had in each case to justify why a break-in should be employed and then outline how agents would conduct it without "any danger or embarrassment to the Bureau." Given the centralized nature of the FBI bureaucracy, Hoover's authorization requirement meant that written records would be created both of requests to conduct break-ins and of his approval. Insofar as all FBI reports were normally serialized and indexed in the FBI's central records system under the name of the individual, organization, or code-named program involved, the automatic indexing of these written requests would potentially render them vulnerable either to court-ordered discovery motions or to congressional subpoenas.

To finesse this problem, Hoover devised a special records procedure. SAC requests for approval to conduct break-ins were to be captioned *Do Not File,* alerting personnel at FBI headquarters that these records should not be serialized and indexed in the FBI's central records system but should, instead, be routed to the FBI director's office or the office of a designated FBI assistant director. No official record would have been created of their existence, and, as a result, they could be safely destroyed. After obtaining FBI headquarters approval, SACs were to "prepare an informal memorandum" to be "filed in [the SAC's] safe until the next inspection by Bureau Inspectors at which time it is destroyed."

The Do Not File system resolved the key problem of accountability—the potential that the courts and congressional committees could otherwise have been able to solicit FBI records that would confirm an illegal investigative activity. Indeed, when members of the so-called Church Committee uncovered this procedure in 1975, they specifically questioned former FBI Assistant Director Charles Brennan about its effect on court-ordered discovery motions. In response, Brennan conceded that this procedure enabled a bureau official to respond to such requests by truthfully affirming that there was "no record" of such a practice in the FBI's central records system, a response that could not be proved false since there would be no gap in the contents of a serialized file. Bureau officials could also truthfully inform the court "that we searched our [official] files and there is nothing to indicate" that an illegal practice had been conducted. Republican Senator Richard Schweiker aptly described the Do Not File procedure as the "perfect coverup" and "nearly total deception."

FBI officials adopted other safeguards to preclude discovery of a practice that even they unqualifiedly described as being "clearly illegal." For one, they carefully screened potential recruits for break-in squads to ensure that they would not panic under stress and were both reliable and meticulous. Those selected for such squads were then specially trained, both in break-in techniques and about needed precautions to avert discovery. Members of break-in squads would first survey the site of the proposed break-in in order to become well acquainted with the subject's normal routine, identify any problems deriving from the location, develop where possible "confidential sources" (janitors or neighbors), and set up a nearby "plant or cover apartment" to monitor "possible movements of the subject." Four agents would conduct a normal break-in, although, when the location posed serious security problems, as many as eight to twelve agents were used. One of the four would act as supervisor, maintaining contact by walkie-talkie with the two agents who entered the building or residence so that he could alert them to the unanticipated return of the subject. The fourth agent tailed the subject. The two agents who entered the site had special tasks: one would photograph the records, and the second would ensure their return to their original place so that the target could not learn that a break-in had occurred and the confidentiality of the records in his or her possession compromised.

FBI agents were monetarily rewarded and received special commendations for their break-in activities. FBI officials furthermore evaluated the attitudes of agents who conducted break-ins. For example, on learning in May 1955 that a New York agent attending a training class had expressed his belief that break-ins were unconstitutional, FBI officials immediately suspended all break-in operations of the New York field office. They then launched an internal investigation to ascertain whether this agent's "mental outlook may be present among other members of that squad" and directed the New York SAC to "determine which of these men should be retained in this type of activity and which should be deleted." In this case, because the resultant investigation established that the offending New York agent was not a member of and had no contact with members of the New York break-in squad, FBI officials lifted the suspension.

The Do Not File procedure, moreover, was an extension of one that FBI Director Hoover had instituted in April 1940 to preclude discovery of the contents of sensitive communications among senior FBI officials generally—and specifically whenever such officials were reporting information "solely for the benefit of the Director which will possibly be seen by the Director and other officials." Such communications were not to be serialized and indexed in the FBI's central records system. To ensure this, they were to be typed on blue paper* and the following instruction printed at the bottom: "This Memorandum is for Administrative Purposes—To Be Destroyed After Action is Taken and Not Sent to File Section." Blue memoranda would "eventually be returned to the dictator to be destroyed or retained in the Director's office." If returned to the sender, they were to be held temporarily in the individual's "personal" office file.

When this memorandum procedure was publicly compromised during a discovery hearing in Judith Coplon's second trial, the practice was discontinued. Thereafter, whenever preparing sensitive communications, FBI officials were to use "personal note or informal memoranda." Prepared on plain white nonletterhead paper, these communications did not contain the printed do not file and destruction orders on the bottom (as did the blue memoranda) but were, nonetheless, distinguishable from those official communications that were to be filed and indexed. FBI Director Hoover soon confronted another problem—the failure of senior FBI officials to have destroyed such records once they were no longer useful. Accordingly, in March 1953, FBI assistant directors and FBI supervisors were ordered to purge their office files on a regular basis—FBI assistant directors every six months, FBI supervisors every ninety days.

Inexplicably, Hoover's 1953 destruction order was not fully honored, leading to the continued existence of some of these sensitive communications. The vast majority, however, were, in fact, destroyed. Hoover himself had maintained two office files. One of these (his so-called Personal and Confidential File) was destroyed by his administrative assistant, Helen Gandy, in the months after his death pursuant to his earlier explicit instructions. The second (his Official and Confidential File), however, escaped destruction

---

* When Justice Department officials required that blue paper be used for intradepartmental communications, the color of the paper was changed to pink.

and was incorporated in the FBI's central records system and remains extant. Three other office files also escaped destruction. These include the Official and Confidential File that FBI Assistant Director Louis Nichols created in 1940 and maintained until his retirement in 1957; portions of the Personal File maintained by FBI Associate Director Clyde Tolson (the extant records cover the years 1965–1972); and a World War II "Do Not File" file maintained by FBI Assistant Director D. Milton Ladd that was subsequently classified 62-116758.

Hoover's belated recognition of the need to institute a "rule with respect to the length of time for which these [office] memoranda should be retained" also led him to devise other records procedures to preclude discovery of the extent of FBI illegal investigative activities and practice of monitoring and recording the personal and political activities of prominent Americans. (Significantly, FBI files on sensitive espionage investigations were included in the official central records system.) Prompting these new rules was (as in the case of the informal memorandum procedure) unanticipated fallout, this time stemming from the discovery proceedings during Judith Coplon's first and second trials.

During Coplon's first trial, Judge Albert Reeves had ordered that the twenty-eight FBI reports found in her handbag at the time of her arrest be submitted as evidence. The public release of these records deeply embarrassed FBI officials as they confirmed that FBI agents wiretapped extensively, monitored the political activities of prominent Americans, and often cited gossip and innuendo. To preclude the recurrence of such embarrassment should FBI reports be released in future trials or should a disgruntled employee or Justice Department official decide to leak accessible FBI reports to the press, Hoover in July 1949 instituted a special "administrative pages" procedure. Henceforth, whenever preparing reports based on their investigative findings, FBI agents were not to include within the text of their report "gossip, rumors or any information that could unjustifiably embarrass an individual or organization," "any verified or unverified information" that was not pertinent to the investigation, and "facts and information which are considered of a nature not expedient to disseminate, or which could cause embarrassment to the Bureau, if distributed." Such information was, instead, to be reported on an "administrative page" to be attached to the back of the report. Had such information been reported in the text of a report, it could not have been safely withheld. But reporting it in an administrative page made withholding it easy—the administrative page was, simply, detached.

When spelling out this new reporting requirement, Hoover cited seven examples of information to be reported on administrative pages. The first involved allegations that "A . . . is a member of the Communist Party and further that A is a man of loose morals, a heavy drinker living with a known prostitute. . . . The allegation of Communist Party membership should be included in the investigative section while the allegation concerning loose morals should be included in the administrative section." The seventh example involved the case of an agent conducting a Mann Act investigation finding "an address book containing data identifying prominent public officials. Unless the names appearing therein are material to the investigation, this material should be placed in the administrative section."

FBI officials reassessed the administrative pages procedure in March 1951, concluding that it was extremely time consuming and could adversely affect future investigations in those cases where the segregated information might be pertinent. They further questioned the premise for segregating such information, that "only the investigative section would be presented" in response to a court order or subpoena. In reality, they then concluded, "an order for the entire file would, of course, make available both" the investigative and the administrative sections. For these reasons, Hoover rescinded the administrative pages procedure on the "understanding that should it become necessary in any case [for an FBI agent] to advise the Bureau of any information which should not be included in the regular investigative report, that such information should be submitted by letter."

The Coplon trial had posed another, more troublesome problem— Coplon's access as a Justice Department employee to FBI reports and the possibility that other Justice Department employees could either leak information to Congress or the press or compromise FBI investigative techniques and strategies. To address this potential threat to his ability to limit public awareness of the FBI's actual operations, Hoover in June 1949 instituted the procedure code-named June Mail. Henceforth, when reporting information obtained through wiretaps, bugs, break-ins, mail covers, mail intercepts, or specially sensitive sources, SACs were to send such information to FBI headquarters in envelopes addressed to the FBI Director and marked *June* and *Personal and Confidential.* SACs were to employ the June Mail procedure whenever reporting information derived from "sources illegal in nature" or from "the most secretive sources, such as Governors, secretaries to high officials who may be discussing such officials and their attitude." When received at FBI headquarters, June Mail submissions were not to be filed in the FBI's central records system but routed to a "separate confidential file" in the FBI's Special File Room, where they were to be maintained "under lock and key." Only those personnel who could demonstrate a need to know would have access to June Mail.

Because of further complications that arose during the course of Coplon's second trial, Hoover in December 1949 refined the June Mail procedure. FBI officials were sharply criticized following the embarrassing disclosure that an agent who had originally denied knowing that Coplon had been wiretapped had, in fact, been a regular recipient of the Coplon wiretap logs. Hoover acted to preclude the recurrence of this embarrassment by explicitly instructing SACs that, when assigning an agent to investigate a case "which might make him a competent witness" should there be a trial, they should ensure that he "have no specific testifiable knowledge of the existence of a technical surveillance [wiretap] in that case."

Similar procedures were adopted to preclude discovery that FBI officials leaked information from FBI files to reporters, columnists, prominent citizens, or members of Congress. FBI files or copies of FBI reports were never to be given or made available to these favored individuals. Instead, the proffered information was to be conveyed in "blind memoranda." Written on plain white, nonletterhead stationary, blind memoranda disguised the fact that the FBI was the source—and were also blind in the sense that the names of the sender and the recipient were not listed. The genius of this procedure was that FBI officials could truthfully deny that a suspected recipient had had access to FBI files or reports and could also truthfully reaffirm the confidentiality of FBI files.

FBI officials even devised a formal system to disguise their responsiveness to written requests for information on specific individuals. The problem, of course, with written requests was that they created records of FBI dissemination practices. Oral requests would have avoided this problem but carried the potential of disrupting the efficiency of FBI operations, requiring untimely meetings or telephone conversations. How this problem was finessed was disclosed when, while researching the papers of Senator Karl Mundt at the Karl Mundt Library in Madison, South Dakota, the historian Kenneth O'Reilly came across a series of letters Mundt had sent to Hoover requesting FBI files. In every case, Hoover refused the request and affirmed the confidentiality of FBI files. Puzzled by a correspondence that ran over decades, O'Reilly questioned Robert McCaughey, the senator's former administrative assistant and the director of the library, about Mundt's seeming obtuseness.

McCaughey denied that Mundt was as obtuse as this correspondence suggested. In fact, he pointed out, an FBI agent always hand delivered Hoover's letter of refusal, brought with him a memorandum summarizing the contents of the requested FBI file, and was fully prepared to answer any questions about the information provided.

Such carefully formulated records procedures minimized the risk of discovery of FBI officials' abusive practices. There remained, however, the potential problem of congressional oversight, a problem complicated both by the fact that FBI officials selectively leaked information to favored members of Congress and congressional committees and by the fact that these recipients frequently breached Hoover's condition of confidentiality. Rather than abandon the practice of selective leaking, FBI officials devised a system whereby they could identify those congressmen who could be trusted insofar as they shared FBI officials' political and bureaucratic agenda—even though this could not ensure that ambitious congressmen would honor the condition of confidentiality.

At first FBI officials based decisions whether to work covertly with a member of Congress on whether a personal relationship had been established with the member or whether, after a review of FBI files, the member's political beliefs and personal character passed muster. By the 1950s, they decided to rationalize this informal practice.

FBI officials might have wanted to maintain an accessible file on each member of Congress. Doing so would, however, have made them vulnerable to criticisms that they were monitoring members of Congress. FBI Assistant Director Louis Nichols soon devised a system enabling them to keep such records without risk of discovery. Beginning in the 1950s, Nichols verbally instructed FBI officials to institute "a systematic review" of all information contained in the FBI's central records system about candidates seeking election to Congress. Such information was to be supplemented by "any information" forwarded by FBI field offices to FBI headquarters and a "summary memorandum" on each congressional candidate produced. This system was further refined when, in 1960, all SACs were ordered to forward whatever information was contained in their field office's files about congressional candidates to the Crimes Records Division. Designated personnel in this division would then produce from this information, supplemented by any information in headquarters files, a "summary memorandum." SAC submissions were to be "by routing slip, not letter," in "sealed envelopes," thereby ensuring that no official record would have been created of them or the fact that they had been solicited. Whenever SACs mistakenly submitted requested information "in formal communications," they were "orally instructed to remove from the files all copies of the material" and resubmit it correctly so that "no record" would be "created in Bureau files." FBI officials at headquarters further understood that, when preparing the "summary memorandum," they were to handle these records "discreetly" and ensure that all information was "submitted on an informal basis" without creating any "formal communications." The underlying reason for these carefully thought out requirements was that the information accumulated and forwarded by field office and headquarters personnel included "allegations of criminal or corrupt practices, subversive activities, and immoral conduct."

Summary memoranda were not files; the reported information was not filed in the FBI's central records system but maintained separately in the FBI's Administrative Review Unit. FBI officials could, thus, truthfully deny that the FBI maintained files or dossiers on members of Congress. In fact, there were no files in the FBI's central records system documenting that FBI agents had monitored the personal and political conduct of members of Congress and had begun doing so when the members were private citizens or active in local and state politics.*

The summary memorandum procedure ensured that FBI officials would be fully informed about a congressional candidate's political views and personal conduct. This did not mean that FBI officials did not retain an interest in the ongoing indiscretions of elected members of Congress. Indeed, Hoover's Personal File, maintained in his office, contained folders on those members of Congress about whom FBI agents had developed derogatory personal and political information. Because this file has been destroyed, its contents cannot be reconstructed. Hoover's extant Official and Confidential File, however, contains one folder that is suggestive of the type of information incorporated in his Personal File. The folder in question consists of a series of reports that the head of the FBI's Washington, D.C., field office sent to the FBI director between June and October 1965. It seems unlikely that no similar reports would have been submitted except during this four-month period, particularly since Hoover's responses to these

---

* Significantly, the summary memorandum procedure was compromised only because, in 1972, records were created when responding to an inquiry whether this separately maintained file should be destroyed. In the course of this review, an FBI analyst described both the origins of the system and the procedures that had been adopted in 1950 and refined in 1960.

reports confirm his keen interest in the reported information and, further, do not suggest that the submission of such reports was unusual.

Hoover responded to these submissions by thanking the SAC for being thoughtful enough to "advise" him on "matters of current interest": "I am glad to have the benefit of this information." The submissions themselves reported that the wife of a congressman was "having an affair with a Negro" and had endeavored "to have an affair with [a male nurse] Indonesian"; that a senator was an "alcoholic" who frequently appeared on the Senate floor "intoxicated"; that a senator was having an affair with a woman employed on the public relations staff of the Sheraton-Park Hotel; that a prostitute had had "sexual intercourse" with a senator on a couch in his office; that a lobbyist had arranged dates with prostitutes for a senator and a congressman and that this prostitute had "made contacts with others on Capitol Hill," including three congressmen; and that a senator had had sexual relations with a male prostitute.

This folder offers no insights into how Hoover and senior FBI officials used this information. Neither do the records describing the origins and purpose of the summary memorandum procedure. In any event, both procedures allowed FBI officials to deny that members of Congress were being monitored.

Interestingly, members of Congress were convinced that Hoover had compiled information about their personal and political activities. During an interview with Ovid Demaris, Congressman Emmanuel Celler, the long-term chairman of the House Judiciary Committee, unqualifiedly observed that the "source of [Hoover's] power derived from the fact that he was the head of an agency that in turn had tremendous power, power of surveillance, power of control over the lives and destinies of every man in the nation. He had a dossier on every member of Congress and every member of the Senate. . . . He held in the palm of his hand the reputation of many people and a good many of the members of the House and Senate and the officials had a lot of skeletons in their closet. A lot of these men were not pure and righteous; they probably committed wrongs too, and it fed Hoover."

Despite these reservations (expressed after Hoover's death), Celler had never initiated hearings into FBI operations—if for no other reason than to ascertain whether the FBI was, in fact, monitoring the personal conduct of members of Congress. Had he done so, Hoover would have denied that the FBI had files or dossiers on members of Congress. Until the 1970s, the only congressional committee that even cursorily oversaw FBI operations was the

House Appropriations Committee during its annual review of the Justice Department's funding requests. And that committee never critically examined how FBI funds were expended and never launched an inquiry or demanded relevant FBI records to ascertain the nature and focus of FBI investigations. This indifference was the result, not of the imperfect lives of members of the committee, but of a liaison relationship that Hoover had established in 1943 with the committee chair, Congressman Clarence Cannon.

In May 1943, willingly acceding to a request for FBI assistance from Cannon, Hoover authorized FBI Assistant Director Hugh Clegg to "help organize and initiate the work" of the committee's staff. At the end of the year, Cannon urged Clegg to remain. Instead, Hoover and Cannon effected an arrangement whereby three FBI agents were assigned to assist the committee, each serving for a three-year period before being replaced. This liaison relationship proved extremely beneficial to FBI officials and ensured a favorable review of FBI appropriations. Cannon and his successors as committee chair were untroubled by this arrangement and, instead, extolled the FBI agents' invaluable "assistance to the Committee." When reflecting in 1971 on this arrangement with then Committee Chair John Rooney, Hoover cited its benefits, noting that Rooney was "very cordially inclined toward the Bureau for that assistance and would respond very readily [to any FBI request]."

From Anticommunism to Law and Order

The sense of crisis generated by the Cold War underpinned the unquestioned public and congressional support for the FBI's crusade against communism,* a sense of crisis that continued to shape the politics of the 1960s and 1970s. Yet the 1960s also witnessed the first challenge to this anti-Communist consensus. Increasingly during this tumultuous decade, radical and many liberal activists rejected the premises of the containment policy and sharply criticized U.S. policy toward Cuba, nuclear weapons testing, the arms race with the Soviet Union, and the Vietnam War. No longer stifled by a politics that equated dissent with subversion, they also demanded an end to inequality based on race, gender, ethnicity, and sexual orientation. The new organizations formed in response to this renewed activist spirit were targeted under a new FBI program code-named COMINFIL (or Communist Infiltration), the stated purpose of which was to "fortify" the government against "subversive pressures."

The goal of this secret program was to uncover the plans and tactics of dissident organizations that covered "the entire spectrum of the social or labor movement." By the end of the 1960s, targeted organizations included those advocating such causes as civil rights (Martin Luther King Jr., the Black Panthers, the Student Non-Violent Coordinating Committee, the Southern Christian Leadership Conference [SCLC]), women's liberation and women's equality (Gloria Steinem, Women Strike for Peace, the National Organization for Women), and gay and lesbian rights (Frank Kameny, the Matachine Society, the Daughters of Bilitis, the Gay Liberation Front) and those critical of the government's economic and foreign policies (John Kerry, Students for a Democratic Society, Clergy and Laity Concerned about Vietnam).

Since the 1940s, FBI officials had regularly briefed the White House about those activists and organizations that they deemed subversive. In addition, they had covertly and on an ad hoc basis leaked information about these organizations and their leaders' plans and personal character to reliable

---

* FBI Assistant Director Louis Nichols in fact described this as "the cause."

reporters, editors, and columnists.* FBI officials refined and rationalized this informal practice of press leaks in 1956, instituting the code-named Mass Media program. Under this program, reporters deemed reliable were provided carefully selected information on the strict condition that they not publicly expose FBI assistance.

This program's methods and advantages are particularly highlighted by the response of FBI officials to a onetime request made by Don Whitehead, the Washington bureau chief of the *New York Herald Tribune*. A former feature writer for the Associated Press, Whitehead had in 1954 written a series of articles about Hoover's directorship of the FBI and then in 1955 solicited FBI assistance related to a proposed article "on the fight against Communism and what the Communists are now doing." The response was unexpected. Already convinced about the lack of a "good" history of the FBI, but having had to scurry to discredit Max Lowenthal's 1950 critical history, FBI officials wanted to make sure that Whitehead would write the desired account before greenlighting the project. They first fully evaluated Whitehead's recent writings, concluding that they "clearly established his reliability." They then launched a "discreet" investigation of his character and associations to certify that he could be entrusted with this "special project." Eventually convinced that he could, they granted Whitehead privileged access to carefully selected FBI records and set aside a special office at FBI headquarters for his use in researching and writing what had grown from an article into a full-fledged book. The finished product was carefully reviewed, with FBI officials offering both suggestions and corrections and FBI Director Hoover personally conveying his "pleasure with the first four chapters" but insisting on specific revisions to chapter 29. Once Whitehead's history, *The FBI Story*, was published in 1956, the FBI's public relations office worked behind the scenes to ensure favorable publicity and reviews and even bought copies in bulk to ensure that it became a best-seller. In 1957, Whitehead's history was turned into a successful Hollywood movie.

Whitehead's history and FBI public relations activities in general were also intended to reinforce the popular perception of the U.S. Communist Party as a "Trojan horse," a dangerous conspiracy that sought to promote Soviet interests through stealth and subversion. To fortify this assessment,

---

* FBI officials divided reporters into two categories: "Special Correspondents," i.e., those deemed reliable, and "Not Contact," i.e., those deemed unreliable. The former were favored with leaks and had their requests for assistance honored.

FBI officials had in 1948 pressured the Justice Department to indict the twelve top leaders of the Party under the Smith Act. Prosecution of the Communist leadership, Hoover counseled Attorney General Tom Clark, could "result in a judicial precedent" establishing that the Communist Party "as an organization is illegal" and, at the same time, promote a public understanding that the "patriotism of Communists is not directed toward the United States but towards the Soviet Union and world Communism."

The Communist leaders were indicted in 1948. The indictment and the resultant trial relied on evidence derived from a review by FBI analysts of Communist publications (primarily Marxist classics) that correlated changes in the American Communist Party's policy positions with changes in the Soviet Union's policy positions. During the trial, testimony from surfaced FBI informants describing the Communist leaders as committed to promoting violent revolutionary change was also introduced—testimony crucial to establishing a violation of the Smith Act's prohibition against organizing or teaching the violent overthrow of the U.S. government. All twelve Party leaders were convicted. Significantly, neither Justice Department nor FBI officials even considered seeking to indict the defendants for having either developed plans to effect a revolutionary overthrow or participated in or recruited others to participate in espionage. Both the convictions and the constitutionality of the Smith Act were, in the 1951 Supreme Court case *Dennis v. United States,* upheld on appeal.

For a time thereafter, FBI officials recommended that similar prosecutions be pursued, these based first on the 1950 Internal Security (or McCarran) Act and then on the 1954 Communist Control Act. The McCarran Act authorized the deportation of alien radicals and barred Communists from employment in defense industries and from securing passports. It required Communist, Communist-front, and Communist-action organizations to register as foreign agents with the specially created Subversive Activities Control Board (SACB), to submit lists of their members to the SACB, and to label their publications as Communist propaganda. It also authorized the detention of "dangerous radicals" during presidentially declared national emergencies. The Communist Control Act extended the McCarran Act's registration requirements to include "Communist-infiltrated" organizations. It specifically denied Communist and Communist-infiltrated organizations the "rights, privileges, and immunities attendant upon legal bodies," including the rights to appear on election ballots and to petition the National Labor Relations Board for union elections and certification.

These laws had expanded the definition of what were considered internal security threats to include membership in proscribed organizations. Yet their passage did not lead to a major increase in prosecutions. A series of Supreme Court rulings in 1956 and 1957, particularly those in *Communist Party v. Subversive Activities Control Board* of 1956, and the follow-up *Albertson v. Subversive Activities Control Board* of 1965 foreclosed this prosecution option. The Fifth Amendment right against self-incrimination, the Court held (when ruling that the McCarran Act was constitutional), meant that the SACB could not compel members of the Communist Party or front groups to register. The Court's initial ruling on the McCarran Act was followed by two 1957 rulings in *Yates v. United States* and *Jencks v. United States* that in effect discouraged FBI officials from proposing future prosecutions.

In *Yates,* the Court in effect reversed *Dennis v. United States* when, reinterpreting, and thereby narrowing, the effect of this earlier ruling, it held that the Smith Act had prohibited, not the mere advocacy of the violent overthrow of the government, but only that advocacy that led to illegal conduct. Any further convictions would, thus, require that the Justice Department (and the FBI) prove that Communist leaders intended to organize a violent revolution. More important, the Court ruled in *Jencks* that defense attorneys had the right to obtain the pretrial statements that government witnesses had made to the FBI—a ruling that would breach the confidentiality of FBI files should the Justice Department produce FBI informers as witnesses in trials of indicted Communist activists. This requirement alarmed FBI officials already troubled by the cost of having to surface FBI informers during trials, thus undercutting their ability to monitor the Communist Party.

To offset this prosecution dilemma, FBI Director Hoover on August 28, 1956, unilaterally instituted a secret disruption program, code-named COINTELPRO–Communist Party. His purpose, informed by his own strong conviction of the need to undermine the Communist movement owing to its "influence over the masses, ability to create controversy leading to confusion and disunity, penetration of specific channels in American life where public opinion is molded, and espionage and sabotage potential," was to contain Communist influence by extralegal means. Through tactics such as sending to Communist Party members anonymous letters intended to provoke factionalism and dissension or leaking derogatory personal and political information about Communist activists to sympathetic reporters and members of Congress, FBI officials attempted to "disrupt" the Communist

Party and "discredit" Communist activists. Hoover's decision to authorize this COINTELPRO marked a major departure in the FBI's role, the abandonment of a law enforcement mission for a course of political containment and the willful reliance on more aggressive tactics in part for the purpose of influencing public opinion.

The increased visibility during the 1960s of the Trotskyite Socialist Workers Party (SWP) led FBI officials to extend the COINTELPRO concept to this radical organization. Hoover's October 1961 decision to institute a COINTELPRO–Socialist Workers Party stemmed again from his concern about the potential influence of radicals on the popular culture, such influence arising in this case from the SWP's attempt to promote "its line on a local and national basis through running candidates for public office and strongly directing and/or supporting such causes as Castro's Cuba and integration problems in the South." Once again the preferred methods of sowing internal dissension and leaking derogatory information to promote hostile public opinion were employed, the latter tactic seemingly irrationally so given the SWP's minuscule membership and the fact that most Americans had never heard of the organization, let alone evinced any sympathy for its candidates or objectives.

The violent resistance of white supremacists to the militant and increasingly more effective tactics of black Southerners when challenging racial segregation precipitated another secret COINTELPRO having the same political containment objective. Under this COINTELPRO–White Hate, instituted on September 2, 1964, FBI agents were to take steps to "frustrate any effort" by the Ku Klux Klan and other white supremacist organizations to "recruit new or youthful adherents." Agents were ordered not to miss any "opportunity" to expose the "devious maneuvers and duplicity" of white supremacists. As in the Communist Party and SWP programs, they were once again to seek "the cooperation of reliable news media sources" and to "capitalize upon organizational and personal conflicts" of the leaders of the targeted white supremacist organizations.

Then, in response to the upsurge in urban race riots in many Northern cities during the 1960s and the concurrent emergence of black nationalist groups that increasingly commanded broad support from many embittered African Americans, FBI officials instituted COINTELPRO–Black Nationalist Hate in August 1967. This secret program's purpose was, again, to "expose, disrupt, misdirect, or otherwise neutralize the activities of black nationalist, hate-type organizations and groupings, their leadership, spokesmen, membership, and supporters, and to counter their propensity for violence and civil disorder."

Finally, this time in response to the dramatic growth in numbers and militancy of radical groups on college campuses and of student opposition to the Vietnam War, FBI officials in October 1968 instituted COINTEL-PRO–New Left. Willing to disseminate "misinformation" in order to "confuse and disrupt New Left activities," FBI agents were under great pressure to devise measures to reduce or contain New Left activists' "violent and illegal activities." FBI officials had by then abandoned any interest in prosecuting New Left activists and, instead, demanded that agents pursue an aggressive disruption strategy. They were to be "alert to opportunities to confuse and disrupt New Left activities by misinformation" and to approach this task with "imagination and enthusiasm if it is to be successful." The adopted tactics ranged from promoting dissension among activists, drafting and sending anonymous letters to their parents calling attention to their illicit sexual activities or use of drugs, and disseminating similar derogatory personal information to "friendly news media."

Hoover had unilaterally authorized these secret COINTELPROs, highlighting how by the 1950s the FBI had become an autonomous agency and FBI officials were emboldened to advance their own political agenda. Nonetheless, when instituting the various COINTELPROs, Hoover was also responding to pressures from the White House. Presidents Dwight Eisenhower, John Kennedy, Lyndon Johnson, and Richard Nixon might not have known about the specific harassment activities undertaken by FBI officials and the underlying propaganda objective of influencing public opinion. They were, however, willing to grant FBI officials broad leeway and never sought to ascertain whether the FBI functioned as a law enforcement agency. The recipients of highly selective briefings, they welcomed the FBI's monitoring of dissident political activities, sharing a common political interest in narrowing the contours of acceptable debate over questions of race and the nation's foreign and internal security policies.

Thus, throughout the 1950s, Hoover regularly briefed the Eisenhower administration about the plans and personal morality of both left- and right-wing activists and also about individuals as prominent as the former first lady Eleanor Roosevelt, the Democratic presidential candidate Adlai Stevenson, Supreme Court Justice William Douglas, the *New York Times* reporter Harrison Salisbury, and the syndicated columnist Joseph Alsop. These briefings elicited no protest from the Eisenhower White House over why the FBI was monitoring and then disseminating information about radical activists and prominent Americans.

The Eisenhower administration was, moreover, fully aware of the conservative ideology governing FBI surveillance activities. This political conservatism, for example, underlay FBI Director Hoover's March 1956 briefing of the Eisenhower cabinet on the "explosive" racial situation in the South. Hoover had then attributed the new militancy of black activists to the Supreme Court's 1954 decision in *Brown v. Topeka* striking down racial segregation in public education as unconstitutional. Moreover, he justified Southern resistance to "mixed education" as stemming from "the specter of racial [*sic*] marriage." At the same time, he sharply criticized the National Association for the Advancement of Colored People (NAACP) for exacerbating racial tensions through its preaching of "racial hatred." Hoover specifically linked civil rights activism with Communist influence, citing how "the Communist Party plans to use [an NAACP] conference [on civil rights] to embarrass the [Eisenhower] Administration and Dixiecrats [Southern Democrats] who have supported it, by forcing the Administration to take a stand [on currently proposed] civil rights legislation, with the present Congress." The Communists, Hoover warned, intended to create a rift between the administration and Southern Democrats, a rift that could "affect the 1956 election."

The NAACP had long sought to mobilize public support to bring about an end to racial segregation and had resorted to lobbying Congress and litigating cases in the courts. That FBI officials depicted these actions as inherently subversive explains their more aggressive response to the militant tactic of direct action adopted by the new civil rights organization formed in 1957 under the leadership of Martin Luther King Jr., the SCLC.

To contain this more fearsome threat, FBI officials did not simply alert presidents but in the 1960s launched another secret program, code-named Racial Matters, to evaluate "Communist influence in racial matters." The premise was that the Communist Party would "interject itself into" and "exploit" "the struggle for equal rights for Negroes." FBI officials were particularly interested in learning about the plans and associations of Reverend King, given his rise to national prominence following his leadership of the Montgomery bus boycott in 1955 and subsequent role in organizing the SCLC. They ordered a massive surveillance effort, including wiretapping King's residence and office and the headquarters of the SCLC and bugging King's hotel rooms during his trips around the country. Uncovering advance intelligence about King's and the SCLC's political plans and public relations strategies and about King's sexual affairs, FBI officials acted aggressively to use this information to contain and discredit King and the SCLC.

For example, in 1964, FBI officials created a composite of tapes recording King's sexual activities that was then mailed anonymously to King's residence, along with an anonymous cover letter threatening to expose his "hideous abominations" and ending: "You are done. There is but one way out for you. You better take it before your filthy fraudulent self is bared to the nation." The letter specifically cited the "34 days left," a reference to the date on which King was to receive the Nobel Peace Prize. King and his wife, Coretta, did read the letter and listen to the composite tape but were not daunted. They were not alone in being unmoved by FBI attempts to discredit King. At the same time as they mailed the composite tape to King, FBI officials approached various reporters (including Ben Bradlee, David Kraslow, and Ralph McGill), offering them the opportunity of listening to another composite. None filed a report publicizing King's affairs. The boldness and crudity of these smarmy attempts to discredit King highlight the extent to which FBI officials went in their efforts to contain those movements and individuals deemed threats to the nation's interests.*

Hoover's efforts to influence the Eisenhower administration were not exceptional and had essentially replicated his earlier efforts to influence the Roosevelt and Truman White Houses. Of course, such efforts were facilitated by all three presidents' interest in the FBI's proffered advance intelligence and the direct access to the White House that Hoover was, as a result, accorded. That direct access was, however, severed when John Kennedy took office. Owing to the unique circumstance that the president's brother was the attorney general, Hoover no longer volunteered political intelligence to the Kennedy White House. After 1961, FBI reports were made only in response to specific requests for political intelligence from the president or the attorney general. For example, in 1961–1962, the White House pressed the FBI to identify the sources of leaked classified information reported in stories appearing in *Newsweek* and the *New York Times*. In response, FBI agents investigated and wiretapped the reporters who authored the stories,

---

* For a reporter to have filed a story about FBI efforts to disseminate damaging information about King or about how the FBI had been monitoring King's personal life would have been risky since it would have been impossible to contradict the FBI's denial. Bradlee did report having been contacted by the FBI to Attorney General Nicholas Katzenbach, who immediately briefed President Johnson. Johnson's response was to alert Hoover to Bradlee's untrustworthiness.

Lloyd Norman and Hanson Baldwin. Also in 1961–1962, the White House asked the FBI to monitor those active in lobbying Congress over pending sugar quota legislation. In response, the FBI wiretapped three Agriculture Department officials, the secretary to House Agricultural Committee Chairman Harold Cooley, and a Washington, D.C., law firm hired by the government of the Dominican Republic to lobby Congress. Subsequently, on learning that Cooley would meet with representatives of the Dominican government in New York City, Hoover had FBI agents bug this meeting as well. In both the Norman/Baldwin and the sugar lobby cases, the White House's motivation was political—in the former case to control the political debate by limiting what information could be published and in the latter to promote its foreign policy objective of forcing a change in the government of the Dominican Republic by ensuring that Congress would reduce Dominican sugar exports to the American market.

Under Presidents Lyndon Johnson and Richard Nixon, Hoover's direct link to the White House was restored, but his personal situation had changed fundamentally. Hoover had reached the mandatory retirement age of seventy on January 1, 1965. He was allowed to continue as FBI director only because President Johnson in July 1964 issued an executive order waiving mandatory retirement. Owing to his insecure status (Johnson's order did not make the waiver permanent), a far less independent FBI director willingly acceded to a series of unprecedented presidential requests for assistance—at the very time when more militant civil rights and anti–Vietnam War activists challenged the president's domestic and foreign policies.

Almost immediately after Lyndon Johnson assumed the presidency, FBI officials sought to exploit the festering personality conflict between him and Attorney General Robert Kennedy, a conflict stemming from Johnson's tense relations as vice president with President Kennedy's liberal White House aides and with the attorney general dating from the 1960 presidential campaign. An accidental president, Johnson had inherited his predecessor's aides and cabinet. Dependent on them at first for advice and political cover, he could not afford to fire all Kennedy holdovers whether on the White House staff, in the Justice Department, or on the staff of the Democratic National Committee.*

---

* Robert Kennedy had served as his brother's campaign manager during the 1960 elections and continued to exercise great influence on the membership of the Democratic National Committee.

FBI officials astutely recognized and tapped into Johnson's distrust of the Kennedy holdovers. During the crucial months of January–March 1964, the FBI director and his liaison to the White House, FBI Assistant Director Cartha DeLoach, regularly briefed the president about the personal disloyalty of these liberal Democrats. On one occasion, they counseled Johnson about the problem posed by "the continued employment of Paul Corbin at Democratic National Committee." Robert Kennedy had appointed Corbin to this post in 1961, and FBI officials alerted Johnson to Corbin's efforts in New Hampshire in early 1964 to promote Robert Kennedy's selection as Johnson's running mate. Hoover and DeLoach further briefed Johnson about how the "Kennedy crowd" in the Justice Department was aggressively promoting a criminal inquiry into the activities of Johnson's former aide, Bobby Baker, "with the avowed purpose of trying to embarrass the President in every way possible" and, thereby, force him to select Kennedy. Hoover also forwarded to the White House detailed reports on the personal background and political activities of holdover Kennedy loyalists Pierre Salinger, Carmine Bellino, William Wieland, Richard Goodwin, and Kenneth O'Donnell. The FBI director continued to stroke Johnson's distrust of Kennedy even after he had resigned the attorney generalship and won election to the Senate. In a series of reports after 1965, Hoover alerted the president to the senator's political plans and objectives, particularly when Kennedy emerged as a forceful critic of the president's domestic and foreign policy initiatives.

Hoover's willingness to further Johnson's political interests underlay his approval of a particularly sensitive operation—the sending of a special FBI squad to monitor the 1964 Democratic National Convention. Headed by Cartha DeLoach, who maintained a direct phone line to the White House, this squad kept the Johnson White House fully abreast of the plans of civil rights activists and their liberal supporters at the convention. It reported on whom these activists were meeting and on their strategies, for example, to ensure the seating of the Mississippi Freedom Democratic Party at the convention, something that Johnson worked hard to frustrate for fear that it would affect his candidacy in the South in the upcoming presidential election.

The president also turned to the FBI for information about the planned activities and strategies of those in the public, Congress, and the media who increasingly after 1965 opposed his decision to commit U.S. air power and troops in Vietnam. He was particularly interested in evidence confirming his critics' suspect loyalty. In 1966, Johnson directed the FBI to monitor the hearings on the Vietnam War held that year by the Senate Foreign Relations Committee. He specifically demanded that the FBI report any information that "sets out the Communist Party line concerning some of the issues" raised by senators during the hearings. In an effort to advance Johnson's political objective of discrediting antiwar members of Congress as acting to further the interests of the Soviet Union, FBI officials from 1966 through 1968 regularly reported on any contacts of members of Congress and congressional staff with Soviet and Soviet-bloc embassies—documented through FBI wiretaps of these embassies. FBI officials were also asked to forward all derogatory information developed by FBI agents that would impugn the loyalty of the antiwar administration critics in the public and the media and, in particular, to brief the president's conservative allies in Congress about those critics' subversive connections. Furthermore, FBI reports detailing such subversive connections were to be prepared so that prowar senators and representatives of both parties could "not only make speeches upon the floor of Congress but also publicly." In one case, FBI officials even drafted a speech to be delivered by Congressman Howard Smith that impugned the loyalty of antiwar activists and then circulated copies of this speech to university presidents and public opinion leaders. FBI officials were also asked to prepare information "to be used by prominent officials of the administration whom the President intends to send in various parts of the country to speak on the Vietnam situation."

The use of the FBI as the intelligence arm of the White House reached unprecedented heights under Richard Nixon. President Nixon's similar desire to discredit and contain dissent led to the inception of a series of abusive initiatives that ultimately unraveled his presidency and, by undermining the secrecy that had heretofore shrouded FBI operations, gave rise to congressional inquiries that ended up exposing the scope and nature of FBI abuses dating as far back as the 1930s.

Not content to await volunteered FBI reports, the Nixon White House sought to assume control over Hoover's practice of reporting on political matters that it would find of interest. Accordingly, in November 1969, the FBI director authorized the code-named INLET program whereby FBI reports, submitted "on an individual basis" since Roosevelt's presidency, were henceforth to be consolidated to ensure Nixon with "high-level intelligence in the internal security field" and any information "which has the qualities of importance and timeliness necessary to secure the President's interest."

"Items with an unusual twist or concerning prominent personalities which may be of special interest to the President or the Attorney General" were particularly sought.

In addition, at the specific request of the Nixon White House, FBI agents began in 1969 to monitor closely and then wiretap seventeen individuals—among them the president's own appointees to the White House and National Security Council (NSC) staffs, senior State and Defense Department employees, and four Washington-based reporters. The original purpose of the operation was to identify the source of a leak to *New York Times* reporter William Beecher that underpinned his articles disclosing that the U.S. military had bombed Cambodia (at a time when White House and Pentagon officials intentionally disguised this escalation in military operations by providing misleading information about U.S. air operations in Southeast Asia to Congress and reporters).

FBI agents were never able to identify the source of the leak. Nonetheless, the wiretaps furthered another purpose, providing valuable political intelligence about the president's principal Democratic adversary, the prospective Democratic nominee Senator Edmund Muskie—obtained through the wiretapping of the NSC staff members Morton Halperin and Anthony Lake. These wiretaps continued after Halperin and Lake had resigned from the NSC and joined Muskie's staff. Their intercepted conversations provided insights into Muskie's plans and concerns and the plans of leading Democrats as well. The sensitivity of this wiretapping operation—both because targeting members of the Washington press corps and prominent officials and because continuing after Halperin and Lake had left the NSC (thereby subverting any claimed national security rationale)—led FBI officials to initiate special procedures to preclude discovery. The names of the individuals whose conversations were wiretapped were not recorded in the FBI's ELSUR index (an index of all intercepted conversations), and the wiretap logs and the FBI reports based on those logs were maintained separately from other FBI wiretap records in the office of FBI Assistant Director William Sullivan.*

Despite the magnitude of this assistance, President Nixon remained dissatisfied over the FBI's failure to confirm the disloyalty of his radical critics. To address this problem, he appointed in June 1970 a secret inter-

---

* When he broke with Hoover and was dismissed in 1971, Sullivan personally delivered the logs to Assistant Attorney General Robert Mardian, emphasizing their "blackmail potential" in Hoover's hands.

agency task force to be directed by White House aide Tom Charles Huston, and composed of representatives from all the U.S. intelligence agencies (the FBI, the NSA, and the CIA), and ordered it to review and evaluate current intelligence-collection methods, recommend any needed changes, and outline how the activities of the various intelligence agencies could be better coordinated to meet the intelligence needs of the White House.

The task force conducted its inquiry in strict secrecy and ultimately recommended that the president authorize a series of "clearly illegal" investigative techniques. These included lifting the current ban on break-ins and mail opening, increasing the use of wiretaps and bugs, authorizing the interception of telegraph and other communications transmitted internationally, and lowering the minimum age of informers to eighteen. The task force also recommended that the president create a permanent interagency intelligence committee that included among its members a White House representative with the authority "to coordinate intelligence originating within this committee."

President Nixon did not directly implement these recommendations. Sensitive to the political risks should it be uncovered that he had directly authorized "clearly illegal" activities, he instead had Huston send out the authorization memorandum under his (Huston's) signature—thereby ensuring presidential deniability. This interest in deniability ironically made the plan vulnerable to the calculated response of FBI Director Hoover.

Better intelligence was only the indirect objective of this proposed plan. The direct objective was countermanding restrictions that Hoover had imposed in 1965–1966 on FBI collection methods. Huston had first learned of this "Hoover problem" from FBI Assistant Director William Sullivan in early 1970 during conversations about the limitations on FBI investigations. Sullivan had then identified why the FBI could not obtain the desired intelligence about radical activists, specifically citing Hoover's 1965–1966 orders imposing restrictions. Sullivan pointed out that these orders imposed numerical limits on FBI wiretaps and bugs, prohibited break-ins and mail opening, and raised the age of informers to twenty-one. Owing to the more skeptical climate of the 1960s, Sullivan explained to Huston, Hoover feared that continuance of earlier FBI practices might lead to his dismissal. For Huston and Sullivan, then, the creation of the interagency task force could advance two complementary purposes: for Huston, enable the intelligence agencies to provide the information desired by the president; for Sullivan, have Nixon in effect countermand Hoover's 1965–1966 restrictions. When the interagency task force was created, however, it operated under the supervision of the heads of the intelligence agencies. This meant that any recommendations must be forwarded through those heads, including the ubiquitous Hoover. On receiving the draft of the task force's final report (which had, in effect, lifted his 1965–1966 restrictions), Hoover insisted on including a series of footnoted objections.

Those objections stemmed not from the illegality of the proposed practices—which Hoover had, after all, utilized until 1965–1966—but from the belief that they would be too risky in the current political climate and that any "leaks to the press . . . would be damaging." Huston downplayed these objections when presenting the report to the president, urging him to hold a "stroking session" with the FBI director and then institute the recommendations by secret executive directive. Nixon's unwillingness to follow this course effectively subverted what has come to be known as the Huston Plan. On receipt of Huston's authorization memorandum, and realizing that the FBI's resort in the future to such activities would appear to have been done without direct presidential authority, Hoover notified Attorney General John Mitchell how he intended to "implement the instructions of the White House." In the future, he advised Mitchell, he "would continue to seek your specific authorization" by each time in writing advising the attorney general that the FBI had conducted the specific "clearly illegal" activity. Counseling Hoover to be patient, Mitchell immediately met with the president, briefing him on the FBI director's plan to create written records, thereby subverting Nixon's strategy of deniability. In response, Nixon recalled Huston's authorization memorandum.

The priority that led FBI officials to focus on containing and discrediting subversives had the further consequence of diverting resources from any serious assault on organized crime—a shift that was particularly striking in view of the fact that, during the 1930s, the FBI's war on gangsters had been instrumental to the creation of the G-man mystique. After 1945, FBI officials lacked the personnel to focus on the emerging threat of a coordinated national crime syndicate, the so-called Mafia. Responding in the early 1950s to questions about the FBI's seeming indifference, Hoover explained: "No single individual or coalition of racketeers dominate organized crime across the country." Although conceding that crime was a serious societal problem, Hoover emphasized that fighting it fell within the purview of local and state police and also reaffirmed his aversion to the creation of a "national police force."

Unfortunately for Hoover, on November 14, 1957, the New York state trooper Edgar Croswell came across a procession of limousines with out-of-state license plates arriving at the secluded Apalachin, New York, estate of the crime boss Joseph Barbara Sr. Establishing a roadblock (ostensibly to determine [under New York motor vehicle law] whether the drivers and occupants had valid identification), Croswell uncovered a gathering of sixty-three reputed crime bosses converging on Apalachin from around the country, a veritable who's who of Italian mobsters—Vito Genovese, Joseph Bonanno, Joseph Profaci, Carmine Galante, Thomas Lucchese, John Scalisi, Stefano Magaddino, Santos Trafficante. Croswell's discovery became a major national news story, with devastating consequences for both Hoover's and the FBI's reputations. That a New York state trooper could uncover a conclave of infamous criminals of Italian descent not only put the lie to Hoover's denial of the existence of a national crime syndicate but also raised questions about the FBI's vaunted efficiency. Were FBI officials completely uninformed about the links among Italian gangsters?

Only days after the Apalachin story broke, Hoover instituted the code-named Top Hoodlum program. FBI field offices were to identify and prepare reports on the activities and associations of the "top 10 hoodlums" in their area and to give these investigations high priority.

The Top Hoodlum program did not, however, bring about a significant increase in federal prosecutions of organized crime leaders. Until the 1970s, FBI agents proved unable to develop evidence that could ensure convictions of known crime bosses, in part because they could neither infiltrate the tightly controlled crime families nor recruit informers from within their ranks. As a result, the Top Hoodlum program evolved into an intelligence operation, one that strikingly resembled earlier FBI operations against subversives. The principal objective became, not to develop evidence to convict, but to contain the identified "top hoodlums." Former FBI Agent William Roemer, who headed the FBI's organized crime task force in Chicago, summarized this purpose: "I spent most of my time attempting to gather information through surveillance techniques to determine who they [organized crime leaders] were corrupting. My prime interest was to use this information to neutralize their efforts." FBI officials had no alternative but to pursue a containment strategy since the surveillance techniques that they were employing were illegal. No information obtained in this way could be used to prosecute the targeted individuals unless it could be laundered through the trial testimony of FBI-recruited criminal informers.

FBI agents did in fact uncover crucial information about the plans of the more infamous crime bosses and were able to confirm the existence of a nationwide organized crime syndicate and identify its leaders. Through a bug installed in September 1959 in a mob hangout in Chicago, FBI agents learned that mobsters acknowledged the existence of a national "Commission" whose leaders included Joe Zarelli (Detroit); Joe Ida (Philadelphia); Joseph Bonnano, Carlo Gambino, Joe Profaci, Vito Genovese, and Thomas Lucchese (all New York); Sam Giancana (Chicago); John LaRocca (Pittsburgh); and Stefano Magaddino (Buffalo). This dramatic discovery was not, however, publicized outside the bureau, even to then Attorney General William Rogers, the bug having been installed without his advance knowledge or approval.

This was not an atypical practice. FBI officials had acted on their own throughout the 1950s and into the 1960s and did not see themselves as accountable to their ostensible superior. This style of operation is captured graphically in their response to the strict rules governing the installation and duration of FBI bugs instituted by Attorney General Nicholas Katzenbach in 1965 and his further practice of informing the courts whenever FBI agents had installed a bug during a criminal investigation. In 1966, for example, FBI Assistant Director James Gale complained: "The Department has successfully prosecuted 15 hoodlums of whom we are aware, but of whom the Department had no knowledge of our microphone coverage. It is seriously questioned whether the Department would have pursued these prosecutions, if they had known of the existence of our coverage, even though no evidence utilized during the course of the trial was of a tainted nature. To elect to advise the Department at this time would probably result in the Department's decision to petition the court for reopening the matter."

Gale's critical commentary speaks volumes about the mind-set of FBI officials and the extent to which secrecy shrouded FBI operations from needed scrutiny. For, despite Gale's disparaging comment, Katzenbach was (as were his predecessors) committed to vigorously prosecuting organized crime. Indeed, on assuming office in 1961, Attorney General Robert Kennedy had instituted a special task force to coordinate a major assault on organized crime.* Recognizing the need for better intelligence, Justice Department

---

* At Kennedy's direction, Justice Department attorneys sought indictments based on the limited authority of federal racketeering laws, a recently enacted antigambling law, and income tax laws. Those targeted included the prominent crime bosses Angelo

officials devised a strategy to pierce the protective shield relied on by organized crime bosses to foreclose discovery of their criminal activities, the oath
of *omerta* and the fear of death should convicted criminals turn informers.
To address this problem, they instituted in the 1960s the Witness Protection
Program, under which informers and their families would be relocated with
new identities after testifying against their former criminal associates.

Joseph Valachi was the best known of these informers. A member of
New York City's Vito Genovese crime family, Valachi was convicted in 1959
of heroin trafficking. While imprisoned, Valachi killed a fellow inmate
whom he suspected was a hit man, fearing that Genovese had marked him
as an informer. He then agreed to cooperate in return for a reduced sentence (on the murder charge) and protection from the mob. Valachi's testimony resulted in the conviction of only one crime associate. His insider's
knowledge of the organizational setup and tactics of what he called *La Cosa
Nostra* did, however, serve a public relations purpose, proving helpful to the
Justice Department's efforts to secure legislation to curb gambling in interstate commerce.

FBI officials had almost invariably resisted surfacing the bureau's highly
placed informers. Nevertheless, Attorney General Kennedy decided in 1963
to allow Valachi to testify during hearings conducted that September by a
Senate subcommittee chaired by Senator John McClellan. Valachi's testimony received wide publicity, including a highly publicized story in *Parade*
magazine, the Sunday newspaper supplement, that began: "La Cosa Nostra,
the secret, murderous underworld combine about which you have been
reading in your newspaper, is no secret to the FBI." The FBI's reputation
had been refurbished.

While Valachi's testimony offset the embarrassment of Apalachin, it did
not mark, just as the Top Hoodlum program had not marked, a breakthrough
in the prosecution of organized crime. The underlying problem—beyond the
FBI's inability to infiltrate crime families or recruit informers—was that its
most productive sources remained illegal investigative techniques. Justice

---

Bruno, Stefano Magaddino, Louis Gallo, Joseph Aiuppa, Sam Giancana, and Carlos
Marcello and the corrupt president of the teamsters' union, James Hoffa. Kennedy's
ambitious effort was, largely, a failure. Only a few targeted figures were convicted and
those only on minor offenses: Hoffa on jury tampering; Louis Gallo and his father on
making false statements on a VA application; and Joseph Aiuppa for violating the Mi-
gratory Bird Act (he possessed more than the legal limit of mourning doves).

Department officials had yet to convince Congress to rescind the 1934 law banning wiretapping, despite having lobbied for such legislation in 1941, 1951, 1953, 1961, and 1962. This state of affairs was, however, soon to change.

By the late 1960s, the combination of an upsurge in urban race riots, militant student antiwar and radical activists' open disdain for the law and traditional moral values, Robert Kennedy's and Martin Luther King's assassinations, and the upsurge of violent crime in the nation's cities had created a new "law and order" dynamic. Southern Democrats and conservative Republicans abandoned their long-held states' rights views, which had underpinned their opposition to expanding federal law enforcement powers, and provided the crucial support that led to the enactment of the Omnibus Crime Control and Safe Streets Act (OCCSS) of 1968 and the Racketeer Influenced and Corrupt Organization Act (RICO) of 1970.

These acts revolutionized law enforcement, consolidating responsibility at the federal level, and, in the process, expanding FBI investigative powers. OCCSS authorized federal assistance to local and state police agencies and made it a federal crime to cross state lines to engage in riots. It also belatedly recognized the reality of the FBI's emergence as an autonomous and powerful agency by requiring Senate confirmation of the FBI director and limiting the director's term of office to ten years (in order to preclude the politicization of the agency). More important, OCCSS repealed the 1934 Communication Act's ban on wiretapping. Wiretaps and bugs could be installed during criminal investigations subject to a warrant from the courts. Congress remained committed, however, to Cold War internal security concerns and qualified the requirement of a court warrant by introducing a rather broad loophole:

> Nothing contained in this chapter . . . shall limit the constitutional powers of the President to take such measures as he deems necessary to protect the Nation against actual or potential attack or other hostile acts of a foreign power, to obtain foreign intelligence information against foreign intelligence activities. Nor shall anything contained in this chapter be deemed to limit the constitutional power of the President to take such measures as he deems necessary to protect the United States against the overthrow of the Government by force or other unlawful means, or against any other clear and present danger to the structure or existence of the Government.

This broad language was challenged during Senate hearings and floor debate as possibly authorizing presidents to wiretap their political critics. Supporters of this section, however, claimed that the language was neutral—

that, rather than conceding that a president had such inherent powers, it simply did not encroach on the president's undefined constitutional powers. The Supreme Court partially resolved this question in 1972 when, in *United States v. U.S. District Court,* it rejected President Nixon's claimed right to authorize warrantless wiretaps during "domestic security" investigations—holding that, because these were essentially criminal investigations, wiretaps could be installed only pursuant to the OCCSS warrant requirement—but it left open the question of the scope of the president's inherent "foreign intelligence" powers.

The OCCSS nonetheless proved to be an invaluable tool and contributed to the sharp increase in the indictments and convictions of organized crime bosses seen during the 1970s and 1980s (most notably in the so-called Pizza Connection case of 1982). This increase in criminal prosecutions was further enhanced by Congress's companion action of 1970 approving RICO. This statute criminalized the acquisition, maintenance, or control of a business funded through illegal activities; the use of a business to conduct an illegal activity; and the use of profits derived from illegal activities in an "enterprise" that involved a "pattern of criminal activity." The statute broadly defined the term *enterprise* as including both legal and illegal businesses and defined *patterns of criminal activity* as involving both state and federal crimes, for example, racketeering, bribery, fraud, and narcotics.

OCCSS's legalization of wiretaps and bugs made it easier for FBI agents to obtain hard evidence of criminal activities. Sophisticated criminals did not create paper trails, and their violent methods made it difficult for FBI agents to infiltrate or recruit informers within their organizations. RICO provided a second avenue of attack as its permissive standards did not require direct proof of a criminal activity, only of the illicit proceedings. It helped FBI agents promote convictions of corrupt politicians and businessmen and disable many long-established crime families that had used legitimate businesses as fronts to launder revenues acquired through gambling, prostitution, narcotics trafficking, and loan sharking operations or milking pension funds. Crime bosses had also started or acquired businesses through illicitly acquired funds. Senior FBI officials moved quickly to capitalize on this new authority and the new politics of crime and, by 1974, had increased to eleven hundred the number of agents assigned to the code-named nationwide Organized Crime Program.

Scandal and Limited Reform

Responding to questions about a June 1972 break-in at the headquarters of the Democratic National Committee (DNC) in the Watergate complex in Washington, D.C., the Senate in 1973 established a special committee to investigate the conduct of the 1972 presidential election. Chaired by Democratic Senator Sam Ervin, this committee held highly publicized hearings in the spring and summer of 1973 that focused on the role of President Nixon and his key aides in the break-in and the ensuing cover-up. The investigation ultimately led to Nixon's resignation in August 1974. As important, however, revelations publicized during the course of the inquiry raised questions about the FBI–Nixon White House relationship.

In June 1972, Washington, D.C., metropolitan police apprehended five men (including the chief security officer of the Nixon reelection committee) who had broken into DNC headquarters, in the process discovering that their purpose had been to install a bug and photograph DNC records. The five were subsequently found to have been recipients of funds contributed to the Nixon reelection campaign and to have been recruited by G. Gordon Liddy and E. Howard Hunt. Liddy, a former FBI agent, had been employed at the Nixon White House in 1971 before assuming a high office in the 1972 Nixon reelection committee; Hunt, a former CIA officer, had also been employed at the Nixon White House in 1971 before becoming a White House consultant.

Although only these seven men were indicted in 1972, questions remained as to whether they had acted alone. By the summer of 1973, doubts had intensified, testimony before and records uncovered by the Ervin Committee confirming that senior White House and campaign aides, and possibly even the president, had been involved in an elaborate cover-up scheme, one purpose of which had been to preclude discovery of illegal activities conducted by White House aides, the FBI, and the CIA from 1969 to 1971 under the direction of senior Nixon administration officials. Indeed, during the course of its inquiry, the committee obtained copies of documents as well as testimony concerning the formulation of the Huston Plan, the activities of the so-called White House Plumbers, and the FBI's wiretapping in 1969–1971 of seventeen individuals. It was becoming evident, not only that senior Nixon administration officials had politicized the FBI, but also that the FBI had extensively employed illegal investigative techniques.

Furthermore, during the February 1973 confirmation hearings before the Senate Judiciary Committee following his nomination by President Nixon as FBI director (J. Edgar Hoover having died in May 1972), L. Patrick Gray III admitted to having destroyed sensitive records that the White House aide John Ehrlichman had turned over to him the previous summer.* These records included the logs of the FBI's wiretapping operation of 1969–1971 relating to the leak to the *New York Times* reporter William Beecher that FBI Assistant Director William Sullivan had maintained in his office until delivering them to the White House in 1971 because of their "blackmail potential." Gray also disclosed that White House Counsel John Dean had been allowed to sit in during FBI interviews of White House aides during the Watergate investigation. Gray's testimony suggested that, at least during the Nixon years, FBI investigations had been shaped by the political interests of the White House.

The Ervin Committee's and the Senate Judiciary Committee's revelations about the FBI's conduct came in the midst of a series of other damaging disclosures. First, in May 1970, it became known that FBI agents had monitored environmental activists involved in planning the 1970 Earth Day activities, including Senators Edmund Muskie and Gaylord Nelson. Next, in March 1971, a group of radical activists broke into the FBI's resident agency in Media, Pennsylvania, and stole thousands of pages of documents that they then photocopied and released to the media and members of Congress. One of the pilfered documents was captioned COINTEL-PRO–New Left, leading the NBC correspondent Carl Stern to file a request under the 1966 Freedom of Information Act for all FBI records pertaining to this secret program. Stern eventually won his suit and, in December 1973, received and then publicized the massive records of this abusive disruption program. Then, in December 1974, the *New York Times* reporter Seymour Hersh disclosed that, during the 1960s and early 1970s, CIA officers had illegally monitored the activities of thousands of antiwar and civil rights activists under the program code-named Operation CHAOS. The final straw came in February 1975, when, during testimony before a House Judiciary Subcommittee, Attorney General Edward Levi disclosed that former FBI Director Hoover had maintained in his office a secret file

* Gray had been appointed acting director on May 3, 1972, serving in that capacity until nominated as FBI director by President Nixon in January 1973. Gray withdrew his nomination as director two months later.

containing derogatory information on prominent Americans, including presidents and members of Congress. The cumulative effect of these revelations shattered the mystique of secrecy that had heretofore immunized the FBI (and the CIA) from critical scrutiny.

Coming as they did after President Nixon's August 1974 forced resignation, these revelations further heightened public doubts about the integrity of administration and intelligence agency officials and the legitimacy of claimed national security and secrecy rationales. Seeking to restore public confidence in the U.S. intelligence community and to contain the growing scandal, President Gerald Ford on January 24, 1975, appointed a special commission chaired by Vice President Nelson Rockefeller. Ford's executive order, however, authorized the so-called Rockefeller Commission to investigate only CIA domestic abuses. This containment strategy failed as both the House and the Senate that same month established special committees (chaired by, respectively, Congressman Otis Pike and Senator Frank Church) to investigate both the domestic and the foreign activities of all the U.S. intelligence agencies—the first such congressional investigations ever. The committees obtained access to formerly secret records and were instructed to determine how the intelligence agencies operated, whether they complied with the law, and what their relationship to the White House was.

The Senate resolution establishing the so-called Church Committee, indeed, authorized a far-reaching inquiry into the FBI's methods and authority and whether FBI operations undermined a democratic system of government based on the rule of law and accountability. The committee was directed to investigate "the conduct of domestic intelligence and counterintelligence operations against U.S. citizens by the Federal Bureau of Investigation"; "the origins and disposition of the so-called Huston Plan"; the "nature and extent of executive branch oversight" of the FBI; the "extent to which United States intelligence operations are governed by Executive orders, rules, or regulations either published or secret, or are in conflict with specific legislative authority"; and "the violation or suspected violation of any State or Federal statute by an intelligence agency or by any person by or on behalf of any intelligence agency of the Federal Government including but not limited to surreptitious entries, surveillance, wiretaps, or eavesdropping, illegal opening of the United States mail, or the monitoring of United States mail."

The broad-based inquiry ensured that a formerly secretive agency would for the first time be subject to an independent review of its operations—its methods, objectives, targets, authority, and relationships with attorneys general and presidents. More important, both the Church and the Pike Committees obtained unprecedented access to records created on the assumption that they would never see the light of day. And that access led to the documentation of the dark side of the FBI's history, exposing the striking difference between the mythical and the real FBI.

For example, congressional investigators uncovered the scope of the FBI's various COINTELPROs—and how this formal program merely centralized the informal practices that had formerly been (and continued to be) directed against such suspected subversives as the civil rights leader Martin Luther King Jr. and the radical attorney Leonard Boudin. More dramatically, they documented the FBI's extensive use of illegal investigative techniques (break-ins, wiretaps, bugs, mail opening) and the questionable authority under which many FBI programs operated. They discovered that presidents and their attorneys general in some cases had no knowledge of the scope and purpose of highly questionable FBI activities and in others sought to avoid meeting their oversight responsibilities. They also discovered that FBI investigations were not confined to criminals or suspected spies but also targeted individuals and organizations engaged in legitimate political activities—and, in the process, confirmed that FBI agents had sought derogatory personal and political information about a broad range of radical and liberal activists, prominent citizens, and journalists. Finally, congressional investigators uncovered a contradictory history—on the one hand, the FBI's authority derived from and FBI investigations responded to requests from attorneys general and the White House; on the other hand, FBI officials operated independently and insubordinately on the basis of their own predilections and were able to exploit the unwillingness of attorneys general to oversee either their conduct or the scope and purposes of their investigations.

A devastating portrait emerged: of an agency that both violated and enforced the law and of an FBI leadership committed to advancing its own political and bureaucratic agenda. These disturbing disclosures contributed to a sharp decline in public support for the FBI. Indeed, public opinion polls taken in 1975 found that only 37 percent of respondents held a "highly favorable" rating of the FBI, a precipitous drop from an 84 percent rating in 1966 and a 71 percent rating in 1970.

For the FBI and its leaders, the years 1970–1975 ushered in an unprecedented crisis of confidence, a crisis that threatened the bureau's future role.

Not only had the G-man mystique been shattered, but FBI officials had also lost control over FBI records at the same time as the agency's current and past practices were subject to critical scrutiny.* The response of FBI officials to the challenge presented by this lost control was, at times, inept, motivated by a concern for damage control. They dissembled and did not always comply with court-ordered discovery motions or congressional requests, their actions reflecting an unfamiliarity with, if not hostility toward, the requirements of a democratic society.

That unfamiliarity is highlighted by the responses of FBI officials to inquiries into FBI break-in practices. For example, in September 1973, attorneys for the Socialist Workers Party (SWP) had filed suit, claiming that the government had violated their client's constitutional rights. During discovery, they asked—having been prompted by the release that summer of records relating to the Huston Plan—whether the SWP had even been wiretapped or been the target of FBI break-ins. They also asked whether it had been targeted under the COINTELPRO program. After first consulting with FBI officials, Justice Department attorneys responded in November, conceding that the SWP had been a COINTELPRO target and had been wiretapped, but denying that it had been a target of FBI break-ins.

This disclosure acquired a new dimension with FBI officials' responses to the Church Committee's inquiry into FBI break-in practices. Through their privileged access to Hoover's Official and Confidential File, committee investigators had learned about the Do Not File procedure instituted by the former FBI director in 1942 to minimize discovery of FBI break-ins. Specifically, they had first discovered in a folder the memorandum of July 1966 authorizing and describing in detail the procedure. They had then discovered in the same folder both Hoover's handwritten order terminating break-ins that month and a follow-up memorandum of January 1967 in which the FBI director had expressed displeasure over the continued submission of break-in requests, admonishing that they "will not meet with my approval in the future." Surprisingly, this strict disciplinarian did not penalize those who clearly had not followed his July 1966 order, the phrasing of his 1967 memorandum simply conveying his unwillingness to approve such requests.

---

* Moreover, Congress had in 1974 approved a series of amendments to the 1966 Freedom of Information Act that undercut FBI officials' ability to withhold requested records, triggering a host of Freedom of Information Act requests by journalists, historians, and political activists.

Church Committee investigators accordingly sought to ascertain how extensively FBI agents had conducted break-ins and whether they continued to do so after July 1966. They specifically requested a statistical enumeration of the number of break-ins conducted since 1942, but only those targeting domestic organizations and activists (to exclude foreign intelligence break-ins), and further only those not authorized (break-ins to install microphones would have been authorized either under Attorney General Brownell's secret directive of 1954 or under the 1968 Omnibus Crime Control and Safe Streets [OCCSS] Act).

When responding, FBI officials began by emphasizing the difficulties affecting their ability to honor the committee's request, citing the highly compartmentalized nature of break-in records. In this, they were indirectly alluding to the intent of the Do Not File procedure to ensure the separate maintenance of break-in request and authorization records at FBI headquarters and field offices in order to permit their undiscoverable destruction. Thus, their response to the committee's statistical request, they emphasized, was based on the "recollections" of knowledgeable FBI officials at headquarters, supplemented by a review of "certain files of the Internal Security Division." With these qualifications, they advised the committee that only 238 break-ins had been conducted between 1942 and April 1968 and that these involved only fourteen targets. The proffered statistics would seem to suggest that, over a twenty-six year period, the FBI's fifty-six field offices had resorted to break-ins only sparingly and, further, that the subjects had been confined to individuals and organizations having a foreign intelligence connection—notably, the U.S. Communist Party.

FBI officials had assumed that they could safely dissemble about past FBI break-ins, an assumption that proved to be unwarranted—much as President Nixon had wrongly assumed that he could safely deny his role in the Watergate cover-up. In Nixon's case, his denial was undercut by the White House aide Alexander Butterfield's unexpected disclosure that a taping system had been installed in the Oval Office in 1971. In the case of FBI officials, their deception was uncovered as the result of the equally unexpected March 1976 discovery that John Malone, the head of the FBI's New York field office, had maintained in a safe in his office the records of break-ins that New York agents had conducted between 1954 and April 16, 1973. For inexplicable reasons, Malone had not complied with the record destruction requirements of the Do Not File procedure. His failure to do so preserved a massive file (amounting to twenty-seven volumes) that documented the number and targets of break-ins conducted by New York agents, identified the agents participating, and contained the specific records of the targeted individuals or organizations that agents had photographed. This discovery triggered three Justice Department responses.

First, Justice Department officials amended their earlier response in the SWP suit to admit that FBI agents had broken into SWP offices ninety-four times between 1960 and 1966. Capitalizing on this admission, on the released FBI records identifying which of their client's records had been photographed, and on the released COINTELPRO–Socialist Workers Party records, attorneys for the SWP prevailed in their suit, receiving a $264,000 settlement for the FBI's violation of their client's privacy and First Amendment rights.

Second, Justice Department officials launched an inquiry into why FBI officials had misled them (and, hence, the court) about the SWP break-ins and, further, why they had misled the Church Committee when claiming that FBI domestic security break-ins had ended in April 1968. Whether or not Justice Department officials found FBI officials' lame explanation convincing, the inquiry established that no other FBI field office (beyond New York) had preserved records of past break-ins and that no current indexing system permitted the expeditious retrieval of information about the targets of past break-ins.

Third, because the Malone file confirmed that, in 1972 and 1973, New York agents had conducted break-ins during an investigation of Weather Underground activists, a practice that fell within the five-year statute of limitations, Justice Department officials accordingly instituted a criminal inquiry that led to the indictment of John Kearney, the FBI supervisor who headed the New York break-in squad (identifiable from the Malone file records). FBI agents nationwide bitterly criticized Kearney's indictment, protesting that he had been following orders. Further investigation led to the May 1977 discovery of thirteen break-in authorization memoranda at FBI headquarters.* Consequently, in April 1978, Justice Department officials dropped the Kearney indictment and indicted, instead, former Acting FBI Director L. Patrick Gray III, former FBI Associate Director W. Mark Felt, and former FBI Assistant Director Edward Miller for having authorized illegal practices. Gray subsequently succeeded in having his trial severed

---

* The phrasing employed in these memoranda ("innovative techniques") purposefully disguised the use of break-ins.

from that of Felt and Miller, arguing that he had been misled and had no knowledge of the Weather Underground break-ins. Conceding the weakness of their case against Gray, Justice Department officials dropped the criminal charges against him in December 1980. Felt and Miller were convicted. But President Ronald Reagan pardoned them on March 26, 1981, on the grounds that "they acted not with criminal intent, but in the belief that they had grants of authority reaching the highest levels of government."*

Probably most significant about the release of the Malone file, however, and therefore worth elaboration, is that it confirms FBI duplicity. As we have seen, not only does the file contradict FBI officials' claims about domestic security break-ins having ended in April 1968, but it also contradicts their claims about overall numbers of both break-ins and targeted individuals and organizations as well as their insinuations that break-ins were confined to foreign intelligence investigations. Ultimately, the various reports and memoranda included in this file confirm that, between 1954 and 1973, agents in the New York office alone had conducted 433 break-ins targeting 250–300 different individuals and organizations.†

As far as targets are concerned, besides the SWP, the Weather Underground, and the Communist Party, these included—at a minimum—the National Lawyers Guild, the Fair Play for Cuba Committee, the Chicago Committee to Defend the Bill of Rights, the American Youth Congress, the American Peace Mobilization, the Washington Committee for Democratic Action, Vietnam Veterans against the War, the International Workers Order, the Nation of Islam, the American Labor Party, *Amerasia*, Students for a Democratic Society, the National Emergency Civil Liberties Committee, the Student Non-Violent Coordinating Committee, the National Committee to Abolish HUAC, the American Association of Scientific Workers, the Joint Anti-Fascist Refugee Committee, the Federation of American Scientists, Russian War Relief, the Independent Citizens Committee for Arts,

---

* The Weather Underground investigation was a high Nixon administration priority. Former FBI Assistant Director William Sullivan claimed that, in response, Hoover had orally authorized the use of break-ins. There is, however, no extant record confirming that either he or President Nixon had known of or authorized the break-ins.

† When releasing the Surreptitious Entry file, the FBI redacted the names of the individuals but not those of the organizations targeted for break-ins, making it impossible to discern whether any or all of these individuals had been the subject of multiple break-ins.

Sciences and Professions, Veterans of the Abraham Lincoln Brigade, the League of American Writers, the American Slav Congress, the Nationalist Party of Puerto Rico, the Chinese Hand Laundry Alliance, the Hellenic American Brotherhood, the National Mobilization to End the War in Vietnam, the Emma Lazarus Federation, *Progressive Labor,* the American Association for Democratic Germany, the Jewish Cultural Society, the Civil Rights Congress, the National Committee to Secure Justice for Morton Sobell, Carol King, Nathan Silvermaster, Stanley Levison, William Remington, Mark Gayn, Emmanuel Larsen, Kate Mitchell, Jennifer Dohrn, Benjamin Cohen, Stewart Albert, Leonard Machtinger, Dorothy Parker, W. E. B. Du Bois, C. Wright Mills, Ursula Wasserman, Jane Keeney, Gerhart Eisler, Bertolt Brecht, Ruth Berlau, Leonhard Frank, Erwin Picator, Ludwig Renn, and Anna Seghers, not to mention the numerous Communist activists targeted under the COMPIC and COMRAP programs.*

As far as post-1968 break-ins are concerned, twenty-eight of these were conducted—three against the Student Non-Violent Coordinating Committee (two in May and one in June 1968), two against the Vietnam Veterans against the War (both in 1971), six against members of Students for a Democratic Society (one in 1971, five in 1972), and seventeen against members of the Weather Underground (two in 1970, twelve in 1972, three in 1973).† And, as far as break-ins being confined to foreign intelligence investigations is concerned, many were, in fact, conducted during the course of criminal investigations, the cases involved ranging from Smith Act, to Mann Act, to bribery, to

* The number of break-ins conducted by the FBI's New York office was not necessarily atypical. M. Wesley Swearingen, a former agent who was a member of the Chicago office's break-in squad during the 1950s and 1960s, admitted in a deposition filed in a suit brought by the American Civil Liberties Union against the FBI and the Chicago police, *ACLU et al. v. City of Chicago et al.,* to having participated in at least five hundred break-ins, a figure that, in his memoir, Swearingen increases to 2,380.

† While FBI officials in 1975 might not have been able to provide fully accurate statistics on break-ins conducted during the 1940s, 1950s, and 1960s, surely they knew that the figures that they originally reported to the Church Committee were gross underestimates, and certainly they would easily have been able to compile accurate figures for the early 1970s, many of the relevant cases—e.g., that of the Weather Underground fugitives—having been very high profile.

The full extent of FBI break-in activity will, however, probably never be known. Another instance of a break-in has since surfaced—that at the office of the radical Revolutionary Union in 1972. And there are likely many others.

interstate theft, to gambling violations. That such break-ins were conducted suggests that one purpose was to obtain information that could be laundered to ensure either a warrant or a conviction. In addition, the Weather Underground investigation was, in fact, a criminal fugitive investigation.

Because the Malone file was discovered only in March 1976, the Church Committee lacked the opportunity to analyze its contents, having by then completed its investigation, the final reports on which were released in April. Inevitably incomplete, the committee's investigation had been hampered by the constraint of having to complete its inquiry in one year and the difficulty of identifying all relevant records of past FBI activities. Still, it did lead committee members to recommend a number of reforms, chief among them being that Congress should enact legislative charters proscribing the authority of the FBI (as well as other U.S. intelligence agencies). The premise of this recommendation was that one source of past abuses stemmed from secret executive directives that either were broadly worded or contravened legislatively proscribed techniques. Committee members also questioned the effectiveness of executive oversight, uncovering numerous examples wherein attorneys general and presidents purposely avoided monitoring FBI (and CIA) activities to ensure their lawfulness.

Released during a presidential election year, the Church Committee reports did not immediately trigger congressional action. Following the 1976 elections and extending through 1980, however, Congress was inundated with a number of different charter bills while the recently established House and Senate Intelligence Committees and the House and Senate Judiciary Committees held hearings on the Church Committee's proposed reforms and other bills introduced by members of Congress. Congress, however, reached no consensus on this matter.

By 1976, liberals and conservatives might have agreed that delimiting the FBI's role should no longer remain an exclusive executive responsibility. They nonetheless differed over the scope and purpose of an FBI legislative charter. Many conservatives objected to liberal proposals laying out precise limits to the FBI's investigative authority, particularly those that would confine FBI investigations to suspected violations of federal statutes. An ongoing (and future) internal security threat, conservatives argued, necessitated that FBI officials have some discretion to initiate investigations of individuals and organizations in cases the sole grounds for which involved the advocacy of either violent or unlawful activities. They proposed that Justice Department officials (and not charter legislation) should decide the limits of FBI intelligence investigations, specifically ensuring that they not involve the monitoring of political activities.

Deliberations in Congress on various charter proposals lasted from 1976 to 1980. Owing, however, to the liberal-conservative impasse and, later, the changed political climate stemming from the Iranian hostage crisis and the Soviet invasion of Afghanistan in 1979–1980, no FBI charter was ever enacted. Meanwhile, Attorney General Edward Levi had, in March 1976, issued new guidelines governing FBI "domestic security" investigations—that is, investigations pertaining to perceived domestic security (formerly termed *subversive*) threats.* These guidelines sought to promote two objectives. First, the attorney general granted FBI officials some latitude to initiate investigations that would not meet a "probable cause" standard, for example, those triggered by political advocacy. Second, he ensured that, because such investigations could potentially intrude on First Amendment rights, they be closely supervised by senior Justice Department officials.

Specifically, under the Levi guidelines, FBI officials could initiate so-called preliminary investigations based on "allegations or other information that an individual or group may be engaged in activities which involve or will involve the violation of federal law." Preliminary investigations were to last no longer than ninety days and were to be limited to confirming or refuting the "allegations or other information." In contrast, so-called full investigations had to be based on "specific and articulable facts giving reason to believe that an individual or group is or may be engaged in activities which involve or will involve the use of force or violence and which involve or will involve the violation of federal law."

The guidelines further required that Justice Department officials monitor and directly approve "domestic security" investigations. Department officials must at least annually "determine in writing whether continued investigation is warranted." By vesting in the Justice Department the responsibility for evaluating whether the standard of criminal conduct had been met, this written authorization requirement in effect precluded the recurrence of an earlier practice wherein attorneys general had deliberately avoided responsibility and had in effect invited FBI officials both to employ illegal investigative techniques (after adopting safeguards to preclude discovery) and to expand beyond anticipating espionage and sabotage to monitor the noncriminal ac-

---

* Levi had concurrently issued secret guidelines governing FBI foreign intelligence and foreign counterintelligence investigations.

tivities of radical and liberal activists who sought to influence public policy and popular culture.

The Levi guidelines, and the climate of suspicion created in the 1970s in the aftermath of the Watergate affair and the Church and Pike Committee hearings, led to a scaling back of FBI domestic security investigations. This did not mean that FBI agents ceased conducting noncriminal "intelligence" investigations or monitoring radical activists and organizations. While the extent to which domestic security investigations were, in fact, scaled back remains unknown, the fact that FBI agents continued to anticipate "subversive" activities is suggested by an agent's response during testimony in *ACLU et al. v. City of Chicago et al.* Questioned by one of the plaintiffs' attorneys, the agent admitted that 258 FBI informers in the Chicago area who had formerly been classified in the category *domestic security* had been reclassified *foreign counterintelligence.*

The FBI experienced other challenges in the 1970s, challenges that led to often-wrenching changes in both personnel and focus. These changes were in part triggered by the broader societal revolution that had in the 1960s given rise to militant civil rights, feminist, and gay and lesbian movements. Demands for equality regardless of race, ethnicity, gender, or sexual orientation commanded increasingly broad public support, with Congress responding by enacting the 1964 Civil Rights Act prohibiting discrimination on the basis of race or gender. Similar concerns led Congress in 1965 to rescind the discriminatory ethnic provisions of the 1924 National Origins Act. This climate of tolerance had, however, dissipated by the late 1960s, having been replaced by a "law and order" backlash that led to Richard Nixon's election to the presidency in 1968. Despite this changed public mood, Nixon recognized that formerly discriminatory practices could not be reestablished and, thus, instituted in 1969 an affirmative action program that gave preference to women and racial minorities in federal hiring practices and the awarding of federal contracts.

The rejection of sanctioned discrimination directly challenged FBI hiring and promotion practices. In 1972, for example, the FBI's agent task force of 8,659 included only 143 minority agents (63 black, 15 Asian, 62 Hispanic, and 3 Native American) and no women. Beginning during the abbreviated tenure of Acting FBI Director L. Patrick Gray III, and continuing under his successors, blacks, Hispanics, Native Americans, and women began to be actively recruited, resulting in a more diverse FBI workforce. By 1992, women composed 11.3 percent of FBI agents (and 12.3 percent of these were minority women), with the number of black agents increasing to 510, Asian to 151, Hispanic to 605, and Native American to 42. The new hiring and promotion policies, however, encountered some resistance within bureau ranks. Venting their frustration over the pace of promotions, moreover, black, Hispanic, and women agents filed a series of class action suits during the late 1980s and early 1990s.

The reduction of and the controversy over FBI "domestic security" investigations and the new politics of "law and order" that led to the enactment of OCCSS in 1968 and the Racketeer Influenced and Corrupt Organization Act in 1970 also led to a shift in FBI priorities—with a heightened interest in the areas of organized and white-collar crimes. Furthermore, following Hoover's death in May 1972, the FBI's senior leadership instituted changes meant to modernize FBI investigative procedures, including the adoption of innovative methods that relied on the latest technology—notably an increased reliance on undercover agents and sting operations and the use of profiling, computers, and DNA analysis.

A Modern Bureau and the Politics of Terrorism

The contradictory politics of the 1960s and 1970s reshaped the FBI's role in the decades after 1980. On the one hand, the "law and order" crisis of the 1960s provided FBI agents with new tools for a successful war on crime, while, on the other, the "abuse of power" crisis of the 1970s heightened public and congressional concerns about secret government and the need for congressional oversight. Then, the manner of FBI officials' responses to a series of publicized incidents in the 1980s and 1990s raised an issue that had not heretofore been central to the public and congressional evaluation of the FBI—that of the bureau's competence and defensive secretiveness. Finally, the collapse of Communist governments in Eastern Europe in 1989 and, then, the dissolution of the Soviet Union in 1991 undercut the anxieties that had lent unquestioned support to foreign intelligence/counterintelligence. A new internal security threat surfaced in the 1980s and 1990s, however, that of terrorism. This threat was perceived to be both domestic and international: the product of the emergence of militant antigovernment militia and white supremacist groups and of Islamic fundamentalist groups, the latter influenced by the internal politics of Egypt, Saudi Arabia, Afghanistan, Bosnia, and Chechnya and by the Israeli-Palestinian conflict.

The FBI's adoption of new investigative techniques (profiling, sting, DNA analysis, and undercover operations) and modern technology (computers), combined with the legalization of wiretapping and the broad conspiracy standards of the Racketeer Influenced and Corrupt Organization (RICO) Act, abetted the new focus of FBI investigations on organized and white-collar crimes. As one result, a series of successful prosecutions delivered a devastating blow to organized crime bosses, particularly in New York City.

The combination of the successful recruitment of criminal informers (aided by the assurances made possible under the Witness Protection Program) and the brazen bravado of FBI undercover agents (notably Joseph Pistone) brought about the conviction of twenty-five hundred organized crime leaders and their associates between 1981 and 1985.

The so-called Pizza Connection case of 1982, brought under the RICO statute, was the most famous of those involved. In this case, an FBI investigation that began in 1979 uncovered an international drug trafficking operation involving members of the Sicilian Mafia and the New York City Bonnano crime family. Morphine bought in Turkey was processed in Sicily, the resulting heroin imported to and sold in New York City, and the illicit funds thereby obtained then laundered through pizza parlors around the country. In 1985, seventeen individuals—including the Sicilian crime boss Gaetano Badalamenti and the New York City crime boss Salvatore Catalano—were convicted of participating in a narcotics conspiracy and continuing criminal enterprise.

Another case, also brought under the RICO statute, led to the convictions of Anthony Salerno (the reputed head of the Genovese crime family); Anthony Corallo and Christopher Furnari (the heads of the Lucchese crime family); Carmine Persico, Gennaro Langella, and Ralph Scopo (the heads of the Columbo crime family); and Anthony Indelicato (a Bonnano family captain). Then, in 1990, twenty-one members of the Patriarca crime family in New England were convicted, as was the New York City crime boss John Gotti in 1992.

FBI agents compiled an equally impressive record in the area of white-collar crime. The most highly publicized of such cases were two involving political corruption. The first of these, an FBI sting operation code-named ABSCAM, led to the arrest and convictions for accepting bribes of seven members of Congress (Senator Harrison Williams and Congressmen Frank Thompson, John Murphy, Richard Kelly, Raymond Lederer, John Jenrette, and Michael Myers) and five local New Jersey police officials. The second, another undercover operation, this one code-named GREYLORD, led to the convictions of more than ninety judges, lawyers, police officers, and court clerks in Cook County, Illinois, for accepting bribes to fix court cases. Among other political corruption cases, Boston police officers and a Philadelphia city commissioner were convicted in 1986, a California state senator in 1989, and ten South Carolina state legislators in 1990.

FBI agents also apprehended American citizens who had been recruited to spy on behalf of the Soviet Union and who in some cases continued their espionage activities following the collapse of the Soviet Union in 1991 and the creation of the Russian Federation. In contrast to the American spies uncovered in the internal security cases of the World War II and early Cold War years, whose motivations were political, these were motivated by mercenary greed. FBI agents, for example, uncovered the espionage activities of the FBI agent Richard Miller in 1984, the former Office of Naval Intelligence officer John Walker (who had also recruited his son, his brother, and a friend) in 1985, Northrop Corporation employee Thomas Kavanagh in 1985, Air Force officer Allen Davies in 1986, and Army tank instructor Daniel Richardson in 1987. Other FBI counterintelligence successes led to the 1985 conviction of Jonathan Pollard (recruited to spy on behalf of Israeli intelligence) and the 1994 conviction of the CIA officer Aldrich Ames (who since 1985 had been providing classified information to the Russians, including the identities of double agents). The FBI's delay in uncovering Ames's espionage activities stemmed, however, from a lack of cooperation on the part of CIA officials—who did not apprise the FBI of Ames's extravagant lifestyle and sloppy work habits, information that could have led to his apprehension much earlier.

The Ames case embarrassed CIA officials, but two widely publicized cases of 2000 and 2001 raised questions about FBI counterintelligence.

The first case involved the Los Alamos scientist Wen Ho Lee. On the basis of what proved to be a false allegation that the Chinese Communists had stolen the secret of the highly classified W-88 missile, an intensive investigation was launched to identify the individual responsible for this security breach. The FBI's focus quickly narrowed to Lee, an Asian American who had frequently traveled to China (to attend authorized international scientific meetings) and had been found to have been in contact while there with senior Chinese officials and Chinese scientists. Given the results of the investigation, FBI Director Louis Freeh in December 1999 recommended Lee's indictment for intent to "injure the United States or . . . to secure an advantage to any foreign nation." The grand jury testimony of an FBI agent, Robert Messmer, was central to Lee's indictment as Messmer asserted that Lee had falsely obtained the use of a colleague's computer by claiming that he wanted to download a "résumé" when in fact he downloaded sensitive files and that Lee then pressured this colleague not to disclose his action.

During pretrial discovery, however, Lee's attorney established that his client had urged his colleague to testify truthfully and had also not misled his colleague by claiming to want to download a résumé. Queried about his earlier testimony, Messmer asserted that it had been a mistake. The outraged presiding judge, James Parker (who had earlier granted the Justice Department's request to hold Lee in solitary confinement in the light of the seriousness of his alleged offense), freed Lee and apologized to the scientist for the jailing. The prosecution's action, Parker asserted, "embarrassed our entire nation and each of us who is a citizen of it." By then, U.S. attorneys recognized the weakness of their case and eventually agreed to a plea bargain whereby Lee pled guilty to having illegally gathered and retained national security data—to further his own research—but not to conduct espionage. As part of the plea bargain, Lee agreed to cooperate fully with government investigators.

While the Wen Ho Lee case had raised questions about ethnic profiling (whether he had been targeted because of his Asian background) and the questionable methods employed to secure an indictment, the second case raised far more serious questions about the effectiveness of FBI counterintelligence. On February 18, 2001, FBI agents arrested Robert Hanssen, a longtime employee in the FBI's counterintelligence division, having observed him deposit a packet at a dead drop in a park in Vienna, Virginia, while a second FBI team recovered $50,000 in $100 bills that Russian operatives had left for Hanssen at a second drop site. On July 6, 2001, Hanssen pled guilty to having delivered six thousand pages of classified documents and twenty-seven computer disks to the Russians over a twenty-year period dating from 1979. The records involved were of sensitive FBI programs, with some identifying Soviet, and then Russian, agents whom the FBI and CIA had recruited as double agents.

Because of the duration of Hanssen's espionage activities, many questioned why he had not been apprehended earlier—particularly in the aftermath of Aldrich Ames's arrest. As we have seen, Ames was found to have compromised many of the CIA's double agents. Nonetheless, Russian officials continued to uncover U.S.-recruited double agents following Ames's arrest in 1994, confirming that the Russians had another mole, one who was likely employed by either the CIA or the FBI. The FBI's investigation into the identity of this second mole, however, focused on another CIA officer; Hanssen was identified only as the result of the defection in 2000 of a Russian intelligence officer who, in return for a $7 million payment, turned over to U.S. officials the Russian intelligence agency's file on Hanssen. To preserve his cover, Hanssen had never disclosed his identity to his Russian contacts and had never met them in person, either when delivering documents or when receiving payment. His Russian intelligence file, however, contained a tape of one of his telephone conversations with a Russian agent. From that tape, FBI agents were able to identify Hanssen's voice.

Then, by closely monitoring his movements and obtaining access to his computer, they were able to establish his complicity in espionage.

Trained as a counterintelligence officer, Hanssen acted to minimize the risk that his espionage activities could be discovered. Nonetheless, a subsequent inquiry conducted by the Justice Department's Inspector General questioned why Hanssen's espionage activities had not been uncovered in the late 1980s. The Inspector General's report disputed the characterization of Hanssen as a "master spy" and concluded that his conduct should have alerted his colleagues to his disloyalty and triggered a polygraph test. Not only did it cite Hanssen's repeated mishandling of classified data — notably a "serious security breach" involving his disclosure of information to a Soviet defector whom he was debriefing and a similar breach involving the disclosure of a sensitive FBI investigation to British intelligence. But it also characterized Hanssen's attempt to give a packet of classified data to a Russian agent in a garage as "remarkable for its recklessness and destructive quality."

The Lee and Hanssen cases seemed to highlight FBI incompetence. They followed three other incidents that similarly seemed to document the questionable professionalism and ingrained insularity (if not duplicity) of senior FBI officials. The first two of these other incidents were the by-products of the establishment in 1983 — in anticipation of possible hostage crises the next year at either the Los Angeles Olympics or the Republican National Convention — of the FBI's Hostage Rescue Team (HRT), composed of agents trained in marksmanship and in the psychology of negotiating with hostage takers.

The FBI's HRT first became enmeshed in controversy during the course of the investigation of Randall Weaver, a right-wing survivalist whom ATF agents suspected of violating federal gun laws, by the Bureau of Alcohol, Tobacco and Firearms (ATF). Weaver was arrested in January 1991, the victim of a sting operation whereby an ATF agent, posing as a gun dealer, bought from him an illegal sawed-off shotgun. Released on his own recognizance following his arraignment, Weaver failed to appear at his scheduled trial date. In August 1992, U.S. marshals were dispatched to arrest the heavily armed Weaver at his remote mountain cabin near Ruby Ridge, Idaho. The attempt ended in a shoot-out that left one marshal and Weaver's fourteen-year-old son dead. ATF officials thereupon solicited the assistance of the HRT.

HRT agents surrounded the cabin. Weaver refused to surrender, however, and, during the resultant siege, one member of the HRT shot and killed Weaver's wife, who had been standing holding her baby next to the cabin door. After holding out for ten days, Weaver finally surrendering, eventually being tried for, and found innocent of, murder in the case of the marshal's death. But the killing of his wife raised the questions whether the HRT had used excessive force and whether it had followed established rules and procedures. Following an internal investigation of the incident, FBI Director Louis Freeh disciplined twelve FBI agents, but not the high-level supervisor at FBI headquarters—Larry Potts—who had been overseeing the operation, for their "inadequate performance, improper judgment, neglect of duty, and failure to exercise proper management oversight."

Freeh's action did not silence criticism of the FBI's performance, and it also generated criticism of the exoneration of high-level FBI officials. The Justice Department's Office of Professional Responsibility conducted its own investigation, which led to disciplinary action against Potts and to the uncovering of another aspect of the case—the destruction by E. Michael Kahoe, the head of the FBI's Violent Crime Section, of the "after action" report prepared in the course of the internal FBI investigation. Kahoe's action, which constituted an obstruction of justice and suggested a purposeful cover-up since it had denied to Weaver's trial attorney a useful report, resulted in his suspension.

The HRT again became enmeshed in controversy during the course of the ATF investigation into the possible illegal possession of firearms and explosives by David Koresh, the charismatic leader of a religious sect, the Branch Davidians, headquartered near Waco, Texas. Rather than attempting to apprehend Koresh during his trips outside the Davidian compound, ATF agents planned a surprise raid for February 28, 1993. Koresh and the Davidians, however, had been tipped off about the raid, with the result that the ATF raiding party became involved in a violent gun battle that left four ATF agents dead and sixteen wounded and six Davidians dead and eleven wounded. Because the heavily armed Davidians had the twin advantages of a fortified compound and the presence in that compound of women and children, ATF officials once again solicited the assistance of the HRT.

HRT agents surrounded the compound in a siege that lasted fifty-one days. Thirty-five Davidians did leave the compound during the course of the siege. But FBI negotiators eventually concluded that Koresh would never surrender, despite his promise to do so, and that continuance of the siege, which involved various harassment tactics, could endanger the lives of the children in the compound. They therefore drafted a plan whereby a fortified combat engineering vehicle would be employed to launch a tear gas assault on the compound. Attorney General Janet Reno approved the plan, and it was executed on April 19, 1993.

The raid proved to be a disaster, the Davidians setting fire to the compound that killed eighty of their number, including twenty-five children. Like Ruby Ridge, it seemingly confirmed that FBI agents had used excessive force, had been too hasty when deciding to forgo negotiations and execute the raid, and had ignored the advice of behavioral experts that Koresh's response was likely to be suicidal. A series of internal Justice Department and congressional investigations was, thus, triggered, but not all doubts were quieted. The continued appeal of conspiracy theories in general and the theory that FBI agents themselves had set fire to the compound in particular—theories that underpinned Timothy McVeigh's truck bombing attack (discussed later in this chapter)—led to the appointment of a special independent commission chaired by former Republican Senator John Danforth.

The Danforth Commission's report refuted the charges that FBI agents had set fire to the compound and had employed force indiscriminately. Nonetheless, the inquiry strengthened public doubts about FBI officials' accountability and siege mentality. Danforth publicly criticized FBI officials for having impeded the commission's investigation, arguing that "it was like pulling teeth to get all this paper from the FBI" and that he had succeeded in obtaining access to desired records only by threatening to secure a search warrant from a federal judge. He added: "I didn't think there was a cover-up of a bad act. I think there was a cover-up of an embarrassment."

FBI heavy-handedness once again became an issue in the aftermath of the 1996 Atlanta Olympics bombing. Responding to press inquiries, FBI officials disclosed that their investigation was focused on the security guard, Richard Jewell, who had discovered the backpack bomb. Jewell's supposed motivation was a desire to appear to be a hero. But, when no hard evidence against him materialized, it became clear that the FBI had got the wrong man. While his indictment in the court of public opinion soon collapsed, Jewell was not officially exonerated until FBI officials linked the Atlanta bombing to the January 29, 1998, bombing of a Birmingham, Alabama, abortion clinic by Eric Rudolph. He was, in consequence, ultimately awarded a hefty defamation of character settlement.

These three incidents suggested that an insular culture of secrecy shaped how FBI officials responded whenever FBI operations became subjected to critical scrutiny. Similar questions had surfaced during the same time period over whether agents fully accepted the FBI's new policy of hiring and promoting women and racial and ethnic minorities. In 1988, Bernard Perez filed a successful class action suit on behalf of more than three hundred Hispanic agents, claiming that they had been discriminated against in assignment and promotion practices. In 1987, the black agent Donald Rochon brought a successful harassment suit exposing the crude racism of white agents in the Chicago and Omaha field offices. And, in 1993–1994, Susan Doucette, Heather Power-Anderson, Bonni Carr Alduendo, and Joanne Misko won victories in their suits charging their superiors with sexual harassment, retaliation when they complained, and discrimination in promotions.

The FBI's reputation suffered a further blow when, in 1995, Frederick Whitehurst publicly debunked the operation of the FBI Laboratory. A chemist employed in the explosives unit of the lab, Whitehurst cited sloppy laboratory procedures and mishandling of evidence by lab employees and inadequate supervision by career employees having no scientific training or expertise. His damning criticisms precipitated an eighteen-month internal investigation of the lab conducted by the Justice Department's Inspector General. The resulting report, publicly released in April 1997, corroborated many of Whitehurst's criticisms, including the sloppy handling of evidence and supervisors' lack of scientific expertise. It also found that laboratory findings had at times been "tilted" to support prosecution and incriminate defendants.

This devastating critique of the professionalism of FBI Laboratory personnel threatened to undermine the prosecution of many past and current cases. Indeed, a follow-up study, released in 2003, concluded that as many as three thousand cases could have been affected by flawed procedures and skewed testimony. The evolving scandal led to the resignation of one lab employee, Jacqueline Blake, who had allegedly improperly tested more than one hundred DNA samples; to the reassignment of three employees working on the Oklahoma City bombing case (and to the decision of U.S. prosecutors trying the case not to call FBI forensic experts as witnesses); to the Houston police laboratory's decision not to place new DNA samples in the FBI's DNA repository; and to a critical review of the FBI's bullet methodology conducted by the National Academy of Science.

The vaunted image of the FBI agent as the highly professional and efficient G-man had given way to an image of the FBI as the Keystone Cops. This unflattering perception received further support with the embarrassing July 2001 disclosure that FBI officials could not locate 449 firearms (including rifles and submachine guns) and 184 laptop computers (one containing classified data) and that FBI computers had not been upgraded, some being four to eight years old and unable to accommodate basic software, making it impossible to conduct full computer searches. These discoveries, the product of an inventory search, were publicized the day after the Senate Judiciary Committee scheduled public hearings on FBI management controls.*

Troubled by this crescendo of embarrassing revelations, the Senate Judiciary Committee convened a series of public hearings—scheduled to run from June through September 2001—to examine the FBI's management and investigative lapses. Introducing the hearings in June, Committee Chair Patrick Leahy articulated the underlying concerns of many in Congress and the public: "Unfortunately the image of the F.B.I. in the minds of many Americans is that this agency has become unmanageable, unaccountable, and unreliable. Its much vaunted independence has been transformed for some into an image of insular arrogance." Before the hearings could run their course, however, they were sidetracked, postponed indefinitely as the result of the September 11 attack on the World Trade Center in New York City. And, where one minute it was questioning FBI competence and insularity, Congress found itself the next minute willingly expanding FBI investigative powers in order to uncover suspected terrorists and terrorist sympathizers.

On the morning of September 11, 2001, nineteen resident aliens of Middle Eastern descent (fifteen of whom were Saudis) commandeered four commercial jets, crashing two of them into the Twin Towers, a third into

---

* This last embarrassment followed two other devastating disclosures during the two previous months. In May 2001, the week before Timothy McVeigh's scheduled execution, Attorney General John Ashcroft reported that, despite earlier assurances from Justice Department officials, over four thousand pages of FBI documents had not been turned over to defense attorneys and, further, that FBI officials had discovered this failure in January 2001 but delayed advising the Justice Department. Then, in June 2001, federal prosecutors charged two former FBI agents—James Hill, a security analyst in the FBI's Las Vegas office, and Michael Levin, a Los Angeles agent—with having stolen and then sold classified information to organized crime bosses and their lawyers.

the Pentagon, and the fourth into a field near Shanksville, Pennsylvania. The nineteen Muslim extremists had been recruited for a suicide mission, planned and financed by operatives of Al Qaeda, the terrorist organization founded by Osama bin Laden. The attack had devastating personal, financial, and psychological consequences—resulting as it did in the deaths of 2,973 people and a cost to the economy of billions of dollars in property and other losses. That nineteen men, armed only with knives and box cutters, could deal such a paralyzing blow to the United States renewed support for an aggressive FBI intelligence initiative and an unprecedented expansion of FBI powers.

On the basis of an investigation that confirmed Al Qaeda's responsibility for the attack, the Bush administration demanded that the Taliban government in Afghanistan turn over for trial bin Laden and the key leaders of Al Qaeda, then headquartered in Afghanistan. The Taliban leaders' refusal to do so led to a U.S. invasion of Afghanistan and the overthrow of the Taliban government. This successful military attack disrupted Al Qaeda operations, training bases being captured and records pertaining to past and planned terrorist activities obtained in the process. At the same time, the administration pressured the Congress to enact the far-reaching USA Patriot Act. The premise of this proposed expansion of federal surveillance powers was that the FBI had been denied the authority that could have allowed its agents to prevent the September 11 attack and would allow it to avert others.

Given the prevailing crisis atmosphere, Congress readily approved the bill, and President W. George Bush signed it into law on October 26, 2001. Although it had willingly granted the FBI broad authority to deal with a pending terrorist threat, Congress had, nonetheless, altered the legislation as originally proposed by adopting a series of "sunset" provisions. For example, some of the expanded surveillance powers would automatically expire in five years unless follow-up legislation were enacted renewing them. The principal expansion, moreover, revised the standard governing "foreign intelligence" surveillance authorized under the 1978 Foreign Intelligence Surveillance Act (FISA). Wiretaps, computer, and other searches would, henceforth, be permitted during investigations having only a "significant" connection with foreign governments or international terrorist movements—no longer would FBI officials have to offer proof of a direct foreign connection. Federal agents could enter homes secretly without producing a search warrant and could obtain access (again without a warrant) to the records of Internet service providers, libraries, bookstores, indeed, any business, whenever investigating individuals suspected of "harboring" or "supporting" terrorists.* Finally, resident aliens could be detained for deportation as suspected terrorists for at least seven days (and in certain situations for as long as six months) without government officials having to specify the charges or present evidence justifying the detention.

Attorney General Ashcroft also reorganized FBI operations and issued new surveillance guidelines. Under the new guidelines, FBI agents could recruit informers and monitor websites, commercial databases, and mosques without having to establish that a violation of a federal statute had been committed or was being contemplated. They were also empowered to do so without authorization from FBI headquarters. Furthermore, Ashcroft and FBI Director Robert Mueller III explicitly affirmed that they were creating a new culture in the FBI, one marked by a shift from law enforcement to terrorism prevention. An unnamed senior Justice Department official explained to the *New York Times:* "We are turning the ship 180 degrees from prosecution of crimes as our main focus to the prevention of terrorist acts. We want to make sure that we do everything possible to stop the terrorists before they can kill innocent Americans, everything within the bounds of the Constitution and federal law." FBI Director Mueller echoed this sentiment, affirming that "we need a different approach that puts prevention above all else" and that this would require "a vibrant, active, aggressive [FBI] headquarters" that was committed to a "proactive" rather than a "reactive" orientation and had the "capability to anticipate attacks."

The announced changes in FBI guidelines, under review since October 2001, were timed to offset the impact of two publicized disclosures of the joint House-Senate Intelligence Committee—convened to investigate the failure to anticipate the September 11 attack—during the summer of 2002 that seemed to suggest that, had FBI officials in Washington been more aggressive, the September 11 terrorist attack might have been anticipated and, perhaps, even averted.

The first involved a recommendation made in July 2001 (two months prior to the September 11 attack) by Kenneth Williams, an agent assigned to the FBI's Phoenix office, that FBI headquarters authorize a nationwide investigation

---

* This broad authority was ostensibly limited by qualifying language: "Such investigation of a United States person is not conducted solely upon the basis of activities protected by the first amendment of the Constitution."

of all Middle Eastern resident aliens attending flight-training schools. The recommendation was rebuffed by FBI headquarters. Of course, in hindsight, it seems prescient. And, at first glance, it seems to highlight the contrast between the "proactive" aggressiveness of FBI agents in the field and the cautious conservatism of FBI bureaucrats imprisoned by a law enforcement mentality.

Closer analysis, however, reveals a different reality. Williams's proposal confirms that FBI intelligence investigations without evidence of a suspected violation of federal statute did not begin with Attorney General Ashcroft's July 2002 announced changes in FBI guidelines. The FBI's Phoenix office had begun conducting them at least a year earlier. It turns out that the investigation out of which Williams's proposal had arisen had been based on nothing more than suspicions, suspicions that had been aroused by the extreme animosity toward the U.S. government and its policies that had been expressed by some Middle Eastern Muslims attending flight schools in the Phoenix area—and, in particular, by Zakaria Soubra, a British citizen of Middle Eastern descent who had specifically advocated a worldwide, unitary Islamic state. Moreover, in his report Williams cited no instance of terrorist planning that would justify launching the recommended nationwide investigation. His suspicions centered on the possibility that Islamic fundamentalists might hijack a commercial aircraft—a practice that had concerned aviation and law enforcement officials since the 1970s. As important, when after the September 11 attack FBI agents did investigate Soubra and the other Middle Eastern resident aliens whom Williams had cited in his July 2001 report, they uncovered no evidence that they intended to mount a terrorist attack or had advance knowledge of the September 11 attack.

However, in the process of singling out Soubra because of his publicly expressed militant views, Williams had missed another Middle Eastern Muslim, Hani Hanjour, who had over a five-year period episodically attended flight-training schools in the Phoenix area. It was Hanjour, not Soubra, who on September 11 piloted an American Airlines jet into the Pentagon. Williams's myopia about prospective terrorists suggests that the failure to have anticipated the September 11 attack was due not so much to the lack of vibrancy or aggressiveness as to misplaced suspicion. His concerns indirectly confirm that an approach that focuses only on ideology will not uncover terrorist conspirators, who were not likely to call attention to themselves (as, indeed, Soubra had).

The second disclosure involved the FBI's detention of Zacarias Moussaoui, a French citizen of Moroccan descent, in August 2001. Instructors at the Pan American Flight Academy in Minneapolis, Minnesota, had reported Moussaoui to INS agents earlier that month, having become suspicious when Moussaoui paid his $6,800 tuition bill in cash and expressed an interest in learning how to fly a Boeing 747 or an Airbus A-300 despite having minimal piloting skills. After confirming that Moussaoui's visa had expired, INS agents turned him over to the FBI on August 16. Agents in the FBI's Minneapolis office thereupon checked into his background and learned from French intelligence that he was a Muslim fundamentalist who believed that it was acceptable for Muslims to kill civilians who harmed Muslims. Having developed no other evidence on their own, the Minneapolis agents requested authorization from FBI headquarters to monitor Moussaoui's computer—as he was in custody, there was no reason to seek authorization for a wiretap. Officials at FBI headquarters rejected this request.

It was not the case, however, that a law enforcement culture had led cautious FBI bureaucrats to miss an opportunity that could have uncovered a planned terrorist operation. FBI officials had not been unduly cautious when rejecting the request to monitor Moussaoui's computer, given their need to obtain approval for such surveillance from the special court established under FISA. Minneapolis agents had cited no evidence of Moussaoui's foreign connection, essential support for any application—in this case because the evidenced proffered by French intelligence involved Moussaoui's strong beliefs about the conflict raging in Chechnya over the Russian military's brutal suppression of Muslim advocates of independence. Moreover, the request came at a time when the FBI's past authorization submissions for foreign intelligence wiretaps had come under critical scrutiny by the FISA court. Indeed, the court had recently chastised FBI officials for having misled it in seventy-five earlier submissions—all ultimately approved—by supplying erroneous information and then, in at least four cases, sharing with agents and prosecutors the information obtained through the less onerous intelligence standards.

The FBI did monitor Moussaoui's computer and traced his telephone records after the September 11 attacks. While the investigation uncovered no evidence that Moussaoui had been in direct contact with any of the nineteen September 11 terrorists, it did establish that he had been interested in learning to fly large commercial airliners and crop dusters. A more intensive investigation subsequently confirmed that Moussaoui had been in contact with Al Qaeda operatives overseas and had received financial assistance from a militant Muslim then living in Europe, Ramzi bin al-Shibh, as had Mohammed Atta and others of the nineteen suicide bombers.

The proposals of the FBI's Minneapolis and Phoenix offices indirectly contradict the rationale articulated by Attorney General Ashcroft either when lobbying for legislation to broaden FBI surveillance powers or when announcing a more proactive approach. In fact, in the 1990s, well before July 2001, FBI officials had established two units at FBI headquarters to co-ordinate terrorist investigations: the Radical Fundamentalist Unit and the Usama Bin Ladin Unit. Despite this interest in identifying terrorist planners and conspirators, FBI agents (such as Williams) had focused on militant Muslims and not on committed terrorists who had an interest in averting discovery and purposefully avoided calling attention to themselves and their plans, for example, communicating through prepaid phone cards and using computers at public libraries.

Interestingly, in the aftermath of the September 11 attack, FBI counter-terrorist agents did wiretap Muslim activists whom they had already been investigating but about whom they had not heretofore developed sufficient evidence to justify a FISA request. The wiretaps produced no evidence that the targeted activists either had advance knowledge of or had conspired with the participants in the September 11 attack. The intercepted conversations did, however, record their elation over it. FBI officials leaked this information to the *New York Times*. Although the resulting story was irrelevant to a legitimate counterterrorism operation, it did serve to alarm a public opinion already embittered by the brutality of militant Islamicists.

As important, how Justice Department officials used the USA Patriot Act calls into question Ashcroft's stated rationale. In September 2003, for example, the attorney general reluctantly released a report disclosing that the Justice Department never sought authorization from the FISA court to obtain information from librarians, bookstores, or other businesses under section 215 of the act. Because they were unable to identify suspected terrorists, FBI agents had been unable to exploit these broad surveillance powers. Another report documents that the Justice Department obtained no terrorist indictments on the basis of information developed under the USA Patriot Act (with the exception of a University of South Florida computer professor, Sami Amin Al-Arian, and then for his moral and financial support of terrorist activities against Israel) but that it did secure indictments in a number of criminal cases involving suspected drug traffickers, blackmailers, child pornographers, money launderers, and corrupt foreign leaders.

Ashcroft's and Mueller's affirmation of a changed culture, moreover, distorts FBI history. FBI officials had abandoned a law enforcement mission as early as the mid-1930s, ever since pressuring FBI agents to conduct intelligence investigations and to rely on a proactive strategy, with the focus of these domestic security investigations shifting to terrorism in 1983. This revamped mission had provoked controversy when the scope and abusive nature of these aggressive tactics first became known in the mid-1970s. In response, Attorney General Levi in March 1976 had issued new domestic security guidelines. Levi's restrictions, however, proved to be of short duration.

As the Republican nominee in the 1980 presidential election, Ronald Reagan campaigned on the need to "unleash" the intelligence agencies—an explicit criticism of the restrictions imposed on the U.S. intelligence agencies by previous administrations. Following the election, the Reagan administration rescinded those restrictions. Executive Order 12333, issued by Reagan in December 1981, rescinded the regulations governing CIA (but also FBI) foreign intelligence and foreign counterintelligence operations imposed by Gerald Ford in 1976 and by Jimmy Carter in 1978. Then, new domestic security/terrorism guidelines issued by Reagan's attorney general, William French Smith, in March 1983 effectively rescinded those instituted by Attorney General Levi in March 1976.

Under the new Smith guidelines, FBI officials could initiate "domestic security/terrorism" investigations whenever "facts or circumstances reasonably indicate that two or more persons are engaged in an enterprise [to further] political or social goals wholly or in part through activities that involve force or violence and a violation of the criminal law of the United States." This more permissive standard empowered FBI agents to "anticipate or prevent crime." Such investigations could be initiated whenever information was uncovered that any individual or organization "advocate[s] criminal activity or indicate[s] an apparent intent to engage in crime, particularly crimes of violence."

Attorney General Smith also rescinded Levi's requirement that Justice Department officials "at least annually" review and determine "in writing" that a continued "domestic security/terrorism" investigation was warranted. FBI officials hereafter had only to "notify" the Justice Department's Office of Intelligence Policy whenever initiating a "domestic security/terrorism" investigation, the oversight role of the attorney general—who "may, as he deems necessary, request the FBI to prepare a report on the investigation"—becoming discretionary.

The new standards were, on the one hand, intended to ensure that FBI agents would not hesitate to monitor the political activities of dissident activists and organizations. Given the heightened U.S.-Soviet tensions triggered by President Reagan's missile-development policies and the new politics of morality underpinning the demands of the so-called Moral Majority, FBI agents in the 1980s initiated investigations of the recently formed "nuclear freeze" movement, which openly opposed the Reagan administration's missile development program, as well as the militant gay organization ACT-UP. Ironically, as one by-product of this intensified surveillance, FBI officials were forced to terminate the Library Awareness Program that had been instituted in 1962.

The Library Awareness Program—under which FBI agents solicited the assistance of university and public librarians to identify those patrons "with Eastern European or Russian sounding names" and any others who copied large quantities of technical information or who placed "microfiches in a briefcase without . . . checking them out"—reflected the security-conscious concerns of the Cold War years. The problem with this secret program was that it targeted those seeking unclassified information in the public domain. It was compromised in 1987 when an outraged Paula Kaufman, the director of Columbia University's academic library, issued a public letter of protest to the American Library Association after being contacted by an agent for information about the library's patrons.

Further compromising evidence about FBI activities surfaced the next year as a result of a Freedom of Information Act request filed by activists associated with the Committee in Solidarity with the People of El Salvador (CISPES), who had long suspected that their organization, which had been formed by liberal religious and political activists in response to the Reagan administration's support of the repressive government in El Salvador, was being monitored by the FBI. These suspicions were, indeed, correct. On the basis of the allegations of a Salvadoran émigré who had infiltrated CISPES that it was supporting international terrorism, FBI officials had from 1981 to 1985 run a massive counterterrorism investigation of the organization but failed to uncover any evidence supporting the allegations. But not only did the relevant files, released in 1988, confirm that FBI agents had investigated CISPES. They also confirmed that they had investigated over one hundred domestic groups opposed to the Reagan administration's Central America policy, including the National Council of Churches, New York City's Riverside Church, students and faculty at eighteen college campuses, the Norfolk (Virginia) Women's Peace Center, the Lutheran Christian Leadership Conference, locals of both the United Automobile Workers Union and the National Education Association, the Maryknoll Sisters, and the Sisters of Mercy.

The released files further confirmed that FBI agents closely monitored political activities. Not only did they seek to identify individuals "actively involved in demonstrations," but they were particularly interested in the political philosophy of CISPES activists—with one agent characterizing the writings of one church leader as evidence of a "mind totally sold on the Marxist-Leninist philosophy." Some agents recommended that FBI officials seek to contain the organization. One zealous agent, for example, deemed it "imperative at this time to formulate some plan of attack against CISPES and specifically against individuals . . . who defiantly display their contempt for the U.S. government by making speeches and propagandizing their cause." Senior FBI officials shared this political concern. Indeed, when another agent concluded that a targeted group was nonviolent and committed to educating public opinion and that "further investigation" did not appear to be "warranted," he was admonished to "consider the possibility" that the group "may be a front organization for CISPES."

The CISPES investigation confirms how FBI investigations of subversive activities (or, in the phrasing of 1976, "domestic security") had by the 1980s expanded to encompass so-called terrorist activities—both foreign-directed and domestic in origin.

Beginning in the 1980s, the FBI monitored a spate of right-wing activists, some espousing an ideology of white supremacy and Christian fundamentalism, others condemning what they believed to be a federal conspiracy to deprive citizens of their constitutional right to bear arms or demanding that the citizenry be prepared to resist either a United Nations or a Zionist conspiracy to impose "a new world order." FBI agents indeed focused on self-described patriots who had formed militia groups (particularly in the Midwestern, the Great Plains, and Western states) and engaged in paramilitary training exercises, modeling themselves after the citizens' militias of the American Revolution. Then, in the 1990s, FBI agents monitored militant antiabortion activists whose strong religious beliefs underpinned their support for violence to protect the "preborn" and Islamic fundamentalists (resident aliens and citizens) who espoused violence against Israel, Egypt, and Saudi Arabia.

The open advocacy of violence and the willingness of identifiable groups and their leaders to act on these beliefs underpinned the sharp increase in FBI "domestic security/terrorist" convictions during the 1980s. One FBI investigation led to the conviction in 1985 of members of a white supremacist group, the Order, for having planned a string of bank robberies to finance a white supremacist revolution. Another led to the arrest in 1996 of members of another militia group, the Freemen, on charges of mail and bank fraud and threatening the life of a federal judge. Then, following the passage in 1994 of the Freedom of Access to Clinic Enterprises Act, criminalizing attacks on abortion clinics and physicians who performed abortions, FBI agents closely monitored and succeeded in identifying those activists who either bombed clinics or killed abortion providers.

The most dramatic of these domestic terrorist attacks occurred on April 19, 1995, the anniversary of the FBI's assault on the Branch Davidian compound near Waco, Texas. That day, Timothy McVeigh orchestrated the truck bombing of the Albert P. Murrah Federal Building in Oklahoma City, Oklahoma, resulting in the destruction of the building, the deaths of 168 (including children at a day-care center), and the injury of 850. Following as it did on two highly publicized 1993 incidents—the indictment of the Islamic fundamentalists who had planned and orchestrated the truck bombing attack on the World Trade Center and the arrest of other Islamic fundamentalists charged with conspiring to blow up the Lincoln and Holland Tunnels and a federal building in New York City—the Oklahoma City attack was at first suspected by many of being the work of Islamic fundamentalists. But the combination of Timothy McVeigh's arrest the day of the bombing by an Oklahoma state trooper (for a license violation) and the FBI's tracking of the identification number of the Ryder rental truck used in the bombing led to McVeigh's indictment and conviction. Further investigation uncovered the role of McVeigh's friend Terry Nichols, who was indicted and convicted for helping plan this terrorist operation.

McVeigh's and Nichols's background as former soldiers embittered by their experiences in the Gulf War of 1991 and their flirtation with the right-wing militia movement provided support for proposed legislation to expand FBI surveillance powers, a bill drafted and vigorously supported by the Clinton administration. Despite the climate of crisis, however, many liberal and conservative organizations and members of Congress* succeeded in watering down what became the Anti-Terrorism Act of 1996. The bill as proposed by the administration would have authorized roving FBI wiretaps, criminalized "material support" of terrorist organizations, granted government investigators access to bank, credit, and financial records, and tagged explosive materials. It would also have expedited the deportation of suspected terrorists through secret proceedings and permitted the introduction of nonreviewable classified information during deportation hearings. Because of concerns that such broad surveillance powers could be abused, Congress dropped the sections extending FBI wiretapping authority, requiring the tagging of explosives, and authorizing warrantless access to bank, credit, and financial records. It did, however, approve the sections criminalizing material support for terrorism and expediting the deportation of resident aliens.

Well before September 2001, then, investigating terrorism had become an FBI priority. Triggered by the 1993 New York incidents, FBI investigations closely tracked the activities of Islamic fundamentalists, whether living in the United States or operating abroad. This interest intensified with the truck bombings in 1996 of the Khobar Towers (which housed U.S. airmen in Saudi Arabia) and in 1998 of the U.S. embassies in Kenya and Tanzania and the suicide attack in 2000 on the USS *Cole*. Moreover, as we have seen, in the 1990s FBI officials established the Radical Fundamentalist and the Usama Bin Ladin Units, counterparts to the CIA's Counter Terrorism Center, created in 1986 to coordinate terrorist investigations within the agency and among members of the U.S. intelligence community.

The principal problem for FBI counterterrorism operatives was not that they lacked sufficient authority or were prisoners of an outmoded law enforcement culture. It was that they knew so little about those activists prepared to engage in terrorist attacks and, especially, that they were unable to distinguish between those willing to engage in terrorist attacks and those simply holding militant Islamicist views.

That inability is dramatically highlighted by the detention of more than twelve hundred resident aliens of Middle Eastern descent that FBI and Justice Department officials initiated in the aftermath of the September 11 attack. These individuals, whose identities were not revealed, were held without

* Opposition ranged from the American Civil Liberties Union to the National Rifle Association and from Senator Edward Kennedy to Congressmen Bob Barr and Tom DeLay.

charge, the only rationale given for their detention being that they either were "material witnesses" who could provide information about the September 11 and planned terrorist attacks, had assisted the September 11 terrorists, or were possible future recruits for other terrorist operations. Of those detained—some for over a year—only ten or eleven were finally determined to have had any relationship to the Al Qaeda terrorist operation. Seven hundred fifty were held solely on immigration charges—principally visa violations. Others were charged with selling or obtaining false documents (driver's licenses, social security cards),* with credit card fraud, with making false statements when applying for passports, with paying imposters to take English-language exams, and with making false declarations to investigators (but *not* about their knowledge of or participation in terrorism).

That FBI and Justice Department policy was driven more by speculation than by hard evidence was made clear by John E. Bell Jr., head of the FBI's Detroit field office, who said: "If you look at the number of people who went through the Al Qaeda training camps, and there are literally thousands who did, it stands to reason that a certain percentage of them are in this country."

Ultimately, despite the broad surveillance powers granted under the USA Patriot Act and the announced new preventative culture, FBI agents proved unable to uncover evidence of ongoing or past terrorist operations. This failure is underscored by statistics on the Justice Department's criminal prosecutions that the Transactional Records Access Clearinghouse obtained through a search of the department's database on crime cases. For example, during the period September 2001–December 2002, the number of criminal referrals actually declined by 23 percent (from over three thousand in the month before September 2001 to just over twenty-three hundred in December 2002). Also, although FBI officials had from October 2001 to March 2002 recommended indictments in ninety-eight terrorist cases, Justice Department attorneys had brought charges in only sixty cases, citing as reasons for their rejection of the others either the "lack of evidence of criminal intent" or the lack of a federal crime having been committed. Moreover, of those sixty cases, only sixteen resulted in convictions. Another study, this one conducted by the General Accounting Office in 2003, found that, although Justice Department officials had claimed to have obtained 288 convictions in terrorist cases during the period June 2002–September 2001, 132 of these had been falsely classified as terrorist

---

* A practice not atypical among illegal immigrants.

related.* These failures seem particularly striking in the light of Attorney General Ashcroft's March 2003 admission that Justice Department officials had personally authorized 170 "emergency" searches (wiretaps and physical entries) without advance court approval.

As in the case of FBI investigations of subversives during the World War II and Cold War eras, FBI terrorist investigations spilled over into the monitoring of political activists. In October 2003, for example, FBI officials authorized the monitoring of demonstrations to be held that month in Washington, D.C., and San Francisco opposing the Bush administration's Iraq war and occupation policies. These investigations were justified as necessary to developing intelligence about whether "violent or terrorist activities are being planned as part of these protests." Insofar as these demonstrations "would be a prime target for terrorist groups," FBI agents were to work closely with local police to identify those "actively involved in trying to sabotage and commit acts of violence." As in the case of the CISPES investigation of 1981–1985, this October 2003 initiative appears to be part of a coordinated nationwide attempt to collect intelligence about dissident political activities.†

The paltry results of the FBI's antiterrorist operations raise the questions, first, whether terrorism can be anticipated and, second, whether such a goal can be achieved by expanding FBI domestic surveillance powers. Two quite different examples of antiterrorist successes indirectly offer answers to these questions.

The first involves the apprehension in 2002 of Khalid Shaik Mohammed and Ramzi bin al-Shibh. Mohammed was the reported chief of Al Qaeda

---

* The Clearinghouse updated its statistics on terrorist cases in December 2003. Of the 6,400 FBI referrals for prosecution, the Justice Department declined 1,554 and filed only 2,001 cases (although 2,845 were pending). Of the 2,001 cases that were filed, only 879 resulted in convictions (although 874 were pending), while 234 were dismissed, and 14 resulted in acquittal. Of those individuals convicted, 506 received no prison sentence, 250 sentences of one year, 100 sentences of one to five years, 18 sentences of five to twenty years, and only 5 sentences of twenty years to life. Not only was the median prison term only fourteen days, but the charges were all for minor offenses (identity theft, document fraud, immigration violations) — hence the light sentences.

† A publicized grand jury inquiry of February 2004 disclosed that FBI and local police were investigating a student group at Drake University and Des Moines peace activists, an investigation triggered by their sponsorship of an anti-Iraq war workshop on the Drake University campus.

operations and the alleged mastermind of the September 11 attack. Bin al-Shibh was to have been the twentieth recruit for the September 11 attack, but he had been unable to gain admission to the United States, having repeatedly been denied a visa, and acted instead as the funding agent for Atta and Moussaoui. Both Mohammed and bin al-Shibh were captured in Pakistan, their apprehension the product of the cooperation and assistance of Pakistani intelligence (in Mohammed's case, the assistance as well of Swiss and German intelligence)—assistance denied to the U.S. intelligence community before the September 11 attacks.* In a response consistent with a law enforcement mission, FBI officials after September 11 both increased the number of FBI agents stationed overseas in foreign liaison offices (so-called legats) and opened new legat offices in Abu Dhabi (United Arab Emirates), Kuala Lumpur (Malaysia), Tunis (Tunisia), Tbilisi (Georgia), and San'a (Yemen).

The second case involves the arrest and indictment of six Yemeni Americans in Lackawana, New York, and their eventual guilty pleas on the charge of providing "material support" to terrorists. Described by Justice Department officials as members of an Al Qaeda "sleeper" cell, the six youthful American citizens (Mukhtar al-Bakri, Sahim Alwan, Yasein Tahar, Yahya Goba, Shafel Mosed, and Faysel Galeb) had taken time out from an April–May trip to Pakistan to attend an Al Qaeda training camp in Afghanistan. An anonymous letter, sent to the FBI before September 11, had alerted FBI agents to the Pakistan trip. After September 11, FBI agents launched an intensive investigation but, despite commanding broad powers authorized under the USA Patriot Act and the advantage of knowing of Al Qaeda's plans (through intercepted overseas communications and records captured in Afghanistan), were unable to confirm that, on their return to the United States, the six had either planned, sought to recruit others for, or obtained the materials essential to launching a terrorist attack. Even FBI agents' knowledge that the six had attended an Al Qaeda camp came only from interviews with a frightened al-Bakri, who nevertheless denied having intended to engage in terrorism. Either this was a case of youthful exuberance turned sour, or (as in the COMRAP case) FBI agents were unable to uncover a planned terrorist operation.

---

* Attorney General Ashcroft unintentionally lent support to this. In speeches given around the country in the fall of 2003 defending the value of the USA Patriot Act, he cited only one example as confirming the act's value—the arrest of Hemand Lakhami, whom the attorney general described as "an alleged arms dealer in Great Britain" who had been arrested for "attempting to sell shoulder-fired missiles for use against American targets."

Peter Ahearn, the head of the FBI's Buffalo office, sought to rationalize this failure, claiming: "If we don't know for sure they're going to do something, or not, we need to make sure that we prevent anything they may be planning whether or not we know or don't know about it." As significantly, the six Yemeni Americans were indicted for having violated the "material support" section of the 1996 Anti-Terrorism Act, further underscoring the broad authority that FBI officials commanded before September 11.

Should FBI surveillance policy, then, be based on the goal of absolute security, requiring a proactive strategy? And would such an approach invariably entail the monitoring of political and personal activities? These questions did not inform the joint House-Senate Intelligence Committee's 2002–2003 investigation, which was highly critical of FBI officials for their failure to have followed up on crucial leads, their "repeated shortcomings," and their undue caution when overseeing terrorist investigations. FBI officials, the committee's report concluded, "should strengthen and improve [the FBI's] domestic capability as fully and expeditiously as possible." It was specifically recommended that FBI and CIA officials assign a higher priority to counterterrorism investigations, improve the training and strategic analysis capabilities of agents assigned to counterterrorism investigations, substantially increase "efforts to penetrate terrorist organizations operating in the United States through all available means of collection," and effect better coordination among all the U.S. intelligence agencies. It was further urged that the Intelligence and Judiciary Committees of both houses of Congress "consider promptly, in consultation with the Administration, whether the FBI should continue to perform the domestic intelligence functions of the United States government or whether legislation is necessary to remedy this problem including the possibility of creating a new agency to perform these functions."

The premises of these recommendations, then, are that absolute security is attainable and that terrorism can be anticipated, highlighting the crisis mentality that has invariably informed and provided the catalyst to FBI intelligence operations throughout the twentieth century and into the twenty-first. Indifferent to a history of both failure and abuse, the joint committee's recommendations imply that expanding surveillance powers and the adoption of more aggressive tactics can ensure security without compromising liberty.* In a sense, this response encapsulates what has been a consistent part of the FBI's history: an unwillingness on the part of Congress and the public to address the problems inherent in the FBI's emergence as an intelligence agency possessing the resources and commanding the latitude to monitor perceived internal security threats.

As early as the controversy of 1907–1908 leading to the FBI's creation in 1908, and again during the scandals of 1924 and 1975 that resulted in the uncovering of FBI abuses of power, some members of Congress and public opinion leaders have raised the concern that a secret national police can abuse power, stifle dissent, and undermine a democratic politics. This concern was, however, never sufficient to lead to the legislative reforms that would preclude future abuses by ensuring that FBI operations would be subject to external scrutiny and not stray over into the monitoring of political activities and personal conduct. This evident unwillingness to institute legislative restrictions stems from two core assumptions: first, that granting FBI officials broad authority is essential to achieving the desired goal of absolute security† and, second, that security considerations should take precedence over the disorder and inefficiency inherent in a democratic politics that questions whether political crimes (be they subversive activities or terrorism) can be anticipated without undermining civil liberties. Until these core assumptions are reconsidered and challenged, the FBI will continue to operate with only very limited oversight and accountability, an arrangement that could, in the extreme, undermine both the spirit and the foundations of our cherished democracy.

* In fact, members of the House and Senate Intelligence Committees succeeded in expanding FBI surveillance powers by inserting a little-noticed provision in the 2004 authorization bill for the intelligence agencies. This provision authorized the FBI to obtain financial records from car dealers, travel agencies, pawnbrokers—in fact, any business—without having to obtain either a court order (either criminal or "foreign intelligence") or a grand jury subpoena. This secret process precipitated protests from six members of the Senate Judiciary Committee (Larry Craig, Richard Durbin, Patrick Leahy, Russell Feingold, Edward Kennedy, and John Edwards), who objected to the failure to hold public hearings or public debate and the exclusion of the Judiciary Committee (given its responsibilities over the FBI).

† The impossibility of achieving this goal of absolute security is indirectly confirmed by the President's Daily Brief of August 6, 2001, the month before the September 11 terrorist attack. Captioned "Bin Laden Determined to Strike in U.S.," this CIA briefing identified various threats and plans of bin Laden to launch terrorist attacks within the United States. The briefing memo concluded by noting that "The FBI is conducting approximately 70 full-field investigations throughout the U.S. that it considers bin Laden-related." Significantly, none of these investigations involved any of the nineteen involved in the 9/11 attack.

Appendices

A. ANNUAL NUMBER OF AGENTS, SUPPORT STAFF, AND APPROPRIATIONS, 1908–2003

Year	Agents	Support Staff[a]	Appropriations ($)
1908	34	None	N.A.[b]
1909	64	None	N.A.
1910	64	9	N.A.
1911	81	33	329,984[c]
1912	158[d]	12	354,596
1913	335	27	415,452
1914	122	39	455,698
1915	219	29	N.A.
1916	234	26	510,000
1917	265	305	617,534
1918	225	268	1,746,224
1919	301	329	2,272,658
1920	579	548	2,457,104
1921	346	294	2,342,751
1922	401	194	1,892,077
1923	401	189	2,166,997
1924	441	216	2,245,000
1925	402	99	2,184,688
1926	380	237	2,294,500
1927	386	208	2,154,280
1928	359	223	2,250,000
1929	339	242	2,250,000
1930	400	255	2,307,720
1931	383	324	2,781,419
1932	388	433	2,978,520
1933	353	422	2,775,000
1934	391	451	2,589,500
1935	568	714	4,626,508
1936	609	971	5,000,000
1937	623	1,064	5,925,000
1938	658	1,141	6,223,000
1939	713	1,199	6,578,076
1940	896	1,545	8,775,000
1941	1,596[e]	2,677	14,743,300
1942	2,987	5,000	24,965,000

Year	Agents	Support Staff[a]	Appropriations ($)
1943	4,591	7,743	38,836,000
1944	4,886	8,305	42,768,000
1945	4,370	7,422	44,197,146
1946	3,754	6,020	37,078,000
1947	3,170	4,692	34,900,000
1948	3,741	5,559	43,900,000
1949	4,005	5,615	48,588,709
1950	4,155	5,789	52,635,919
1951	4,962	6,573	69,947,000
1952	6,451	8,206	90,665,000
1953	6,459	7,525	84,400,000
1954	6,073	7,558	77,000,000
1955	6,269	8,128	81,002,000
1956	6,246	7,866	93,826,000
1957	6,185	7,590	95,510,000
1958	6,147	7,839	105,562,000
1959	5,988	7,285	112,111,000
1960	5,889	7,862	114,600,000
1961	5,899	8,062	125,550,000
1962	5,968	8,147	127,216,000
1963	6,045	7,942	135,925,000
1964	6,142	8,220	146,900,000
1965	6,336	8,533	161,080,000
1966	6,508	8,948	169,100,000
1967	6,675	9,399	182,325,000
1968	6,703	9,320	194,986,000
1969	7,177	9,233	219,670,000
1970	7,600	10,428	256,857,000
1971	8,548	11,130	294,565,000
1972	8,659	11,252	336,116,000
1973	8,767	11,357	358,915,000
1974	8,658	11,122	392,294,000
1975	8,441	10,846	449,546,000
1976	8,619	11,405	485,950,000 [f]
1977	8,149	11,203	513,377,000
1978	7,931	11,547	553,954,000
1979	7,800	10,780	584,483,000
1980	7,857	10,562	621,942,000
1981	7,751	10,582	680,723,000
1982	7,885	11,234	767,009,000
1983	8,340	11,362	854,254,000
1984	8,760	12,013	1,063,936,000
1985	8,925	11,940	1,160,388,000

Year	Agents	Support Staff[a]	Appropriations ($)
1986	9,012	12,541	1,156,143,000
1987	9,434	12,910	1,303,989,000
1988	9,640	13,570	1,401,492,000
1989	9,599	13,463	1,439,100,000
1990	9,851	12,729	1,684,444,000
1991	10,314	13,369	1,697,121,000
1992	10,479	14,118	1,927,231,000
1993	10,273	13,834	2,007,423,000
1994	9,785	13,538	2,038,705,000
1995	10,285	13,797	2,138,781,000
1996	10,702	14,602	2,307,201,000
1997	11,271	16,039	2,837,610,000
1998	11,545	16,311	3,041,875,000
1999	11,681	16,775	2,993,128,000
2000	11,399	16,218	3,106,155,000
2001	11,122	15,715	3,566,275,000
2002	11,507	15,612	4,200,000,000
2003	11,776	16,080	4,300,000,000

a. Support staff includes supervisors and administrators at FBI headquarters and FBI field offices, clerks, secretaries, forensic scientists, craft and maintenance workers.

b. Not available.

c. Prior to 1924, Congress did not specifically appropriate funds for bureau personnel and operations, although it did appropriate funds to promote the Justice Department's "detection and prosecution of crimes." This, and the succeeding figures through 1924, might overstate or understate bureau expenditures: overstate in that not all such funds were necessarily allocated to the bureau; understate in that some bureau operations may have been funded through other Justice Department appropriations.

d. Prior to 1917, bureau personnel were not broken down into agents and support staff, and the agent figure therefore includes clerks, secretaries, and technicians.

e. FBI employees assigned to the Special Intelligence Service to conduct foreign intelligence operations in South America were included in the agent and support staff categories for the years 1941–1947.

f. Prior to 1976, the federal government's fiscal year ran from July 1 through June 30. In 1976, the fiscal year was changed to run from October 1 through September 30. As in the case of other federal agencies and departments, Congress approved a transitional appropriation of $128,741 to fund FBI operations for the period July 1–September 30, 1976.

B. FBI DIRECTORS, 1908–2003

Finch, Stanley (1908–1912). A career Justice Department employee, Finch was appointed the first head of the recently established Bureau of Investigation in July 1908. In 1912, Finch resigned as bureau director to accept appointment as special commissioner in the Department of Justice for the prosecution of White Slave Traffic Act cases. As bureau director, Finch took a particular interest in organized prostitution and played an important role in lobbying Congress to enact the White Slave Traffic (or Mann) Act in 1910.

Bielaski, A. Bruce (1912–1919). Having served as Finch's assistant, Bielaski was promoted to bureau director in 1912, heading the bureau during the World War I period until he was forced to resign owing to the controversy surrounding the bureau's role in the so-called slacker raids of 1918.

Flynn, William J. (1919–1921). The former head of the U.S. Secret Service, Flynn saw his directorship marred by controversy over the bureau's role in the mass dragnet raids leading to the arrest and deportation of alien radicals in 1919 and 1920—the 1919 raid involving the Union of the Russian Workers and the 1920 Communist and Communist Labor Party members (the so-called Palmer raids).

Burns, William J. (1921–1924). The former head of a private detective agency, Burns served as bureau director until fired by Attorney General Harlan Fiske Stone in May 1924 over the bureau's controversial role in monitoring congressional critics of the Harding administration calling for an investigation of the Teapot Dome affair.

Hoover, J. Edgar (1924–1972). On graduation from law school in 1917, Hoover accepted first an appointment in the alien registration section of the Department of Justice, then an appointment to head the Radical (renamed the General Intelligence) Division in 1919. Hoover then compiled massive files on political activists and played a leading role in executing and planning the mass dragnet raids of 1919 and 1920. Hoover was appointed assistant bureau director in 1921 and, despite his role in both the Palmer raids and the bureau's investigation of the Teapot Dome affair, director in May 1924. Hoover continued as director until his death in May 1972. Inheriting a scandal-ridden agency, Hoover instituted administrative and personnel reforms to improve the professionalism and efficiency of the bureau. His actions in creating the Fingerprint Division, the FBI Laboratory, and the FBI National Academy enhanced the bureau's public image and improved local and state law enforcement. Hoover's astute sense of public relations—and cultivation of the print media, radio, and Hollywood—promoted a popular image of the FBI agent as the "G-man." He then successfully exploited popular fears of first German and then Soviet espionage both to ensure an increase in FBI appropriations and personnel and to undercut any demands for congressional oversight. Hoover's broad definition of *subversive activities* underpinned the FBI's massive monitoring of political and personal activities and led to the institution of abusive programs such as COINTELPRO. The scope of these abuses did not become known until after his death. To avert future scandals and ensure greater efficiency, Hoover instituted strict rules and created a highly centralized bureaucracy. His success as FBI director stemmed from the crucial contributions of three aides—Clyde Tolson, Louis Nichols, and Cartha DeLoach. Hoover's close friend and confidante, Tolson acted as Hoover's gatekeeper, ensuring that the director's rules and priorities were enforced and briefing Hoover on important cases and developments. In contrast, first Nichols and then DeLoach served as Hoover's liaison to the media and Congress, both promoting the bureau's image and warding off potential criticisms.

Gray, L. Patrick, III (1972–1973). A former assistant attorney general in the Justice Department's civil division and at the time acting deputy attorney general, Gray was appointed acting FBI director in May 1972 following Hoover's death. Formally nominated as FBI director in January 1973, Gray removed his name from consideration in April 1973 (under legislation enacted in 1968, FBI directors had to be confirmed by the Senate). Questions had already arisen during confirmation hearings about his relationship with the Nixon White House and his handling of the FBI's investigation of the Watergate affair, and Gray publicly admitted to having destroyed records given to him by Nixon White House aides.

Kelley, Clarence M. (1972–1978). A former FBI agent and then senior FBI official, Kelley had resigned from the FBI in 1961 to become police chief of Kansas City. His tenure as FBI director occurred during a period of public and congressional skepticism, triggered first by the Watergate affair, then by Church and Pike Committees revelations of past FBI abuses. Kelley acted to restore public confidence in the FBI's professionalism, reoriented FBI investigative priorities, instituted new techniques, and promoted greater diversity in bureau personnel. Kelley was forced to resign in 1978 following revelations that he had used FBI employees to remodel his home.

Webster, William H. (1978–1987). A federal judge in Missouri at the time of his appointment as FBI director, Webster served until 1987, when he accepted an appointment as the director of the Central Intelligence Agency. As FBI director, Webster continued and refined Gray's and Kelley's reforms to focus on white-collar and organized crime and to enhance bureau diversity.

Sessions, William S. (1987–1991). A federal judge in Texas at the time of his appointment, Sessions was fired by President Bill Clinton in 1991 in response to criticisms of his violations of bureau rules and federal laws—for having bureau personnel provide personal services to himself, his wife, and a key assistant and using federal funds for personal trips. Sessions's administrative style and efforts to promote diversity provoked opposition within bureau ranks at FBI headquarters and field offices and proved to be key to the revelations leading to his firing.

Freeh, Louis J. (1991–2001). A former FBI agent, prosecutor, and federal judge, Freeh during his tenure as FBI director instituted a series of changes meant to address the problems of organized crime (international in character), the end of the Cold War and the collapse of the Soviet Union, and the emergence of a new domestic and international threat of terrorism (highlighted by the truck bombings of the World Trade Center in 1993 and the Albert Murrah Building in 1995). His tenure was marked by controversy—the Ruby Ridge, Waco, Timothy McVeigh records, Robert Hanssen, Richard Jewell, and Wen Ho Lee incidents. Freeh resigned as FBI director in May 2001, months before the September 11, 2001, terrorist attack.

Mueller, Robert S., III (2001–). A career prosecutor (who had served variously as assistant U.S. attorney and U.S. attorney in Boston and San Francisco, with brief stints as assistant attorney general and acting deputy attorney general in the Justice Department), Mueller was nominated as FBI director in July 2001. He did not formally assume office until the week before the September 11, 2001, terrorist attack. Mueller moved quickly to reorganize FBI operations, increasing the number of agents assigned to terrorist cases, and instituting new rules to govern counterterrorism investigations. His tenure has been marked by calls from some in Congress and in the media to strip the FBI of its counterterrorism and counterintelligence responsibilities.

A Note on Sources

It would have been impossible to write a serious history of the FBI before the mid-1970s. Until then, not a single FBI record had been deposited at the National Archives, while FBI officials obtained archives approval in 1975 to destroy all closed FBI field office files and in 1977 to destroy three files relating to the FBI's Sex Deviate program. Moreover, when discovering in the 1950s and 1960s that FBI reports were accessible at the Roosevelt presidential library (in the diaries of former Secretary of the Treasury Henry Morgenthau) or at the National Archives (in the accessioned records of the Departments of State and Justice and the Customs Bureau), FBI officials successfully pressured archives officials to withdraw these records.

This wall of secrecy was first breached in 1974–1976. In 1974, Congress enacted a series of amendments to the 1966 Freedom of Information Act (FOIA) making it possible for researchers to obtain FBI records. Then, in 1975–1976, in their reports and hearings the so-called Church and Pike Committees either reprinted hundreds of FBI records or quoted and cited hundreds of others. The combination of these developments has made it possible for researchers to identify specified records essential to filing FOIA requests.

While the 1974 amendments to the FOIA have proved to be the most effective way to research the FBI's history, the act nonetheless poses certain insurmountable problems.

First, researchers seeking FBI files must pay processing fees of ten cents per page. Given the volume of records created since the bureau's establishment in 1908, these costs effectively preclude any individual from being able to fund the acquisition of the millions of pages of relevant FBI records. Researching the history of the FBI requires a strategy of identifying the most important and representative files.

Second, while the FBI must release all records relating to a specific FOIA request, to make such records requests a researcher must know how FBI officials created and then maintained records. A requestor can identify the files of a named individual or organization but might not know the names of special code-named programs (COMPIC, COMRAP, ABSCAM). Furthermore, all records pertaining to an identified individual or organization were not all filed and indexed under that individual's or organization's name. Some were maintained in the secret office files of senior FBI officials (and most of these office files have been destroyed). Others were maintained in other files, not all of which are cross-referenced in the FBI's index to its central records system. For example, the FBI's file on the House Committee on Un-American Activities (HUAC) does not contain all records relating to the FBI-HUAC relationship. Some are extant in the FBI's files on Alger Hiss, others in the code-named COMPIC file—and conceivably still others are included in the FBI's files on Richard Nixon, Robert Stripling, or other, unknown code-named programs. Furthermore, in my effort to understand the relationship between the FBI and the Justice Department, I requested all FBI files on named attorneys general, but the released files offer limited insights. Conceivably, this relationship can be understood by researching the files on both proposed and rejected prosecutions of major cases or otherwise unidentifiable files in the FBI's 66 (Administrative Matters) classification.

Third, FBI officials can withhold in whole or in part records under FOIA's specified exemptions: information that is national security classified, reveals FBI sources and methods, relates to internal FBI rules and procedures, or violates the privacy rights of individuals. When processing FOIA requests, FBI personnel have interpreted these exemptive provisions broadly, even capriciously. Having filed multiple FOIA requests, I have been struck by the variances in processing of the same report included in different files—having information withheld in one case but not in another. Because I have also successfully appealed FBI redactions, I have also discovered how FBI personnel have either capriciously or purposefully withheld releasable information. For example, when processing my request for FBI Director Hoover's Official and Confidential File, FBI personnel at first released only 6,000 heavily redacted pages of this 17,700-page file. Having been granted five appeals over twenty years, I have by now had released to me approximately 17,000 unredacted pages. More revealingly, FBI personnel withheld in their entirety six documents when releasing the Fred Black folder in this file, on the grounds of the sources and methods and personal privacy exemptions. My successful appeal led to the discovery that the withheld memoranda pertained to a specially sensitive initiative—FBI Assistant Director Cartha DeLoach's contact with Supreme Court Justice Abe Fortas (a close confidante of President Johnson) seeking Fortas's and Johnson's intercession involving a Justice Department brief to the Court that had political implications for President Johnson's conflict with then Senator Robert Kennedy.

The inevitable result is that a comprehensive history of the FBI cannot be written, despite the release of numerous FBI files to researchers interested in writing biographies of prominent personalities, the history of specific internal security and criminal cases, or the history of a specific period. I have accordingly sought, not to be comprehensive, but to explore the major programs and priorities that have shaped the FBI's history, as defined either by senior FBI personnel or in response to congressional and presidential pressures. My hope is that this brief history will encourage others to build on my findings—on the further premise that they will have access to FBI records that in the immediate future will have been deposited at the National Archives.

I have based this brief history on research into FBI reports and administration responses in the records currently accessible at various presidential libraries (Roosevelt, Truman, Eisenhower, Kennedy, and Johnson), on the congressional hearings and reports on FBI programs and procedures conducted since 1975, and on the growing volume of books and articles that focus on aspects of the FBI's history either directly or indirectly (through biographies of prominent personalities). Rather than cite the extensive secondary literature and congressional hearings and reports that I have consulted, I refer readers to the annotated bibliography that I have compiled on relevant books, articles, congressional hearings, and microfilmed collections, published in *The FBI: A Comprehensive Reference Guide,* ed. Athan Theoharis with Tony G. Poveda, Susan Rosenfeld, and Richard Gid Powers (Phoenix: Oryx, 1999), 385–96.

My principal sources, moreover, have been FBI records that I have personally obtained through the FOIA. These records are currently accessible at the Marquette University Archives or in the FBI Reading Room.

The most helpful have been the extant secret office files created by senior FBI officials. These include the Official and Confidential File of FBI Director J. Edgar Hoover, the Official and Confidential File of FBI Assistant Director Louis Nichols, the Personal File of FBI Associate Director Clyde Tolson, and the World War II "Do Not File" file of FBI Assistant Director D. Milton Ladd, now classified 62-116758.

I have also obtained a number of key policy files and the records of known sensitive FBI programs. These include the June Mail file, the Surreptitious Entries file,[1] the National Security Electronic Surveillance index card file,[2] the SAC Letters file,[3] Bureau Bulletins,[4] minutes of the FBI Executives' Conference,[5] selected FBI Manuals of Instruction,[6] the Record Destruction file, the Dissemination of Information file, the Access to FBI Records and FOI/PA policy files, the American Legion Contact Program file, the House Committee on Un-American Activities file, the Senate Internal Security Subcommittee file, the Responsibilities Program file, the COIN-TELPRO files, the Senator Joseph McCarthy files, the COMPIC file, and the COM-RAP file.

In addition, I have obtained FBI files on specified organizations, public officials, prominent Americans, and reporters and columnists. The files on organizations include those for the American Civil Liberties Union, the Workers Party, the Committee on Public Justice, the Southern Christian Leadership Conference, America First,

---

1. Created in 1981, this file includes the break-in records that FBI Assistant Director John Malone retained in his office safe, supplemented by memoranda relating to the Justice Department inquiry into whether other FBI field offices still maintained break-in records and why FBI officials had misled Justice Department attorneys, the court in the Socialist Workers Party case, and the Church Committee.

2. A card file identifying the subjects of FBI wiretaps and bugs and the dates of their installation and termination. The released file contains only those index cards relating to closed investigations and only cards of organizations, the FBI having withheld on personal privacy grounds the index cards when the subject was a named person.

3. Directives sent by the FBI director to all special agents in charge recounting changes in rules and procedures and other administrative matters.

4. Policy directives issued by the FBI director to be read by FBI agents and posted in FBI field offices.

5. The Executives' Conference was composed of senior FBI officials at FBI headquarters. It reviewed recommended changes in policy and administrative matters. Its recommendations were subject to the approval of the FBI director.

6. The handbook on rules and procedures given to FBI agents, to be consulted as guidelines for conducting and reporting the results of investigations.

the Women's International League for Peace and Freedom, the War Resisters League, the National Negro Conference, and the Revolutionary Communist Party (formerly the Revolutionary Union). The files on public officials include those for the U.S. Supreme Court, Harland Fiske Stone, Robert Kennedy, Thomas Clark, Herbert Brownell, J. Howard McGrath, Robert Jackson, William Donovan, Edward Tamm, Thomas Walsh, Burton Wheeler, James McGranery, Adolf Berle, Homer Cummings, Vincent Astor, John Carter, Ernest Gruening, and Gerald Nye. The files on prominent personalities include those for Thomas Corcoran, Alger Hiss, Felix Frankfurter, Henry Grunewald, Victor Kravchenko, Theodore Hall, Saville Sax, Charles Lindbergh, Albert Kinsey, Ralph van Deman, William Parker, James Haggerty, Walt Disney, John Cronin, Albert Einstein, Val O'Farrell, John Henry Faulk, Jesse Jackson, Paul Robeson, Burt Lancaster, Paul Corbin, Orson Welles, Lana Turner, John Wayne, Humphrey Bogart, and Allen Ginsburg. The files on reporters and columnists include those for Courtney Ryley Cooper, Walter Winchell, George Sokolsky, Westbrook Pegler, Don Whitehead, Henry Suydam, Harry Overstreet, Lyle Wilson, David Lawrence, Fulton Lewis Jr., Howard Rushmore, David Sentner, Fulton Oursler, and Frederick Woltman.

Index